THE
ESSENCE
OF THE
HOLY DAYS

THE ESSENCE OF THE HOLY DAYS

Insights from the Jewish Sages

AVRAHAM YAAKOV FINKEL

JASON ARONSON INC.

Northvale, New Jersey
London

This book was set in 11 pt. Schneidler by Lind Graphics of Upper Saddle River, New Jersey, and printed by Haddon Craftsmen in Scranton, Pennsylvania.

Library of Congress Cataloging-in-Publication Data

Finkel, Avraham Yaakov.
   The essence of the holy days : insights from the Jewish sages / by
Avraham Yaakov Finkel.
     p. cm.
   Includes bibliographical references and index.
   ISBN 0-87668-524-6
    1. Fasts and feasts–Judaism–Meditations. 2. Fasts and feasts–
Judaism. 3. Parables, Jewish. 4. Rabbinical literature.
   5. Judaism–Customs and practices. 6. Parables, Hasidic.
   I. Title.
   BM690.F4625 1993
   296.4'3–dc20   93-1228

Manufactured in the United States of America. Jason Aronson Inc. offers books and cassettes. For information and catalog write to Jason Aronson Inc., 230 Livingston Street, Northvale, New Jersey 07647.

This book is dedicated to the memory
of my dear father,
Reb Yehoshua Mattisyahu (Max) Finkel ע״ה,
who inspired me with his deep love of Torah.
Admired and cherished by all who knew him,
he radiated warmth and kindness.
He left a bountiful legacy of Torah values
to four generations of his offspring.

CONTENTS

Contents

ACKNOWLEDGMENTS

Odecha bechol libi, "I thank You with all my heart" (Psalm 138:1).

With deep gratitude to *Hashem*, I offer this work in which I attempt to capture the unique spirit and flavor of the *Yamin Tovim*, their times of boundless joy as well as their moments of solemn contemplation.

Drawing on the writings of great rabbis, representing a wide spectrum of Jewish thought, I have assembled and translated teachings, insights, and anecdotes that convey the majestic motifs of the Festivals in kaleidoscopic variety. Since many of these books are not readily available, and most of these comments have never been translated into English, these treasures of wisdom and wit have been inaccessible to most readers.

By presenting these selections, I hope to stir a sense of excitement and place the reader in the spiritual frame of mind pertaining to each *Yom Tov.*

A special word of gratitude is due my good friend Arthur Kurzweil, the talented and courageous Vice President of Jason Aronson Inc., who originated the idea for this book. A man who knows the pulse beat of the reading public, he offers them the best in Jewish literature. His glowing enthusiasm is a constant source of encouragement to me.

I am thankful to Janet Warner, who proficiently and meticulously edited this book, and to Muriel Jorgensen, Editorial Director, for superbly guiding the production process. My thanks also to Nancy D'Arrigo for the exquisite cover design, and to the entire dedicated staff of Jason Aronson Inc.

Many thanks to Rabbi Eliyahu Meir Cohen, librarian of Central Torah Library of Agudath Israel of Borough Park, who was very helpful in locating copies of hard-to-find books.

My deepest thanks to my mother for her encouragement and her interest in the progress of the book. May *Hashem* grant her *arichas yamin veshanim*.

My special thanks to my children and grandchildren for taking a lively interest in my work. They are a source of genuine *nachas* .

Most important, I would like to thank my dear wife, Suri, for her love, patience, and devotion. Her constructive criticism and wise suggestions were invaluable.

INTRODUCTION
The Jewish Festivals

Living in the modern world, contemporary man is aimlessly adrift in a vast ocean of cultural emptiness. Tossed by the crosscurrents of conflicting doctrines, he is searching for direction, trying to find meaning in his existence. On a desperate quest for the truth, he attempts to discover his identity and find his niche in the scheme of things.

The Jew is different. He knows where he is coming from, why he is here, and where he is going. Each year on Passover, on a journey through time, he is transported back to his origins. He labors as a slave under Pharaoh's cruel taskmasters, relives the wonders of the Exodus, and experiences the exhilaration of freedom. On Shavuot, the Jew is catapulted to a rendezvous at Mount Sinai, where he is launched on a trajectory toward his destiny: to perfect the universe through the Almighty's sovereignty. On Sukkot, he experiences the exquisite joy and fulfillment of knowing that he is on the right track and that God is on his side, protecting him and watching over him.

And if, in a moment of forgetfulness, the Jew should stray off course and be in danger of missing his mark, he is not irretrievably lost. For on

Rosh Hashanah and Yom Kippur, he is offered an opportunity to square things and make a midcourse correction to get back on track again.

But lofty concepts alone are not sufficient to mold the Jewish personality. Ideas must be translated into action, and it is by means of tangible symbols that the Torah's objectives become firmly anchored in the consciousness of the Jew. On Passover, he actually tastes in the *matzah* and the bitter herbs the redemption from bondage; on Shavuot, he actually receives the Torah amid thunder and lightning as that portion in the Torah is read during the service; on Sukkot, God's protective shield becomes palpable as he dwells in the shade of his *sukkah*; on Rosh Hashanah, the penetrating sounds of the *shofar* arouse him to mend his ways, and when he fasts on Yom Kippur, he senses the cleansing renewal that is inherent in divine forgiveness. The *mitzvot* that are associated with the holidays lift the Jew out of the doldrums of his mundane life and bring him closer to God. The Festivals tell the Jew who he is, what his purpose in life is, and where he is going.

Mo'ed, the Hebrew word for "festival," literally means "coming together," for on the Yamim Tovim, a Jew has an encounter with his Creator. This encounter is a mutual endeavor, for God meets us halfway: "Turn back to Me, and I will turn back to you, said the Lord of Hosts" (Malachi 3:7). If we but take the first step, God will respond a thousandfold, as it is written, "If you only make an opening for me as small as the point of a needle, then I will open for you a gate as wide as the portal of the Temple" (*Pesikta Rabbati*, ch. 15; *Shir Hashirim Rabbah* 5:3).

And so, on each of the holidays, we shed our worldly garb and embark on a voyage that transcends the confines of time and space, a journey "to behold the sweetness of God" (Psalm 27:4). And as the stars appear in the evening sky, we take the initiative by getting into the spirit of the *Yom Tov*. Surrounded by our loved ones at the sparkling, festive table, the *Yom Tov* candles shining brightly, we raise our cups and intone the *Kiddush*. Our joy is boundless as we feel God's infinite goodness descending on us. It is the moment of *mo'ed*, the loving encounter between the Creator and His people. And the more intensely we experience the Festivals, the greater are the spiritual joy and uplift we derive from them.

The sages of all ages have captured the essence of the holidays and illuminated them. Each in his own unique way found new meaning and inspiration in the *Yamim Tovim*. Their comments come in a multi-faceted variety, ranging from novel interpretations of the plain meaning of the scriptural text to profound kabbalistic expositions, spanning the writings of the Talmud, *Rishonim*, *Acharonim*, *Mussar*, *Chasidut*, and contemporary commentaries. By offering a selection of such insights, along with a brief summary of the laws and the historical background of each holiday, I hope to contribute to a better understanding of the Festivals and enhancement of the *Yom Tov* atmosphere. Most of all, I hope to whet the reader's appetite for exploring the Festivals in the Codes and in the *masechtot* (talmudic tractates) pertaining to them.

I pray that we may soon see the fulfillment of the verse "Bring us to Zion, Your city, in glad song, and to Jerusalem, home of Your Sanctuary, in eternal joy" (from *Mussaf* for the Festivals).

Leshanah habaah birushalayim!

Next year in Jerusalem!

Note to the Reader

Sources are cited in abbreviated form in text. For complete source information, see the Bibliography. For biographical information about the authors quoted in text, see the Appendix.

1

YAMIM NORA'IM:
DAYS OF AWE

Unlike the three Pilgrimage Festivals, which commemorate momentous events in the history of the Jewish nation, the *Yamim Nora'im*, the Days of Awe, are not directly linked to milestones of the past. Their message is directed primarily at the personal history of each individual Jew. Man's life history is determined by a set of behavioral patterns he has adopted, ingrained habits that have become second nature to him. Insidiously, and against man's better judgment, the seductive powers of laxity and self-indulgence have taken hold and set him on the wrong course.

We all are aware of our failings, but like addicts, we feel incapable of changing. It would take a supernatural power to break the structure of our lives.

The *Yamim Nora'im* tell us that there exists just such a supernatural force: *teshuvah*, repentance. *Teshuvah* is indeed supernatural, because it was created even before the cosmos came into existence, "Before the mountains were born . . . You said, 'Repent, O sons of man' " (Psalm 90:3). Because *teshuvah* predates even Creation, it is not subject to the laws of nature, which decree that time marches on inexorably, thunder follows lightning, death follows life, and punishment follows sin.

Teshuvah negates the laws of nature. It proclaims: time *is* reversible, the past *can* be undone, a wasted life *can* be restored; "God is close to all who call Him – to all who call Him with sincerity" (Psalm 145:18). And miraculously, *teshuvah* has the power to transform man, to wipe out his shortcomings. But more than that, sincere *teshuvah* has the ability to convert wrongdoings into *mitzvot*.

The hundred jarring blasts of the *shofar* wake us from our stupor, make us realize how far we have gone astray, and cause us to break the patterns of the past, rearrange the broken pieces of our soul, and create a new personality.

On Yom Kippur, God accepts our *teshuvah*, forgives our missteps, cleanses and purifies our souls, and seals us for a good and bountiful year. Reborn and revitalized, we march toward the future, our hearts bursting with love of God and love of our fellows. This passionate love comes to a climactic expression in the exuberant celebration of the Festival of Joy, the *Yom Tov* of Sukkot. The *Yamim Nora'im* in conjunction with Sukkot gives us the spiritual boost to nurture us through the long winter, until Passover and Shavuot provide the next uplift, in an everlasting cycle of joy and inspiration.

✖✖✖✖✖✖✖✖✖✖✖✖✖

Elul: Preparing for the Days of Awe

Ever since the dawn of Jewish history, the month of *Elul* has been a favorable time for bringing about a reconciliation between God and His people. It is a time when God is especially receptive to our prayers and our *teshuvah*, more so than at any other time of the year.

Historically, the forty days that span the first day of *Elul* and Yom Kippur have been associated with divine pardon and benevolence. When Moses, upon coming down from Mount Sinai, saw the people of Israel dancing around the Golden Calf, he shattered the Tablets of the Law he was carrying. He thereupon ascended the mountain and pleaded for divine mercy for Israel. God responded by telling Moses to "carve out two stone tablets just like the first ones" (Exodus 34:1). This happened on the first day of *Elul,*[1] and after a sojourn of forty days on the mountain, Moses came down with the second set of tablets, on the tenth of *Tishrei,* as a token that God had forgiven the sin of the Golden Calf. This manifestation of supreme divine pardon has been imprinted on the Jewish calendar for all time, marking these forty days as a period of self-examination, repentance, and forgiveness.

※※※※※※※※※※※

Acronym of *Elul*

Although God welcomes our prayers at any time of the year, the month of *Elul* is the most opportune time for repentance, because during that month, God is more accessible. This divine nearness is alluded to in the initials of the words אני לדודי ודודי לי, *Ani Ledodi Vedodi Li,* "I am my Beloved's, and my Beloved is mine" (Song of Songs 6:3). Joined together, these four letters form the word *Elul,* signifying that *Elul* is an auspicious month for returning to God in love.

In a similar way, the initials of את לבבך ואת לבב, *Et Levavecha Ve'et Levav,* "[God will remove the barriers] from your heart and from the hearts of your descendants" (Deuteronomy 30:6), also form the word *Elul.* The acronym comes to teach us, says the *Sefat Emet,* that the merit and the favor that a *baal teshuvah* gains benefit not only himself but all the generations that will come after him, for by changing his own life, he is charting a course of Torah observance for all his descendants.

In a similar vein, the word אריה, *aryeh,* lion, in the verse "A lion has roared, who will not be afraid?" (Amos 3:8) is the acronym of the names of the days on which we are summoned to do *teshuvah: Elul, Rosh Hashanah, Yom Kippur,* and *Hoshanah Rabbah.* The preceding verse, which states, "When a ram's horn is sounded in a town, do the people not take alarm?" offers clear evidence that "the lion's roar" is indeed a call to *teshuvah.*

※※※※※※※※※※※

Sounding the *Shofar* during *Elul*

It is a universally accepted custom to blow the *shofar* after the morning service on every weekday during the month of *Elul*. Only one series of *tekiah, shevarim, teruah, tekiah* is sounded. However, on the day before Rosh Hashanah, the *shofar* is not blown, in order to make a distinction between the *shofar* blowing of *Elul*, which is based on Jewish custom, and the blowing on Rosh Hashanah, which is mandated by the Torah.

Various reasons are given for blowing the *shofar* during *Elul*. According to one opinion, the custom is designed to confound Satan, who takes the blowing of the *shofar* as a sign that Rosh Hashanah has arrived. For it is on Rosh Hashanah, the Day of Judgment, that he brings charges against the Jewish people before the Heavenly Throne. When he hears the *shofar* sounds during the entire month of *Elul*, he becomes confused and does not know when to present his accusations.[2]

Another view has it that the custom originates in early Jewish history. When Moses went up Mount Sinai to receive the second tablets on the first day of *Elul*, the *shofar* was sounded in the camp to announce to the people that Moses had ascended the mountain, so that they would not again make the fatal mistake of worshiping an idol. The custom of blowing the *shofar* during *Elul* has been instituted in commemoration of Moses' ascent.[3]

❈❈❈❈❈❈❈❈❈❈❈❈❈

Recitation of Psalm 27: *Hashem Ori Veyish'i*

Beginning with the second day of Rosh Chodesh *Elul* through Shemini Atzeret, Psalm 27 is recited after the morning service.

The relevance of this psalm to the High Holidays is based on its first verse, "A psalm of David; God is my light and my salvation" (Psalm 27:1). The *Midrash* expounds, "God is my light"–on Rosh Hashanah–"and my salvation"–on Yom Kippur. Verse 5, which states, "For He will hide me in His shelter," is an allusion to Sukkot, the festival when we dwell in the *sukkah*, the symbol of divine protection.

Rabbi Moshe Alshich offers the following explanation of these verses: on Rosh Hashanah, God illuminates the road to repentance; on Yom Kippur, He gives us salvation by forgiving our sins. After He has pardoned us, He shelters us from our enemies who seek to destroy us.

Another reason for reciting this psalm during *Elul* can be found in verse 13, "Had I not the assurance that I would enjoy the goodness of the Lord in the land of the living." The first word of this verse, לולא, *lule*, is *Elul* spelled backward.[4]

✖✖✖✖✖✖✖✖✖✖✖✖✖

To Live in the House of God

Perhaps the most moving passage in Psalm 27 is the verse "One thing I asked of God, that I shall seek: to live in the house of God all the days of my life, to behold the sweetness of God, and to contemplate in His Sanctuary" (Psalm 27:4).

What is the meaning of the two apparently redundant phrases, "One thing I asked of God, that I shall seek"?

The *Maggid* of Dubna explains it with a fitting parable: A father whose sick son refused to take any nourishment called the doctor, who prescribed a medicine. The boy adamantly rejected the potion and grew steadily weaker. At wit's end, the doctor pleaded with the boy, asking him to take just one spoonful. The boy replied, "I'll take the medicine if you promise not to pressure me to take any more medicine or food." When both the doctor and the father assured the boy of this, he took the spoonful of medicine. Whispering into the father's ear, the doctor said, "You'll see, now that he took the medicine, his health will improve, and you won't have to push him anymore to eat; he himself will be demanding food."

David is saying, "One thing I asked of God, this I shall seek." All I am asking God is that He give me a pure heart. Once I have a pure heart, I will seek by myself "to live in the house of God all the days of my life, to behold the sweetness of God, and to contemplate in His Sanctuary."

Ohel Yaakov

※※※※※※※※※※※※※※

No Ulterior Motive

"One thing I asked of God, that I shall seek: To live in the house of the Lord all the days of my life, to behold the sweetness of God, and to contemplate in His Sanctuary" (Psalm 27:4).

Rabbi Eliyahu Lapian asks, "Isn't it quite obvious, if you are asking something of God, that is what you are seeking!" Why the seeming repetitiveness?

One who asks for a loan doesn't borrow the money just to keep it in the house. One needs the money for a certain purpose, either to invest it in a business or to buy a house or for a similar objective.

By contrast, King David, the author of Psalms, said, "One thing I ask of God, and I have no ulterior motive. My request is all I desire, no more, no less: To live in the house of God all the days of my life, to behold the sweetness of God. . . ."

Lev Eliyahu

※※※※※※※※※※※※※※

To Behold God

Job, after suffering a series of calamities and being stricken with a debilitating affliction, cried out, "And after my skin is destroyed, then without my flesh I shall see God" (Job 19:26).

Rabbi Uri of Strelisk expounded the phrase, "without my flesh I shall see God" as follows: "If man would completely divest himself of his corporeality and rise above his physical nature, then he would be able to behold God."

Imrei Kadosh

❀❀❀❀❀❀❀❀❀❀❀❀

Selichot: Prayers of Supplication

Beginning with the Sunday before Rosh Hashanah, we rise early for the *Selichot* service. If Rosh Hashanah should fall on a Monday or Tuesday, so that there are fewer than four days on which to say *Selichot*, we begin a week earlier. In many communities, the first *Selichot* service is held on *Shabbat* night after midnight.

❀❀❀❀❀❀❀❀❀❀❀❀

Thirteen Attributes of Mercy

The central feature of the *Selichot* service is the recitation of the Thirteen Divine Attributes of Mercy. This is the prayer God taught Moses after the people of Israel had committed the dreadful sin of worshiping the Golden Calf. Moses tried to gain atonement for their crime, and God responded by revealing to him the Thirteen Attributes of Mercy, adding, "Whenever the people of Israel will sin, let them perform this service of the Thirteen Attributes, and I will forgive them." Furthermore, God made a covenant with Moses that the prayerful recitation of the Thirteen Attributes of Mercy will not go unanswered (*Rosh Hashanah* 17b).

Rabbi Moshe Alshich comments: "God did not say, 'Let them *recite* this service,' but 'Let them *perform* this service,' for forgiveness does not depend merely on words. It is performance that counts. If a person emulates God's qualities, then his iniquities are forgiven."

Following are the Thirteen Attributes enumerated in Exodus 34:6, 7, with Rashi's interpretation:

1. Lord–I am He who is compassionate before man sins, although I know that he will sin again;
2. Lord–I am compassionate after a person sins and repents;
3. God–This too is an attribute of mercy;
4. Compassionate–He has mercy on the poor;
5. and gracious–He is kind to the wealthy;
6. Slow to anger–He is patient and not quick to exact retribution, in the hope that the guilty will repent;
7. Abundant in loving-kindness–He acts with loving-kindness toward those who lack merit;
8. and truth–He rewards those who fulfill His will;
9. He remembers deeds of love for thousands of generations– He remembers the deeds of love a person does before Him to the thousandth, even the two thousandth, generation;
10. Forgiving sin–He forgives sins that one commits willfully;
11. and rebellion–He forgives sins one commits in the spirit of rebelliousness;
12. and error–He forgives sins that were committed unintentionally;
13. and who cleanses–He will clear those who repent but will not clear those who do not repent.

The verse continues: " . . . but keeps in mind the sins of the fathers to their children and grandchildren, to the third and fourth generations" (Exodus 34:7).

This passage gives rise to a fundamental question: Why do children have to suffer for the sins of their fathers?

The Damesek Eliezer answers: This verse must be understood quite differently. By keeping in mind the sins of their fathers, God is performing an act of kindness to the children. He thereby diminishes the children's guilt when they violate His laws. God takes into account that the children's wrongdoing is their parents' fault. They are to blame. The children are only following in their sinful footsteps.

Lesson from a Peasant

Once during the month of *Elul*, Rabbi Mordechai of Lechovitz, while traveling, stayed with his disciples at a country inn. There he over-heard a peasant telling his friend, "Listen, fellow, if you don't work your head off during this month, you won't have a thing to eat all year."

Turning to his disciples, the *tzaddik* exclaimed, "Brothers, did you hear what this simple peasant just said? Think about it!"

Or Yesharim

❋❋❋❋❋❋❋❋❋❋❋❋

Serve Yourself

A *chasid* came to Rabbi Mordechai of Lechovitz, asking the rabbi to teach him the proper way to serve God. The *rebbe* replied, "God does not need your service. Do we not say in the *Shemoneh Esrei* of *Ne'ilah*, 'If man is righteous, what can he give You?' Instead of asking me to teach you how to serve God, you should ask me to teach you how to serve yourself. For it is *you*, not God, who benefits from your prayer, your *mitzvot*, and your Torah."

Or Yesharim

❋❋❋❋❋❋❋❋❋❋❋❋

The Fish Are Trembling

Said Rabbi Moshe of Kobryn, "When I was a boy, I once was playing with my schoolmates during the month of *Elul*. My older sister scolded me, 'Do you think it is right to play today? Don't you know that it is *Elul*, the season when even the fish in the streams are shuddering with awe of the upcoming Judgment Day?'

For a long time I sat there, dumbstruck with fear and trepidation. Her poignant words seared my soul. They are still ringing in my ears even today."

❊❊❊❊❊❊❊❊❊❊❊❊❊❊

Every Day Is *Elul*

Rabbi Yisrael Salanter was wont to say, "Consider every day as if it was an *Elul* day, and *Elul* itself is of course *Elul*."

❊❊❊❊❊❊❊❊❊❊❊❊❊❊

Finding the Way

Rabbi Chaim of Sanz told the following parable to his *chasidim*: A man was lost deep in a forest for several days, unable to find the way out. Suddenly, he saw another man at a distance. Joyfully he made his way toward the stranger, thinking, "At last I shall find the way out."

He asked the man, "My friend, tell me which is the right way. I have been wandering about in this forest for days." Said the other fellow, "I don't know the way out either. I too am lost. But one thing I can tell you: don't take the way I've been taking, for it will lead you astray. And now let us look for a new way out together."

Said Rabbi Chaim, "So it is with us. One thing is certain: we should abandon the way we have been following thus far, for that leads us astray. But let's look for a new way together."

Darkei Chaim

❊❊❊❊❊❊❊❊❊❊❊❊❊❊

Teshuvah for the Entire Year

Once on the eve of Rosh Hashanah, before going to the synagogue, the Chidushei Harym said to his *gabbai* (right-hand man, secretary, and ambassador), "Right now we can do *teshuvah* for the entire year that has passed. You see, the *Gemara*[5] says that one day counts as a whole year, and a portion of a day counts as an entire day.[6] So, if we do *teshuvah* at this hour, it is considered as a full day, and the day counts as an entire year, so it is as if we had been immersed in *teshuvah* all year long."

Siach Sarfei Kodesh

Better Yourself

Rabbi Bunam of Pshis'cha once said, "The need for self-improvement I learned from a Polish nobleman on the timber market in Danzig. Once, when I was still a lumber dealer, I came to the timber market in Danzig wanting to buy a large quantity of timber from a count who owned large tracts of woodland. I was unwilling to pay the price he was asking and made a counteroffer. During the lengthy negotiations that followed, the nobleman kept saying in Polish, 'You've got to better yourself!' What he meant was that I should raise my bid. I did increase my offer, and the deal was struck. This taught me an important lesson: if you want to reach your goal, you must constantly improve yourself."

Siach Sarfei Kodesh

Even before *Selichot*

Rabbi Levi Yitzchak of Berditchev, the great defender of the Jewish people, once spent the night at a roadside inn. He overheard a thief in the adjoining room telling his companion about his exploits the night before.

"Who is like Your people Israel!" exclaimed the *rebbe*. "It is still weeks until *Selichot*, yet this man has already begun to confess his sins."

Sifran shel Tzaddikim

Standing before God

The weekly portion of *Nitzavim* is always read on the *Shabbat* before Rosh Hashanah. It is a portion that makes us mindful of the approach of the Days of Awe. Its rousing opening words: "Today you are all standing before God your Lord" (Deuteronomy 29:9) summon us to prepare for the Day of Judgment by doing *teshuvah*.

Nitzavim foretells the time when the people of Israel will return to God and obey Him: "You will do everything that I am commanding you today; you and your children will repent with all your heart and with all your soul" (Deuteronomy 30:2).

Like a Lamp

The Baal Shem Tov uses a beautiful analogy to explain the concept of *teshuvah*: When you enter a dark room carrying a burning lamp, the darkness vanishes without leaving a trace. So too a *baal teshuvah*, a returnee to Torah observance, even though until now he lived in the total darkness of sin, when the light of Torah begins to shine in his soul, all the darkness is gone.

Sefer Baal Shem Tov, Nitzavim

2

ROSH HASHANAH: DAY OF JUDGMENT

Rosh Hashanah, the Jewish New Year, is observed on the first and second days of *Tishri*. It is called the *Yom Hadin*, the Day of Judgment, and marks the beginning of the Ten Days of *Teshuvah*, which culminate in Yom Kippur. It is a solemn season, a time of self-examination, when we reflect on our mistakes of the past and deeply regret our offenses against God and the hurts we may have inflicted on others. We want to return to our Father in Heaven, ask His forgiveness, and resolve to make amends, to improve our conduct, and not to repeat the errors of the past; in short, we do *teshuvah*. With infinite love, God welcomes our sincere repentance, and on Yom Kippur, the climactic close of the *Yamim Nora'im*, He grants us forgiveness, and in the Book of Life, seals us for life during the coming year.

The Torah describes Rosh Hashanah as "a sacred holiday for remembrance and sounding [of the ram's horn]" (Leviticus 23:24 and Numbers 29:1). Surprisingly, no explicit mention is made of the essential feature that on this day God sits in judgment and decides the fate of all mankind for the forthcoming year. The Torah conceals this fact in order to make us concerned about our wrongdoing all year long, so that we will not put off doing *teshuvah* until Rosh Hashanah.

The sages of the Talmud derive the judgment aspect of Rosh Hashanah from the scriptural verse in which Moses describes the Promised Land to the generation of the wilderness as "a land that is constantly under God your Lord's scrutiny; the eyes of God are on it at all times, from the beginning of the year until the end of the year" (Deuteronomy 11:12). Focusing on the phrase "from the beginning of the year until the end of the year," the sages expound, "On Rosh Hashanah – the beginning of the year – judgment is rendered concerning all events that will occur until its end." On this day, God determines "who will live and who will die, who by water and who by fire, who by sword, who by beast, who by famine, who by thirst . . . who will rest and who will wander, who will live in harmony and who will be harried, who will be degraded and who will be exalted" (*Mussaf* prayer for Rosh Hashanah).

(For a detailed discussion of all the laws pertaining to Rosh Hashanah and the sounding of the *shofar*, the *Shulchan Aruch, Orach Chaim* 581–603 and *Kitzur Shulchan Aruch* 128–130 are available in English translation.)

Meireishit: From the Beginning

The phrase "from the beginning of the year until the end of the year" also contains a fascinating allusion identifying Rosh Hashanah with the first day of *Tishri*. In the Torah, the word *meireishit*, "from the beginning," is written in an abbreviated form, מרשית, without an *alef*. If we rearrange the letters of מרשית, we may read it as מתשרי, *miTishri*, "from *Tishri*," a hint that the new year begins in *Tishri*.[1]

Day of New Beginnings

The month of *Tishri* occurs in the autumn of the year, at a time when the harvest of the previous year has been gathered in and we take stock in order to close the books. It is an appropriate time for reevaluating the past, planning the future, and making a fresh start.

Since the dawn of history, *Tishri* has been a time for new beginnings. According to Rabbi Eliezer, God created Adam on the first day of *Tishri* and thereby completed the creation of the universe. Furthermore, the Patriarchs, who were the first to introduce monotheism to a pagan world, were born in *Tishri*.

On Rosh Hashanah, God accorded special remembrance to Sarah, Rachel, and Hannah. They had been childless for many years, and on that day God took note of their plight and they conceived.

On Rosh Hashanah, Joseph was freed from prison, where he had been confined on false charges. His release marked the beginning of his rise to power and glory as the viceroy of Egypt.

On Rosh Hashanah, six months before the Exodus, the redemption of our ancestors in Egypt began with the end of their bondage and their harsh labor. In the month of *Nisan*, they were redeemed, and in *Tishri*, they will be redeemed in time to come.[2]

※※※※※※※※※※※※※

Day of Judgment

The Talmud tells us that on Rosh Hashanah three books are opened before God: one for the wholly virtuous, one for the out-and-out evildoers, and one for those in-between. The virtuous are immediately inscribed and sealed in the Book of Life; the out-and-out evildoers are immediately inscribed and sealed in the book of death. The fate of those in between is held in the balance from Rosh Hashanah until Yom Kippur. If they repent and are found worthy, they are inscribed for life; if they are found unworthy, they are inscribed for death.

Rosh Hashanah 16b

※※※※※※※※※※※※※

Inscribe Us in the Book of Life

Once, when Rosh Hashanah fell on a *Shabbat*, Rabbi Levi Yitzchak of Berditchev declared, "Master of the Universe, You forbid us to write on *Shabbat* except in order to save a life. So write us down in the Book of Life, since otherwise even You may not write on *Shabbat*."

Sefer Hachasidut

❈❈❈❈❈❈❈❈❈❈❈❈❈

Sign of the Zodiac

The zodiac sign for the month of *Tishri* is Libra, or the Scales, which is an indication that during that month the deeds of all mankind are weighed in the balance in order "to repay every man according to his ways, with the proper fruits of his deeds" (Jeremiah 17:10).

Kad Hakemach

❈❈❈❈❈❈❈❈❈❈❈❈❈

Divine Scales of Justice

Each individual has merits and sins. If one's merits exceed his sins, he is a *tzaddik*, a righteous man; if his sins exceed his merits, he is a *rasha*, an evildoer. If both are equal, he is a *beinoni*, an in-between person.

The same applies to each country. If the combined merits of its citizens exceed their sins, it is considered a righteous country. If their sins exceed their merits, it is a wicked nation.

And the same applies to the entire world.

If a person's sins exceed his merits, he dies immediately because of his wickedness. Likewise, if a nation's sins exceed its merits, it perishes instantly. The same holds true for all mankind; if their sins exceed their merits, they face immediate destruction. However, this judgment is not a quantitative one but a qualitative one. There are individual noble acts, which outbalance many sins. Conversely, there are individual sins, which outweigh many meritorious deeds. This determination is made through the perception of the all-knowing God, for He alone knows how to assess merits as opposed to sins.

Each person should therefore consider himself during the entire year half-meritorious and half-guilty. Likewise, he should regard the entire world as half-meritorious and half-guilty. If he commits one sin, he tips the scale of guilt for himself and for the entire world and causes its destruction. If he performs one *mitzvah*, he tips the scale of merit for himself and for the entire world and rescues himself and all mankind.

Hilchot Teshuvah, ch. 3[3]

Rosh Hashanah: A Day of Rejoicing

The dominant theme of Rosh Hashanah is that God, the King of the universe, is reviewing and judging the deeds of all mankind. Although this fateful connotation tends to cast the worshiper into a grave and somber mood, the *Yom Tov* should be celebrated in a festive spirit.

And so we read in the Book of Nehemiah that Ezra the Scribe, on the first Rosh Hashanah after his return from the Babylonian Exile, read from the Torah to a large assemblage gathered on the main square of Jerusalem. Listening to the words of the Torah, all the people began to weep. Ezra then exhorted them, "This day is holy to the Lord your God: you must not mourn or weep. Go, eat choice foods and drink sweet drinks, and send portions to whoever has nothing prepared, for the day is holy to our Lord. Do not be sad, for your rejoicing in God is the source of your strength" (Nehemiah 8:9, 10).

Confusing Satan

Why does Rosh Hashanah fall on the first day of *Tishri*? The reason is that Satan denounces Israel before the Heavenly Throne, charging, "Israel has sinned."

The Holy One, blessed is He, replies, "Do you have witnesses to support your allegations?"

Satan then is forced to say, "There is no one to testify on my behalf. Shall I bring the sun and the moon? I can find only the sun, since the moon is covered [on the first of the month]. The sun alone cannot testify, since it is written, 'A case can be valid only on the testimony of two witnesses' " (Deuteronomy 19:15). But when the moon becomes visible between Rosh Hashanah and Yom Kippur, and Satan now wants to bring his charges, the Holy One, blessed is He, tells him, "It's too late. My children have repented already."

Machzor Vitry

❋❋❋❋❋❋❋❋❋❋❋❋❋

Man's Sustenance

The Talmud in *Betzah* 16a relates, "A man's entire sustenance for the year is fixed in advance on Rosh Hashanah." Rabbi Yosef Yozel Hurwitz of Novardok, discussing this text, said, "If you don't believe this *Gemara*, and you exert yourself and make strenuous efforts to earn more and increase your income, you are just like a man riding on a train who, in his eagerness to reach his destination, is pushing against the wall of his compartment in order to make the train go faster."

❋❋❋❋❋❋❋❋❋❋❋❋❋

Rosh Hashanah Greetings

On the first night of Rosh Hashanah after the *Maariv* (evening) service, we wish one another *Leshanah tovah tikateiv vetechateim*, "May you be inscribed and sealed for a good year."

✹✹✹✹✹✹✹✹✹✹✹✹✹

Apple Dipped in Honey

After the *Kiddush* of the evening meal of Rosh Hashanah, it is customary to eat a sweet apple dipped in honey. The *berachah* over the fruit of the tree is recited, and after eating of the fruit we say, "May it be Your will that You inaugurate for us a good and sweet year."

A pomegranate – a fruit that is full of seeds – is eaten, accompanied by the prayer that God may multiply the merits of our good deeds. Headmeat, preferably of a ram, to commemorate the Binding of Isaac, or fish heads are eaten, and the wish is expressed that "we may be the head and not the tail."

Minhagei Maharil

✹✹✹✹✹✹✹✹✹✹✹✹✹

Yoma Arichta: One Long Day

According to *Halachah*, the two days of Rosh Hashanah are considered a *yoma arichta*, one long day. This being so, how can we say the *berachah* of *Shehecheyanu* during the *Kiddush* on the eve of the second day?

The problem is solved by placing on the table a fruit that has not yet been eaten that season or by putting on a new garment. Normally,

when eating a new fruit or putting on a new garment, one would
have to say the *berachah* of *Shehecheyanu*. In this instance, we say the
Shehecheyanu during the *Kiddush* or when lighting the candles but have
in mind the new fruit or the new garment as well. If a new fruit or a
new garment is not available, the *Shehecheyanu* should nevertheless be
recited.

Shulchan Aruch, Orach Chaim 601:2

❋❋❋❋❋❋❋❋❋❋❋❋❋

The King

It happened one year that Rabbi Aharon of Karlin led the *Shacharit*
(morning) prayer on Rosh Hashanah. When he intoned the opening
word, *Hamelech,* "The King," he suddenly trembled, his voice broke,
and he fainted. When he recovered, he explained that he had been
reminded of an incident that is related in the Talmud (*Gittin* 56a): after
the Roman legions had laid siege to Jerusalem for three years, Rabbi
Yochanan ben Zakkai appeared before Vespasian, commander of the
Roman forces, and said to him, "Peace unto you, O King." Replied
Vespasian, "You deserve the death penalty. For if I am a king, why
have you not come to me until now?" Therefore, continued Rabbi
Aharon, when I began to sing *Hamelech,* "The King," I was overcome
with awe, for God is a King, and I have not come before Him until now
in *teshuvah.*

Seder Hadorot Hechadash

❋❋❋❋❋❋❋❋❋❋❋❋❋

Psalm 130

Many communities recite Psalm 130, "Out of the depths I call You, O
God" throughout the Ten Days of Repentance. The psalm is emi-

nently fitting for this period because it is a plea to God for mercy and forgiveness. Following are several commentaries on Psalm 130.

Out of the depths I call You, O God (Psalm 130:1).

Malbim: Out of the depths I call You—why is the word "depths" written in the plural? A person may be well off materially, but spiritually at a very low ebb. We supplicate God out of the depths, because we are depressed both spiritually and physically.

Out of the depths I call You, O God (Psalm 130:1).

Rabbi Yerachmiel of Pshis'cha explained the plural form of "depths," telling the following parable: A traveler had lost his way in the desert and was left without food or water. After wandering about for days, he found a container of food, but to his great disappointment, it was empty.

Soon thereafter he met another traveler. With renewed hope, he approached the man and begged him for food. The traveler, taking him for a robber, turned his horse around and prepared to ride off. The wanderer fainted. This second disappointment was too much for him to bear; there was no one else to whom he could turn. The rider noticed his misery and revived and fed him.

Said the *rebbe*, "When we appeal to God, we should be impelled by two depths: the depth of remorse for our transgressions and the depth of our recognition that God is the only Source of our help."

Tiferet haYehudi

My Lord, listen to my voice, let Your ears be attentive to my cry for mercy (Psalm 130:2).

My Lord, listen to my voice—A person who is in a tranquil frame of mind can put his prayers into words. But when he is overcome with anguish, he utters a wordless cry to God: "Listen to my voice."

Pri Tzaddik

I yearn for my Lord, among those longing for the dawn, those longing for the dawn (Psalm 130:6).

Redak: I yearn for my Lord, among those longing for the dawn–I am not hoping for a redemption that is vague and uncertain. My hope is based on certainty; I am like those who are longing for the dawn that is sure to come.

Yours is the power to forgive, so that You may be feared (Psalm 130:4).

Rabbi Mordechai of Lechovitz: A man whose sins have not been forgiven will find that his transgressions form an impenetrable barrier that separates him from God. But when his sins have been pardoned, this barrier is removed so that he can come closer to God and understand what it means to be in awe of God.

When God forgives us, He removes the wall that separates us from Him and enables us to be in awe of Him.

Or Yesharim

✹✹✹✹✹✹✹✹✹✹✹✹✹✹

Faith Is the Answer

In the repetition of the *Shemoneh Esrei (Amidah)* of *Shacharit*, we chant: "His concealment is uprightness; His advice is faith. His accomplishment is truth."

Commented Rabbi Baruch of Mizhbozh:

"*His concealment is uprightness*–the fairness of God's behavior is hidden from man, who cannot understand how God rules the world;

His advice is–the only solution is,

faith–to believe that

His accomplishment is truth–that His deeds are fair and upright."

✹✹✹✹✹✹✹✹✹✹✹✹✹✹

Why Does God Hide Himself?

Rabbi Uziel Meisels expounded: *His concealment is uprightness*–God hides Himself from man, but He does so for a very good reason. If God displayed His mighty miracles for everyone to see, it would not take an act of faith to recognize Him, and a believer would not be rewarded for unquestioning belief.

His advice is faith – but God conceals His powerful deeds, making it appear as though events can be attributed to natural causes, luck, or an accident. In so doing, He offers us the free choice to believe in chance and materialism or to see God as the Prime Mover of history and of all that happens in the universe, so that He can reward us for having faith in Him.

Tiferet Uziel

❋❋❋❋❋❋❋❋❋❋❋❋❋

Hidden Spark

The Chidushei Harym explained the words in the Rosh Hashanah hymn: "Give praise to the One Who tests hearts on the day of judgment; to the One Who reveals the depths in judgment."

Deep in the heart of every Jew, yes, even of the most estranged among them, there is a spark of Jewishness that has remained pure and perfect. On Rosh Hashanah, when life is renewed, this spark is reawakened and invigorated. This, then, is the meaning of the words, "To the One who reveals the depths in judgment": on the Day of Judgment, when God tests our hearts, this deeply hidden Jewish spark is ignited and revealed.

Siach Sarfei Kodesh

❋❋❋❋❋❋❋❋❋❋❋❋❋

Why Don't We Recite *Hallel*?

Hallel, the Psalms of Praise we recite on every *Rosh Chodesh* and *Yom Tov*, is not said on Rosh Hashanah. Why is it omitted?

The Talmud relates that the ministering angels said to the Holy One, blessed is He, "Master of the universe, why does Israel not sing hymns of praise before You on Rosh Hashanah and Yom Kippur?" Said He to them, "Can the King sit on the throne of judgment with the books of life and death open before Him, and Israel sing songs of praise?"

Rosh Hashanah 32b

✹✹✹✹✹✹✹✹✹✹✹✹✹

Sounding of the *Shofar*

The *Midrash*, quoting Rabbi Yehoshua ben Korchah, says the *shofar* was created specifically for the good of Israel.

It was with the blowing of the *shofar* that the Torah was given to Israel, as it is stated, "The sound of the *shofar* grew louder and louder" (Exodus 19:19).

With the blowing of the *shofar*, the wall of Jericho fell down, as it is written, "When the people heard the sound of the *shofar* . . . the wall collapsed" (Joshua 6:20).

The blowing of the *shofar* will proclaim the coming of *Mashiach*, as it is written, "And the Lord will manifest Himself to them [Israel] and His arrow will flash like lightning; My Lord God will sound the *shofar* . . ." (Zechariah 9:14).

It is the *shofar* that the Holy One, blessed is He, will blow when He gathers in the exiles, as it is stated, "And in that day He will blow on the great *shofar*; and the strayed who are in the land of Assyria and the expelled who are in the land of Egypt will come and worship the Lord on the holy mountain, in Jerusalem" (Isaiah 27:13).

And so it is written, "Cry with a full throat, without restraint; raise your voice like a *shofar*!" (Isaiah 58:1).

Tanna deBei Eliyahu Zutta 22

✹✹✹✹✹✹✹✹✹✹✹✹✹

Why Do We Blow the *Shofar*?

The Torah commands us to sound the *shofar* on Rosh Hashanah, stating, without giving a reason, "It shall be a day of the sounding of the ram's horn" (Numbers 29:1).

And it is written, "Blow the *shofar* at the moon's renewal, at the time appointed for our festive day. Because it is a decree for Israel, a judgment day for the God of Jacob" (Psalm 81:4–5).

In the Talmud we read: Why do we sound the horn of a ram? Because the Holy One, blessed is He, said: Blow me a ram's horn that I may remember for you the binding of Isaac, the son of Abraham, and I shall consider it as though you bound yourselves before Me (*Rosh Hashanah* 16a).

❊❊❊❊❊❊❊❊❊❊❊❊❊

Wake Up from Your Sleep!

The Rambam offers the following rationale for the *mitzvah* of blowing the *shofar*: Although the blowing of the *shofar* is a biblical decree [and must therefore be observed whether or not you know the reason for it], there is an allusion in it. It tells you: Wake up from your sleep, you sleepers! Arise from your slumber, you slumberers! Examine your deeds! Return to God! Remember your creator! Those of you who forget the truth in the futilities of the times and spend all year in vanity and emptiness, look into your soul, improve your ways and your deeds. Let each of you abandon his evil ways and his immoral thoughts.

Hilchot Teshuvah 3:4

❊❊❊❊❊❊❊❊❊❊❊❊❊

To Confound Satan

The Talmud (*Rosh Hashanah* 16b) states that we blow the *shofar* "in order to confuse Satan, the Accuser."

Rashi explains that when the Accuser hears the sounds of the *shofar* and realizes with how much love Israel is performing this *mitzvah*, he becomes dumbfounded, unable to denounce them.

Rabbi Pinchas Horowitz comments that according to the Talmud (*Yoma* 86a), when Israel returns to God out of love, all their sins are transformed into merits. Continues Rabbi Pinchas: The main purpose of blowing the *shofar* is to arouse the people to *teshuvah*. When Satan sees Israel's great devotion to the *mitzvah* of *shofar*, he understands that their *teshuvah* is done out of love. He becomes confused but realizes that all the failings of which he is about to accuse Israel will be turned into merits, and the more faults he finds, the greater will be their merit. Therefore, when Satan hears the sounding of the *shofar*, he is speechless.

✶✕✶✕✶✕✶✕✶✕✶✕✶✕✶

A Broken Heart

One year, the Baal Shem Tov appointed his disciple Rabbi Zev Kitzes as the caller of the *shofar* sounds on Rosh Hashanah and asked him to learn the kabbalistic meanings behind those sounds. Reb Zev immersed himself in studying the mystic thoughts and wrote them down on a slip of paper. When it was time to call the *shofar* tones, he searched everywhere for the slip of paper but it was gone. He tried to remember the profound meanings, but his mind went completely blank. Heartbroken and with tearful eyes, he called the sounds, without thinking of any of the mystic meanings behind them.

After the service, the Baal Shem Tov said to him, "In the Palace of the King there are many rooms, and the keys to the rooms are the mystic thoughts we think when we perform a *mitzvah*. But all mystic thoughts in the world are nothing compared to a broken heart."

Or Yesharim

❊❊❊❊❊❊❊❊❊❊❊❊❊

Mitzvah of Hearing the *Shofar*

The one who blows the *shofar* recites the blessings:

"Blessed are You, Lord our God, King of the universe, who has sanctified us with His *mitzvot* and commanded us to hear the sound of the *shofar*."

"Blessed are You, Lord our God, King of the universe, who has kept us alive, sustained us, and brought us to this season."

Rabbi Yisrael of Chortkov comments: Prayer is something very personal. Every person prays with an individual degree of intensity, concentration, and emotion that is different from his fellow's. This opens the door to arrogance and pride, since a man might haughtily say, "I grasp the deeper meaning of this prayer," or "I pray with a fervor that has the spirituality of angels."

We must remember that the blessing over the *shofar* reads, "Who has commanded us to *hear* the sound of the *shofar*." The *mitzvah* of *shofar* is not fulfilled with sounding the *shofar* but with *hearing* it, and everyone, old and young, rich and poor, hears the same blasts. There is no envy or rivalry, no pride or snobbery. The *shofar* unites the Jewish nation.

Ginzei Yisrael

❊❊❊❊❊❊❊❊❊❊❊❊❊

Saved by the *Mitzvah* of Blowing the *Shofar*

The story is told that on one Rosh Hashanah, Rabbi Elazar Rokeach of Amsterdam was aboard ship, sailing to *Eretz Yisrael*. At night, a storm blew up, the ship sprang a leak, and the water started pouring in. While the passengers began bailing water feverishly, Rabbi Elazar stayed engrossed in prayer and meditation. When it became apparent that the ship was about to go down, someone warned the rabbi of the impending danger. "If so," replied the rabbi, "let us prepare to sound the *shofar* at dawn." At the first ray of sunlight, the rabbi blew the *shofar*. Immediately the storm subsided, and the damage could be repaired.

When Rabbi Simchah Bunam of Pshis'cha heard this story, he commented: Rabbi Elazar did not blow the *shofar* to save himself. Not at all. Rather, when he heard of the mortal danger that confronted them, he wanted to perform the *mitzvah* of blowing the *shofar* one last time before he died. It was the merit of this *mitzvah* that saved him and the other passengers from certain death.

Simchat Yisrael

✶✶✶✶✶✶✶✶✶✶✶✶✶✶

Torah Reading on Rosh Hashanah

On the two days of Rosh Hashanah, the Torah reading is from Genesis, chapters 21 and 22, which tell the story of the *Akeidah*, the Binding of Isaac. The reading of the first day begins with the birth of Isaac, because it was on Rosh Hashanah that his mother Sarah was remembered by God, and she conceived.

The *haftarah* of the first day is read from the first chapter of 1 Samuel, which relates the birth of the prophet Samuel, whose mother, Hannah, like Sarah, was remembered by God on Rosh Hashanah.

On the second day of Rosh Hashanah, we read the *Akeidah*, one of the major themes of Rosh Hashanah, to evoke Abraham's act of supreme self-sacrifice, in the hope that it may stand us in good stead as we are being judged. For the *haftarah*, we read the prophecy of Israel's ultimate redemption, as it is proclaimed in the thirty-first chapter of Jeremiah, which contains the stirring verses:

Thus says the Lord:
A cry is heard in Ramah—
Wailing, bitter weeping—
Rachel weeping for her children.
She refuses to be comforted
For her children, who are gone.
Thus says the Lord:
Restrain your voice from weeping,
Your eyes from shedding tears;
For there is a reward for your labor, says the Lord:
They shall return from the enemy's land.
And there is hope for your future, says the Lord:
Your children shall return to their country.
Truly, Ephraim is a dear son to Me,
A child that is dandled!
Whenever I speak of him,
My thoughts would dwell on him still.
That is why My heart yearns for him;
I will surely have compassion on him, says the Lord.

Jeremiah 31:14–19

✳✳✳✳✳✳✳✳✳✳✳✳✳✳

He Refused to Blow the *Shofar*

It happened one Rosh Hashanah that Rabbi Levi Yitzchak of Berditchev mounted the *bimah* (central podium). He raised the *shofar* to his lips preparing to blow but then placed it back on the reader's lectern and said in a defiant tone of voice, "Master of the universe, do You think that I am going to blow for You? Let the leader of the evil empire that oppresses us with its harsh decrees blow for You! Let Ivan blow the *shofar!*"

After a brief pause, speaking softly, the *rebbe* continued, "But dear

God, I cannot help myself. Since I love You so ardently, I will set aside
my will in favor of Your will."

Migedolei Hachasidut

※※※※※※※※※※※※※※

Sounds of the *Shofar*

The Torah describes Rosh Hashanah as *Yom Teruah*, a day of the
sounding of the [ram's] horn. Thus, *teruah* is the primary sound, and it
is always preceded and followed by *tekiah*, a long, clear blast. The
mitzvah requires that three sets of *tekiah–teruah–tekiah* be sounded.

Concerning the *teruah* sound, uncertainty arose whether it is a
moaning sound, consisting of three short, broken blasts, called *shevarim*;
or a sobbing sound, consisting of nine very short staccato blasts, which
we call *teruah*; or a combination of the two: *shevarim–teruah*.

In order to satisfy all three alternatives, we blow three series of
tekiah–shevarim–tekiah, three series of *tekiah–teruah–tekiah*, and three series of *tekiah–shevarim/teruah–tekiah* – a total of thirty blasts, which are
blown after the Torah reading. In addition, thirty more blasts are
sounded during the *Shemoneh Esrei (Amidah)* of *Mussaf*. It is customary to
blow another forty sounds after *Mussaf* to complete a total of one
hundred sounds. The final sound is a *tekiah gedolah*, a long, drawn-out
tekiah, which is reminiscent of the long blast of the *shofar* that signaled
the end of God's revelation on Sinai: "When the ram's horn sounds a
long blast, they will be allowed to go up the mountain" (Exodus
19:13).

※※※※※※※※※※※※※※

Tekiah–Shevarim–Teruah–Tekiah

Rabbi Aharon II of Karlin offered the following poignant interpretation of the various sounds. He said, "God created man upright and

flawless. Man, however, through his sins, became warped and twisted. But by returning to God in *teshuvah*, he is straightened out again."

This thought is reflected in the sounds of the *shofar: tekiah–shevarim–teruah–tekiah*. The first *tekiah*, a straight, clear sound, represents man's original rectitude and virtue. The broken *shevarim* sound is indicative of the spiritual breakdown that comes as a result of his sinning. This is followed by the sobbing *teruah* sound, which mirrors his brokenheartedness, inner turmoil, and deep remorse, the forerunners of repentance. The culmination is reached in the steady tone of the final *tekiah*, which signifies the inner tranquillity of the *baal teshuvah* whose missteps have been forgiven.

Bet Aharon

❈❈❈❈❈❈❈❈❈❈❈❈❈

Secret Code

You can compare the sounds of the *shofar* with a secret code that two friends are using in order to prevent outsiders from reading their correspondence. In the same way, on Rosh Hashanah, when we are on trial, God does not want Satan the Accuser to know our requests. He therefore devised for us the secret code of the *shofar* sounds, which only He can decipher and understand.

Tiferet Uziel

❈❈❈❈❈❈❈❈❈❈❈❈❈

Malchuyot, Zichronot, Shofarot

In the *Mussaf Shemoneh Esrei (Amidah)* of Rosh Hashanah, three special sections have been inserted, which are devoted to the main themes of the day. They are *Malchuyot* (God is King), *Zichronot* (God remembers and judges), and *Shofarot* (the *shofar*). In the section of *Malcuyot*, we accept God as our sovereign King and as Ruler of the entire universe. In the section of *Zichronot*, we affirm our belief in divine providence, that all of man's deeds are remembered by God and that man is rewarded or punished according to his actions; furthermore, we ask God to remember the act of supreme self-sacrifice of the *Akeidah*, when Abraham bound his son Isaac on the altar in unquestioning obedience to God's command. In the section of *Shofarot*, we relive the Giving of the Torah on Mount Sinai, which occurred amidst thunder and lightning and powerful blasts of the *shofar*, and we anticipate the final redemption and the coming of *Mashiach*, when "the Lord God will blow the *shofar*" (Zechariah 9:14).

Each of the three sections is composed of an introduction followed by ten scriptural verses that express the central idea of the section: three of the verses are from the Torah, three from the Writings, three from the Prophets, and a concluding verse, again from the Torah. Each section concludes with a paragraph that summarizes the theme and ends with a *berachah*.

In the *chazzan*'s repetition of the *Shemoneh Esrei* (*Amidah*), the *shofar* is blown at the end of the each of the three sections.

❈❈❈❈❈❈❈❈❈❈❈❈❈

Accept God as Your Master

The Holy One, blessed is He, said, "Recite the *Malchuyot* in order to make Me the Sovereign over you" (*Rosh Hashanah* 16a).

Rabbi Eliyahu Lapian elaborates on this: "The emphasis in this phrase is on the words 'over you.' A man may proclaim God the Ruler over all the upper and nether worlds, including the universe and the entire earth, yet he will fail to make Him his own personal Master. It is for this reason that God says, 'Make Me the Sovereign *over you*,' meaning, 'Don't forget to enthrone Me also as King over yourself.' "

Lev Eliyahu

✳✳✳✳✳✳✳✳✳✳✳✳✳

Avinu Malkeinu/Our Father, Our King

During the Ten Days of Repentance, beginning with Rosh Hashanah and ending with Yom Kippur, the *Avinu Malkeinu* prayer, comprised of numerous requests for human wants, is recited twice a day, after the *Shemoneh Esrei* of *Shacharit* and of *Minchah*. On *Shabbat*, however, it is omitted.

The Talmud (*Taanit* 25b) relates how the prayer originated. One year a severe drought ravaged *Eretz Yisrael*, and despite all fervent prayers, not a drop of rain fell. Then Rabbi Akiva approached the *amud* (*chazzan*'s lectern) and prayed, "*Avinu Malkeinu*, our Father, our King, we have sinned before You. Our Father, our King, have compassion on us." Immediately it began to rain.

When the sages saw that this prayer formula, beginning with *Avinu Malkeinu*, was answered, they added other requests as the need arose, and they ordained that these verses be recited during the Ten Days of Penitence.

Siddur Rashi 180

✳✳✳✳✳✳✳✳✳✳✳✳✳

Treat Us with Charity

In many congregations, the entire prayer *Avinu Malkeinu* is recited responsively, except for the last verse, which is said quietly. This verse reads: Our Father, our King, be gracious with us and answer us, though we have no worthy deeds; treat us with charity and kindness, and save us.

Why are all the verses but the last said aloud, whereas the last is said in an undertone?

The *Maggid* of Dubna explains it with an apt parable: The keeper of a small shop went on a buying trip to a large wholesale house in the big city. Entering the huge warehouse, he loudly announced the order he was placing: "I need one hundred yards of velvet, two hundred yards of pure silk, one hundred yards of wool, and an order of buttons and thread." Immediately the entire order was filled and neatly packed in boxes. When the invoice was presented, the shopkeeper quietly whispered into the merchant's ear, "Sir, I don't have a penny to my name right now. Would you take a promissory note?"

We, too, approach God loudly, asking Him to fulfill our personal requests for life, good health, prosperity, redemption, salvation, and so on. However, after we finish loudly reading the list of our wants, we quietly and in hushed tones add, "Be gracious with us and answer us," for we are penniless; "treat us with charity and kindness," and please accept our promissory note.

Ohel Yaakov

Remembering and Forgetting

Rabbi Yisrael of Rizhin expounded on the verse in the *Mussaf* liturgy, "For You remember all forgotten things, and there is no forgetfulness before Your Seat of Glory."

He asked, Why does this phrase stress the obvious fact that the Creator has a good memory and does not forget anything?

His answer: The words "You remember all forgotten things" come to tell you that God remembers those things that man forgets. If one performed *mitzvot* and good deeds but forgets them, expecting no reward, then God remembers those forgotten things. Conversely, if one sins but forgets the transgressions and does not repent, then God remembers also those forgotten things.

Simchat Yisrael

❋❋❋❋❋❋❋❋❋❋❋❋❋

Akeidah

May You remember the Binding that our father Abraham performed on his son Isaac . . . (from the *Mussaf* prayer).

Why does the *Akeidah*, the story of the Binding of Isaac, hold such preeminence in Jewish thought, literature, and liturgy? Have not thousands of Jewish parents throughout Jewish history chosen a martyr's death for their children rather than see them abandon their faith?

Each new concept and ideology has a forerunner, a pioneer who breaks a new trail for others to follow. Cain was the first murderer in history; Nimrod introduced the idea of idol worship into the world. Just as evil is initiated by one pioneer of evil, so is a movement for good launched by one pioneer of virtue. Abraham was the trailblazer of the belief in God, paving the way for millions of believers to follow in his footsteps. Abraham's spirit of unquestioning faith and self-sacrifice, manifest in the *Akeidah*, was ingrained in all future generations to become an innate character trait, a genetic feature as it were, of the Jewish people. This fact makes the *Akeidah* an event of great overriding significance.

Pardes Yosef

❋❋❋❋❋❋❋❋❋❋❋❋❋

Vision of the Golden Calf

Abraham then looked up and saw a ram after it had been caught by its horns in the thicket (Genesis 22:13).

The sages of the *Midrash* comment that Abraham saw in a prophetic
vision that someday the people of Israel would worship the Golden
Calf. He pleaded that when this fateful day arrived, God would recall
the self-renouncing dedication he and his son Isaac had demonstrated at
the *Akeidah* and have mercy on Israel. The ram that was caught in the
thicket is symbolic of Israel's being caught in the thicket of the sin of
the Golden Calf.

Rabbi Shimshon of Ostropole[4] discovered a fascinating allusion to
that thought. In the Hebrew alphabet, the letters of the word סבך,
s'vach, thicket, are followed by the letters of עגל, *eigel*, calf (the *samach* is
followed by the *ayin*, the *beit* by the *gimel*, and the *kaf* by a *lamed*), an
indication that Abraham saw the people of Israel caught in the thicket
of the Golden Calf.

※※※※※※※※※※※※※※

The Wicked and the Good

Rabbi Tzvi of Ziditchov explained the verse in the Rosh Hashanah
hymn "And All Believe," which reads, "He is good and He does good
to the wicked and the good." He remarked that the text should be
reversed. It should say God does good to the good and to the wicked.
Why are the wicked mentioned before the good?

He answered, God does good to those unassuming people who in
their humility think that they are wicked, and He does good even to
those arrogant people who consider themselves to be at the pinnacle of
virtue and perfection.

Sifran shel Tzaddikim

※※※※※※※※※※※※※※

Good to All

Rabbi Simchah Bunam of Pshis'cha explained the phrase "He is good
to the wicked and the good" as follows: "God is good to those who are

sometimes wicked and sometimes good; in other words, He is good to all of us."

Kol Simchah

❊❊❊❊❊❊❊❊❊❊❊❊❊

Language of Heaven

In the *Shemoneh Esrei (Amidah)* of Rosh Hashanah, we say, "For You, O God, are truthful and Your word is truthful." This comes to tell us: In heaven there is only truth, and truth is the language of heaven. Thus, the prayer of a man who is insincere is not accepted. For this man's language, the language of falsehood, is not understood in heaven.

Lev Eliyahu

❊❊❊❊❊❊❊❊❊❊❊❊❊

Like a Fly

Said Rabbi Eliyahu Lapian, "Our sages compare the evil inclination to a fly. What does this mean? Just like a fly will leave a place that is clean and flit to an area that is soiled, so will the evil inclination attach itself firmly to a person who is contaminated by sin."

Lev Eliyahu

❊❊❊❊❊❊❊❊❊❊❊❊❊

Story of Rabbi Amnon

One of the best-known *piyyutim* (liturgical compositions) of Rosh Hashanah and Yom Kippur is the *Unetanneh Tokef*, a moving description of God sitting in judgment of all mankind. It was written about a thousand years ago by Rabbi Amnon of Mainz. The following story related in *Or Zarua* forms the background of the prayer.

Rabbi Amnon of Mainz was one of the great scholars of his generation, a wealthy man and a descendant of a prominent family. He was also a handsome man. The lords and the bishop demanded that he convert to their religion, but he paid no attention to them. Although they urged him day in and day out, he would not listen. One day, after the bishop again tried to prevail upon him, Rabbi Amnon said, "I wish to take counsel and to reflect on this matter for three days." He said this only to put the bishop off.

As soon as the rabbi left the bishop, he regretted having allowed himself to utter a word of doubt, as though he needed to take counsel whether to deny the Living God.

So he went home and would neither eat or drink, until he fell ill. All his friends and relatives came to console him, but he refused to be comforted and said, "I will go down to the grave mourning because of what I have said." He was ashamed at having given the impression that he even considered abandoning his God.

On that third day, the bishop sent for the deeply troubled and distraught Rabbi Amnon, who said, "I will not go." His tormentor continued to send many more and higher-ranking dignitaries, but Rabbi Amnon still refused to go to the bishop. Thereupon the bishop ordered Rabbi Amnon forcibly brought before him. "What is this, Amnon?" the bishop said. "Why did you not come to answer me at the end of the time you yourself set to think it over?"

Rabbi Amnon replied, "I will pronounce my own sentence. Let the tongue that spoke falsely to you be cut out," for Rabbi Amnon wanted to sanctify God because of the way he had spoken.

The bishop answered, "No, I will not have your tongue cut out, for it spoke well. But I will instead chop off the feet that did not come to me at the time you set, and the rest of your body I will punish also."

At the tyrant's command, they chopped off Rabbi Amnon's hands and feet. As each limb was cut off, they asked, "Will you be converted?" Each time he answered, "No." When they finished tormenting him, the evil man ordered Rabbi Amnon to be sent home together with his severed limbs at his side. He was appropriately called Rabbi Amnon [the faithful one, from the word *emunah*, faith], for he had faith in the Living God and willingly suffered extreme anguish for the sake of his belief.

When Rosh Hashanah arrived a few days later, Rabbi Amnon asked to be carried to the synagogue and his stretcher set down next to the *chazzan*. When the *chazzan* reached the *Kedushah* (Sanctification), Rabbi Amnon said to him, "Stop, and I will sanctify the Name of God." Then he cried in a loud voice, "And so the *Kedushah* prayer shall ascend to You." He continued with *Unetanneh tokef kedushat hayom*, "Now let us relate the power of this day's holiness. It is true that You alone are the One who judges, proves, knows, and bears witness." When he finished, his soul left his pain-wracked body, for God had taken him. To him applies the verse "How abundant is the good that You have in store for those who fear You" (Psalm 31:20).

Three days after Rabbi Amnon's death, he appeared in a dream to Rabbi Kalonymos ben Rabbi Meshullam, taught him the hymn prayer *Unetanneh Tokef*, and ordered him to send it to all parts of Jewry so that he would be remembered by it. Rabbi Kalonymos did so, and the hymn was inserted as an integral part of the Rosh Hashanah and Yom Kippur liturgy.

Or Zarua, Hilchot Rosh Hashanah

꧁꧂꧁꧂꧁꧂꧁꧂꧁꧂꧁꧂

Fear of the Angels

Rabbi Shalom Rokeach of Belz commented on the phrase in the hymn *Unetanneh Tokef*, "The great *shofar* will be sounded . . . and angels will hasten; a trembling and terror will seize them."

Asked Rabbi Shalom, "Why are the angels terror stricken on Rosh Hashanah? What are they afraid of? What sin have they committed?"

The Belzer *rebbe* replied, "God gave the angels the task to defend the Jewish people and find excuses for their misdeeds. On Rosh

Hashanah the angels are being judged whether or not they scrupulously fulfilled their assignment. This is the reason for their anxiety."

Dover Shalom

※⊗※⊗※⊗※⊗※⊗※⊗※

Tashlich

It is a universally accepted custom to recite the *Tashlich* after the *Minchah* service. It is said near a river, a spring, a lake, or the sea. We recite the last three verses of Micah and symbolically cast our sins into the water, as it is written, "You will cast all their sins into the depths of the sea" (Micah 7:19).

Reciting the *Tashlich* near a body of water recalls the *Akeidah*, the Binding of Isaac. According to the *Midrash*,[5] Satan tried to prevent Abraham from carrying out God's will and turned himself into a roaring river. Undaunted, Abraham and Isaac entered the raging waters, and when the water came up to their necks, Abraham cried out, "Deliver me, O God, for the waters have reached my neck" (Psalm 69:2). God rebuked the river, and they were saved.

Minhagei Maharil

※⊗※⊗※⊗※⊗※⊗※⊗※

Like Fish

It is customary to say the *Tashlich* near a river or lake where there are fish, because we are compared to "fish caught in a fatal net" (Ecclesiastes 9:12). The fish will remind us that we are enmeshed in the fatal net of judgment and death. That awareness will prompt us to do *teshuvah*.

Nagid Umetzaveh

※⊗※⊗※⊗※⊗※⊗※⊗※

Strategy of the Evil Inclination

The Baal Shem Tov told the following parable: A man asked a landlord for permission to live in his house. When he was turned down, he asked permission to knock a nail into the wall. This request was granted. He then hammered the nail into the wall but continued to dig up the foundation of the house until the place was a shambles. The *yetzer hara* (the evil inclination) behaves in the same fashion. If one allows it to enter and gain a small foothold, it will destroy one completely.

Siach Sarfei Kodesh

****

Smashing Your Ego

The Chidushei Harym commented on the verse "It shall be a day of *teruah*, 'blowing the horn' to you" (Numbers 29:1). The word *teruah* is related to the root *ra'a*, which means "to smash."[6] Bearing this in mind, we may translate "a day of *teruah* to you" as "a day on which you smash your 'you.' " In other words, Rosh Hashanah is a day on which you shatter your ego and your selfishness.

Siach Sarfei Kodesh

****

Eye of a Needle

During a discourse on the subject of *teshuvah*, Rabbi Simchah Bunam of Pshis'cha said, "The *Midrash* teaches that God exhorts us, 'My children, if you make an opening in your hearts for Me no bigger than the eye of a needle, then I will make an opening for you as wide as the gateway to the Sanctuary.' "[7]

The *rebbe* continued, "I say to you, this small opening in your heart that God is asking you to make should not be just a scratch on the surface; it should go through and through."

Siach Sarfei Kodesh

(The underlying thought of this *Midrash* is that if we make even only a small but sincere effort to return to God, He will receive us with open arms, and our modest endeavors will be crowned with undreamed-of success.)

※※※※※※※※※※※※※

Greatness of a *Baal Teshuvah's* Prayer

It happened one Rosh Hashanah that Rabbi Levi Yitzchak of Berditchev, the great advocate of the Jewish people, before uttering the *berachot* over the sounding of the *shofar* put down the *shofar* and waited. A long time passed, but the blowing of the *shofar* did not begin.

"*Rabbotai*, dear friends," explained the *rebbe*, "in the back row near the door there sits a Jew who lived all his life among Gentiles. He would dearly love to pray, but he does not know how. So he said, 'Dear God, You know all prayers, but I know only the twenty-two letters of the *alef-bet*. I am going to recite for You: *alef, bet, gimel, dalet* . . . and I ask You to combine the letters and make prayers out of them.'

"At this moment," Rabbi Levi Yitzchak concluded, "God is busy forming into prayers the letters this *tzaddik* has uttered. We must wait patiently."

Agadah uMachashavah beYahadut

※※※※※※※※※※※※※

Break Your Stubborn Heart

Rabbi Nachman of Bratzlav used the following parable to explain *teshuvah*, the central idea of Rosh Hashanah.

A king sent his son abroad to study the sciences of the world. After mastering all the sciences, the son returned home. The father, eager to test his son's wisdom, asked him to transport a large rock to the top of a mountain. Straining every muscle, the son arduously rolled the rock to the summit. Thereupon he proudly reported to his father that after laboring with all his might, he had managed to roll the rock to the peak. In response, the father shook his head and said, "For this I had to send you to the great universities? If you had broken up the rock into small pieces, you would have been able to carry it up effortlessly!"

It is the same with us. God wants us to lift up our hearts to Him, which are as rigid and heavy as a flinty rock. The only way we can do it is by shattering our hearts of stone and smashing them into small pieces through *teshuvah*.

Likutei Moharan

3

TEN DAYS OF
TESHUVAH

During the seven days between Rosh Hashanah and Yom Kippur, a serious mood of repentance takes hold, blended with optimism born of a newfound closeness to the Creator. The special insertions in the *Shemoneh Esrei* (*Amidah*), the prayer *Avinu Malkeinu* (our Father, our King), and *Selichot* (penitential prayers) are recited every day. Rabbi Mordechai Ashkenazi, in his halachic compendium known simply as the *Mordechai*, mentions that there were people who would take it upon themselves to fast during these days, eating only in the evenings.

The additional prayers evoke in us an awareness that our actions of the past year are being weighed on the heavenly scales of justice. One virtuous act can tilt the balance toward life. Mindful that "repentance, prayer, and charity remove the evil decree,"[1] we take the time to do serious soul-searching, which leads to *teshuvah*; we pray with more concentration and fervor; we increase our gifts to charity; and we show a kinder attitude toward our family and neighbors.

Fast of Gedalyah

The day after Rosh Hashanah, the third of *Tishri*, is *Tzom Gedalyah*, the Fast of Gedalyah. The fast, which is observed from daybreak until nightfall, commemorates the murder of Gedalyah ben Achikam on the third of *Tishri* in 423 B.C.E.

After the destruction of the First Temple in 423 B.C.E., King Nebuchadnezzar exiled the Jewish people to Babylonia. However, a small number of Jews, "the poorest in the land" (Jeremiah 40:7), remained in *Eretz Yisrael*. The Babylonian ruler appointed Gedalyah as governor of *Eretz Yisrael*, where he was assassinated by Yishmael ben Netanyah.[2] Because Gedalyah's death brought about the end of the last Jewish settlement in *Eretz Yisrael*, the day of his death was instituted as a public fast, for "the death of a *tzaddik* [righteous man] is equivalent to the destruction of the Bet Hamikdash."[3] The Fast of Gedalyah is mentioned by the prophet Zechariah, who calls it "the fast of the seventh month" (Zechariah 7:5 and 8:19).

✳✳✳✳✳✳✳✳✳✳✳✳✳✳✳

Shabbat Shuvah

The *Shabbat* before Yom Kippur is called *Shabbat Shuvah* or *Shabbat Teshuvah* (repentance) because its *haftarah* begins with the words *Shuvah Yisrael*, "Return, O Israel, to the Lord your God" (Hosea 14:2). Because of the serious message, it is customary that the rabbi or an outstanding member of the community is called up to read this *haftarah*.

It is the custom for the rabbi to deliver a *derashah* (sermon) on *Shabbat Shuvah*, which usually consists of a halachic discourse on a theme relating to the oncoming Yom Kippur and a homily that gently prods congregants to improve their ways and inspires them to do *teshuvah*.

✳✳✳✳✳✳✳✳✳✳✳✳✳✳✳

Sermon

When the great *tzaddik* Rabbi Yechezkel of Shiniava happened to be in the city of Ujhel, he was invited to deliver a sermon on *Shabbat*. Everyone came to listen to his *derashah*. Standing in front of the pulpit, Reb Yechezkel said, "*Rabboisai* [my masters], please listen to me. I once delivered a *derashah* in this very place, and my motives were not purely for the sake of heaven. It certainly is a grave sin to have other things in mind when you are addressing a congregation, and I want to do *teshuvah*. Our sages have said, 'The sure sign that your *teshuvah* is complete is when you have the opportunity to do the same transgression in the same place where you first committed it, and you avoid it' [*Yoma* 86b]. Therefore I have come to do *teshuvah* in this very place. And I ask the Holy One, blessed is He, to forgive me."

Deeply moved by the *rebbe*'s words, the people were aroused to examine their deeds and do *teshuvah*.

Mekor Chaim

Overt and Covert Satan

Rabbi Yosef Engel, who in 1906 became the rabbi of Cracow and who wrote many works on *Halachah* and Kabbalah, explained the *Gemara* in *Yoma* 20a, which states: The numerical value of the word *haSatan*, "the Satan," amounts to 364 (*hei* = 5, *sin* = 300, *tet* = 9, *nun* = 50). This is an indication that for 364 days of the year, Satan (the evil impulse) has the capacity to entice people, but on one day, Yom Kippur, he is powerless.

Rabbi Engel posed a question: Why does the *Gemara* compute the numeric value of *haSatan*, "*the* Satan" and include the article *ha*, "the," in the calculation? Why not simply "Satan"?

He answered: There are two kinds of Satan, or *yetzer hara* (evil impulse): the overt one, which openly seduces man to sin and fans the flames of his desire until he is unable to resist, and the covert *yetzer hara*, which cunningly conceals the sin, draping it in a robe of virtue. The covert *yetzer hara* tricks a person into thinking that he is not committing a sin at all, but rather that he is performing a *mitzvah*. This is the worst kind of *yetzer hara*; it is the source of all the hypocrisy and duplicity in history. By invoking the name of religion and ideology, millions of people have been wiped out. Everyone falls victim to this covert *yetzer hara*; it beguiles both the good and the bad, the individual and society. The *Gemara* says: haSatan, "*the*" Satan, because only the overt *yetzer hara*, the one that everyone recognizes, is the Satan that is powerless on Yom Kippur. The covert, insidious *yetzer hara* operates 365 days a year – even on Yom Kippur.

Otzerot Yosef

※✕※✕※✕※✕※✕※✕※✕※✕※✕※✕

Erev Yom Kippur: Eve of Yom Kippur

The day before Yom Kippur has the character of a semi-*Yom Tov*. It is a *mitzvah* to eat two festive meals on this day. Indeed, Rabbi Chiya said, "One who eats on *Erev* Yom Kippur is considered by the Torah as meritorious as if he fasted on both the ninth and the tenth of *Tishri*" (*Rosh Hashanah* 9a).

Charity is given liberally because the merit of charity protects one from evil decrees.

The *Kapparot*, the practice of waving a chicken around one's head, is an ancient custom dating back to the days of the *Geonim* (589–1038 C.E.). It is designed to make us aware that we are on trial and that we really deserve the fate of the chicken but that our repentance and good deeds can save us from this penalty. During the ceremony, in which others substitute money for the chicken, the appropriate verses are recited. The chicken or the money is then given to the poor.

After the conclusion of the *Shemoneh Esrei (Amidah)* of *Minchah*, the *Viduy* confession is said.

It is a widespread custom for parents to bless their children on *Erev*

Yom Kippur. It is the time to ask the forgiveness of people one has hurt and to forgive those who ask our forgiveness.

It is customary for men to immerse themselves in a *mikveh* on *Erev* Yom Kippur.

Orach Chaim 606:4; *Mishnah Berurah*, par. 17–18

❋❋❋❋❋❋❋❋❋❋❋❋

Twice as Much

Said Rabbi Aharon of Sadigora: "It is written in the *Gemara*: 'One who eats on *Erev* Yom Kippur the Torah considers as meritorious as if he fasted on the ninth and the tenth of *Tishri*' (*Rosh Hashanah* 9a).

"This proves that serving God through good deeds is twice as effective as serving Him spiritually. For if you do the *mitzvah* of eating on *Erev* Yom Kippur, it is considered as though you fasted both on the ninth and the tenth of *Tishri*–two days. But in matters of the spirit, such as studying and praying, one good thought never counts for two."

Kedushat Aharon

❋❋❋❋❋❋❋❋❋❋❋❋

How Can You Sit Down to Eat?

The Torah considers one who eats on *Erev* Yom Kippur as meritorious as if he fasted on the ninth and the tenth of *Tishri* (*Rosh Hashanah* 9a). Rabbi Elimelech of Lizhensk wondered: Why are the meals of *Erev* Yom Kippur considered as a form of fasting, as if you had afflicted yourself?

He replied: If you ponder the holiness of the upcoming Yom Kippur day, you are overwhelmed with awe. In that frame of mind, how can

you possibly indulge in eating? Can you think of a greater ordeal than
to sit down to a meal at a time like this?

Bet Rebbi

✳✳✳✳✳✳✳✳✳✳✳✳✳✳

Take Appetite Suppressant Pill before
Yom Kippur?

The following *she'eilah* (halachic question) was submitted to Rabbi
Mordechai Yaakov Breisch of Zurich, Switzerland, *Chelkat Yaakov*
2:58.[4]

Question: The doctors have developed a pill that, when taken in the
morning, prevents hunger pangs all day. Each capsule contains about
two hundred small time-release granules that desensitize hunger
feelings. Is it permitted to swallow such a capsule before Yom Kippur
so as not to suffer from hunger during the fast? Do we have to be
concerned that the Torah states, "You must afflict yourselves"?
(Leviticus 23:27).

Responsum: In my opinion, this is plainly permissible. Because the
capsule is taken before the onset of Yom Kippur and not on Yom
Kippur itself, it is comparable to eating all one can take before Yom
Kippur so that the time of digestion will last longer. As long as the food
has not been digested, you don't feel hungry. Would it enter anyone's
mind to prohibit this? The present case is analogous to this. The
capsule contains tiny granules. The outer shell dissolves in the digestive
juices of the stomach, releasing the small granules, which consecu-
tively counteract hunger feelings. The same happens with food. Some
foods digest faster than others. It certainly is not forbidden to eat foods
that are slow to digest. On the contrary, Rashi states (*Yoma* 81b),
"Prepare yourself on the ninth day of *Tishri* so that you will be able to
fast on the tenth (Yom Kippur)." And in *Rosh Hashanah* 9a, it says,

"The more you eat before Yom Kippur, the better." Care should be taken, however, to make certain that the capsule does not contain any forbidden ingredients.

✹✹✹✹✹✹✹✹✹✹✹✹✹

Immersion in the *Mikveh*

The Sochatchover *rebbe* offered the following explanation for immersing oneself in a *mikveh* on *Erev* Yom Kippur:

It is stated in *Yoma* 85b, "Just as a *mikveh* purifies the contaminated, so does the Holy One, blessed is He, purify Israel."

God set boundaries for all his creatures: fish cannot live on dry land, and land animals cannot survive in the sea.

Therefore, when one immerses himself in the water of a *mikveh* he is, as it were, shedding the shackles of his former self to become a totally new being. As one enters the water, he ceases to be the tainted person he was before immersion and is purified. In the same way, when the Jewish people do *teshuvah*, they tear themselves loose from their former state of sinfulness. They become attached to God and thereby are redeemed and cleansed from their sins.

Siftei Tzaddikim

✹✹✹✹✹✹✹✹✹✹✹✹✹

Seudah Mafseket

In the afternoon, following the *Minchah* service, the *Seudah Mafseket* (the meal before the fast) is eaten. It is a festive meal with solemn overtones, for it is an expression of joy over the divine forgiveness that is soon to be granted. Another reason for the feast is that we eat and drink in order to be physically strong enough to concentrate on our prayers and on self-examination while fasting on Yom Kippur.

The *Seudah Mafseket* should end before twilight, because the fast of Yom Kippur must begin while it is still daytime, on the ninth of *Tishri*. The fast is extended on the next day so that it ends after nightfall. It is the custom to wear a *kittel* (a white robe), which conveys a sense of purity, on Yom Kippur. Because the dead are clothed in a *kittel*, it reminds the wearer of his mortality, which tends to make him humble and contrite (*Orach Chaim* 610:1, 4).

❊❊❊❊❊❊❊❊❊❊❊❊❊

Best Deal

Rabbi Yosef Yozel of Novardok said: Our sages teach us (*Rosh Hashanah* 86b) that he who repents out of love has all his sins counted as *mitzvot*. So you see, *teshuvah* is the best possible deal one can make, because it turns all your losses into profits; your transgressions are converted into merits.

Madregat Ha'adam

4

YOM KIPPUR

Yom Kippur, the holiest day on the Jewish calendar, is the culmination of the Ten Days of *Teshuvah*, which begin with Rosh Hashanah. It was on this day, the tenth of *Tishri* of the year 2449 of Creation, that Moses came down from Mount Sinai bearing the second tablets, after God had forgiven Israel for the sin of worshiping the Golden Calf. This act of divine pardon marked the tenth of *Tishri* for all time as the Day of Atonement and reconciliation with God. It is the day on which God purifies us from all our errors, forgives our missteps, and turns His ear to our pleas. The Torah sums it up in the words, "And it shall be to you a law for all time: In the seventh month, on the tenth of the month, you shall afflict yourselves and not do any work, both the native born and the proselyte who joins you. For through this day He will atone for you, to cleanse you from all your sins; before God you shall cleanse yourselves" (Leviticus 16:30).

(For a comprehensive treatment of all the laws of Your Kippur, the *Shulchan Aruch, Orach Chaim* 604-624 and *Kitzur Shulchan Aruch* 131–133 are available in English translation.)

Five Afflictions of Yom Kippur

On Yom Kippur we must abstain from five forms of physical pleasure: eating and drinking, washing and bathing, applying lotions, wearing shoes containing leather, and having marital relations.[1] All work prohibitions that apply to *Shabbat* must be observed on Yom Kippur also. In fact, Yom Kippur is called *Shabbat Shabbaton*, a *Shabbat* of *Shabbats*. Eating or drinking a quantity greater than the size of a date is punishable by *karet* (premature death). Of course, in a case of *pikuach nefesh*, where fasting would present a potential threat to life, eating is clearly permitted.

The five afflictions correspond to the five books of the Torah, which we accept without allowing our physical pleasures to deter us from fulfilling its commandments; to the five senses, with which we keep the commandments or commit transgressions; and to the five services ordained for Yom Kippur: *Maariv, Shacharit, Mussaf, Minchah,* and *Ne'ilah.*

Teshuvot Maharil

By fasting on Yom Kippur and spending the day engrossed in prayer, we resemble angels, who have no natural functions and who continually sing hymns of praise to God.

Rabbi Samson Raphael Hirsch explains that by giving up the sensual pleasures of life and refraining from work on Yom Kippur, we are living for twenty-four hours as if we were dead. We are thereby affirming that this would be the fate we deserved if God had not granted us forgiveness for our past. Without God's gift of atonement, we would have forfeited both our right to live (symbolized by the five afflictions) and our right to create (symbolized by the work prohibition).

Hirsch, *Commentary on the Pentateuch*, Leviticus 23:27

Power of *Teshuvah*

The indispensable condition for attaining atonement is *teshuvah*, repentance. It is God's priceless gift to man, enabling him to rise after he has stumbled and fallen down, to wipe the slate clean and return to God after he has gone astray. *Teshuvah* is one of the fundamental concepts of Judaism; the sages of the Talmud tell us that *teshuvah* came into being even before the world was created.[2] The implication is that before Creation, God envisioned the possibility that man would commit evil and He provided in advance the remedy of *teshuvah*, by which man could be reconciled with his Creator.

Because *teshuvah* existed before the creation of the world, it is not subject to the rules and standards by which the world operates. The worldly rules dictate that every offense must be punished, every sinner must be penalized, and no transgression can be repaired without retribution and suffering. God in His great mercy granted us *teshuvah*, which transcends the rigid principles of law. He gave us Yom Kippur, a day on which we are purified from all our errors and our mistakes are forgiven.

The sages of the Talmud said that *teshuvah* is so magnificent, it has the potential of propelling the *baal teshuvah* to the immediate nearness of God, in fact, as close to God as the Heavenly Throne. Furthermore, they said, it brings healing to the entire world, and it advances the redemption (*Yoma* 86a,b).

✖✖✖✖✖✖✖✖✖✖✖✖✖✖✖✖

Teshuvah for Love and for Fear

The sages of the Talmud state that a person is motivated to do *teshuvah* by one of two reasons. The repentance may be induced either by fear of divine punishment (*teshuvah miyirah*) or by love of God and a desire to become attached to Him (*teshuvah me'ahavah*). The sages tell us that a person who repents out of fear has his intentional sins counted as errors, but he who does *teshuvah* out of love, which is the highest form of *teshuvah*, has his sins counted as virtues (*Yoma* 86b).

How can this be understood? Rabbi Eliyahu Dessler (1892–1953) in his work *Michtav Me'Eliyahu*, volume 2, page 80, explains that the person who today repents out of fear of divine punishment did not have this fear yesterday when he committed his transgression; otherwise, he would not have sinned willfully. Thus, he sinned only because he did not realize God's exaltedness. Therefore, in God's accounting, while the sin is not entirely wiped out, it is counted as unintentional.

The person who repents out of love recognizes the gravity of his wrongdoing and the depth of sinfulness to which he has sunk. As he contemplates that it is God Himself who in His mercy accepts his *teshuvah* and descends into the cesspool of his sin to cleanse him[3] and lift him out of the morass of his defilement, a feeling of passionate love of God wells up in his heart. The more he has sinned, the greater is his remorse and the more ardent is his attachment to God. Each sin, thus, becomes a powerful catapult that launches him to ever loftier spiritual heights, and God therefore considers every sin of his a virtue. He gains a closeness to God that only a *baal teshuvah* is capable of achieving. His nearness to God is unexcelled: "he ranks higher than even an accomplished *tzaddik*" (*Berachot* 43b).

The high esteem in which a *baal teshuvah* is held may also be explained by the fact that the *baal teshuvah* has experienced the satisfaction of forbidden appetites and lusts yet was repelled by them and overcame their captivating attraction; the *tzaddik* whose entire life was devoted to Torah never was exposed to the enticing taste of transgression. This is also the underlying thought of the following selection.

※※※※※※※※※※※※※※

Discovering the Straight Path

Rabbi Dov Ber of Mezritch, the Great *Maggid*, said, "A person who always walks on the straight path does not feel any enjoyment in it. He does not know there is a crooked path. But the person who has at first walked on the crooked path and then finds the straight route is elated with his discovery. In the same way, the *baal teshuvah* (returnee) appreciates righteousness more than the *tzaddik* who has never sinned."

Maggid Devarav LeYaakov

❊❊❊❊❊❊❊❊❊❊❊❊❊

God's Answer

Wisdom was asked; What shall be done to a sinner?
Wisdom replied: May misfortune pursue him (Proverbs 13:21).
Prophecy was asked: What shall be done to a sinner?
Prophecy replied: The sinner shall die (Ezekiel 18:4).
The Torah was asked: What shall be done to a sinner?
The Torah replied: Let him bring a sin offering.
God was asked: What shall be done to a sinner?
God replied: Let him do *teshuvah* and and he shall be forgiven.

Yalkut Shimoni, Tehillim Psalm 25, par. 702

❊❊❊❊❊❊❊❊❊❊❊❊❊

I'd Rather Not Die

Rabbi Shmelke of Nikolsburg once said: "If I had the choice I'd rather not die. For in the World-to-Come there are no *Yamim Nora'im*, no Days of Awe. And how can a Jewish soul exist without a Rosh Hashanah and a Yom Kippur? What good is life without *teshuvah*?"

Shemen Hatov

❊❊❊❊❊❊❊❊❊❊❊❊❊

Once in Seventy Years

Said Rabbi Yisrael Salanter[8] "If Yom Kippur, the day a person's sins are forgiven, would occur only once every seventy years, we would have reason to be overjoyed. How much more elated should we be, now that this holy day occurs every year."

Or Yisrael

❊❊❊❊❊❊❊❊❊❊❊❊❊

First Priority

Rabbi Yisrael of Koznitz said, If you want to return to God and do *teshuvah*, don't try to mend your mistakes. Instead, strive to distance yourself from your weaknesses. Begin by running away from the *yetzer hara* [evil impulse] that is pursuing you and do your best to serve God with love and awe.

Your situation may be compared with that of a wounded soldier who is being chased by the enemy. If he stopped to nurse his wounds, the enemy would catch up with him and slay him. He must run for his life until he is certain that he is safe from his pursuers. Only then can he attend to his injuries.

In the same way, a *baal teshuvah* must start out by distancing himself from his wrongdoings and from the conditions and the environment that breed sin. Later, when he feels that he can control his negative tendencies, he can begin to make amends for his sins.

Devarim Areivim

❊❊❊❊❊❊❊❊❊❊❊❊❊

Little Sins Are More Dangerous

Once Rabbi Elimelech of Lizhensk, while deeply engrossed in critical self-assessment, reproached himself, "I am the worst person alive."

A *chasid* who had overheard him asked, "How can you say such a thing? Have you ever committed a serious transgression?"

Replied Rabbi Elimelech, "It's the little sins I am worried about; they are worse than the grave transgressions. If you stab yourself repeatedly with a small, thin needle, you get accustomed to the pain. Then, when you are struck with a heavy iron, it does not hurt so much." [Each wrongful act conditions a person to further wrongdoing and dulls the conscience, so that ultimately one becomes indifferent to the most serious transgressions.]

Ohel Elimelech

Turn Around

Rabbi Nosson David of Shidlovtza said, "It is written, 'As east is far from west, so far has He removed our sins from us' (Psalm 103:12). When you stand facing east, all you need to do is turn around to face west. In the same way, a sinner needs only a small mental about-face to be far removed from his transgressions."

Holy Sparks Inside of Sin

Said the great *Maggid*, Rabbi Dov Ber of Mezritch: "Sparks of divine sanctity dwell even in sin. Without them, sin would be unable to exist. Now what kind of holy sparks could dwell inside of sin? The sparks of *teshuvah* (repentance). The moment you repent and turn away from sin, the sparks that were in it are raised to the higher worlds."[4]

Siach Sarfei Kodesh

Like a Burning Candle

The Baal Shem Tov commented on the verse "You will return to God your Lord" (Deuteronomy 30:2).

He said, "When you are entering a dark room holding a burning candle, the darkness vanishes without a trace. The same thing happens to a man who repents. He may have sinned, committed the most grievous transgressions, and perverted his soul, yet when he does *teshuvah*, he becomes a new man and his past is wiped clean. This is implied in the present verse: 'You will return to God your Lord.' By returning, you will draw closer to God your Lord."

Degel Machaneh Efraim

The Berditchever's Plea

It happened one *Kol Nidrei* night, as the entire congregation was assembled in the House of Prayer, that Rabbi Levi Yitzchak of Berditchev passed through the long rows of benches, bending down and searching beneath all the seats.

"Rabbi," the people asked, "what are you looking for?"

"I am looking for a Jew who is drunk," the rabbi replied, "but there doesn't seem to be one."

Rabbi Levi Yitzchak, the great champion of the Jewish people, then mounted the platform in front of the ark and declared:

"Master of the universe, look down from heaven and see. Who is like Your people Israel, the only holy nation on earth? You have commanded us to eat and drink today, the eve of Yom Kippur. If such a command were given to the nations of the world, then toward evening many of them would be intoxicated, quite a few would be rolling in mud and slime, and several would be bruised and maimed. Not so Your people of Israel. Today they fulfilled your command; they ate, drank, and feasted. Yet, well before it became dark they rushed to the synagogue, not one drunk, not one unsteady. They are all holy and pure, and all are prepared to accept the afflictions of Yom Kippur, confess their sins before You, and return to You wholeheartedly. Your children deserve that You forgive and pardon all their transgressions. Inscribe and seal them immediately in the Book of Life for a good life and a good year, a year of redemption and salvation."

Eser Orot

5

KOL NIDREI: EVENING SERVICE

Before the sun sets, Jews assemble in the synagogue to begin the Yom Kippur evening service. A solemn mood descends on the worshipers, who are filled with awe of God and radiate cordial feelings of friendship toward one another. Tonight all Israel is united, and any thought of divisiveness is banished from the heart.

The service opens with the *chazzan*, flanked by the rabbi and a leading member of the congregation, reciting, "With the approval of the Omnipresent, and with the approval of the congregation . . . we sanction prayer with the transgressors."

The formula for this declaration dates back to sixteenth-century Spain, when the Jews of that country were forced to convert to Christianity. Many publicly professed to accept Catholicism while secretly continuing to observe Judaism. When discovered, these so-called Marranos, or *Anussim*, were burned at the stake by the Spanish Inquisition after being cruelly tortured. Throughout the year, the Marranos did not dare participate in any public worship, but on Yom Kippur they risked their lives to assemble for prayer and to ask for

God's forgiveness for their seeming apostasy all year. Originally, the rabbis had these Marranos in mind when formulating this declaration, but it applies to all transgressors, assuring them that their sincere prayers will be heard together with the prayers of all Israel.

Indeed, transgressors are permitted to participate in the Yom Kippur service, because the sages teach that "a fast day in which sinners do not take part is no fast" (*Keritot* 6b). The sages find a reference to this in that one of the ingredients of the incense that the High Priest brought into the Holy of Holies to atone for Israel was *chelbena* (galbanum), which itself has an offensive odor. Just as *chelbena* was blended into the incense, so should transgressors be admitted to Yom Kippur services, for the Name of God is glorified when sinners repent and want to join with the righteous and emulate them.[1]

The *chazzan* then chants the *Kol Nidrei* three times in the moving ancient melody. The first time, he sings softly, like a supplicant who hesitates to enter the king's palace to plead for his life. The second time, as he gathers confidence, his voice gains strength. The third time, he chants loudly, as someone who approaches his king like a friend.[2]

Kol Nidrei is a declaration by which personal vows are canceled. For example, if someone had undertaken to fast on certain days and is unable to carry out the vow, *Kol Nidrei* nullifies the oath. However, *Kol Nidrei* annuls neither vows that affect other persons nor promises and oaths that were given to someone else, to a court, or to a government.

Kol Nidrei impresses on our mind the seriousness with which the Torah views both the fulfillment of one's commitment and the keeping of one's word. The requirement to annul a resolution we cannot keep and to do this at the advent of the most solemn day of the year makes us mindful of the importance of being faithful to our word.

❋❋❋❋❋❋❋❋❋❋❋❋❋❋

God, the Forgiver and Pardoner

A *baal teshuvah* (returnee to Torah observance) once tearfully confessed to the Rizhiner that he had gravely sinned in the past, and even after having done *teshuvah,* occasionally lapsed into his former missteps. "How can I expect God to accept my *teshuvah* time and again?" he asked.

The *rebbe* consoled him, "In the *Shemoneh Esrei* (*Amidah*) of Yom Kippur we say, 'For You are the Forgiver of Israel and the Pardoner of the tribes of *Jeshurun* [the Jewish people].' Why doesn't the text simply read, 'You *forgive* Israel and *pardon* the tribes of *Jeshurun*'?

"The words *solchan,* 'Forgiver,' and *mochalan,* 'Pardoner,' signify that God forgives constantly because it is His nature to forgive and to pardon, unlike the words *solei'ach* and *mocheil,* 'forgive' and 'pardon,' which can apply even to a callous person who on rare occasions displays compassion.

"God is the Forgiver who pardons a backsliding *baal teshuvah* each time he repents. He is a Forgiver by nature, because mercy is one of the divine attributes."

Yeshuot Yisrael

He Forgives Our Iniquities

Rabbi Elimelech of Rudnick said, "In the *Amidah* of Yom Kippur, we say, 'Blessed are You, God, the King who pardons and forgives our iniquities . . .'; but how can we say with such certainty that God will forgive us? Could this not be a *berachah* in which we uttered the name of God in vain?"

He answered with a parable: "A man came home carrying a bag of apples. His bright little son, craving to eat the appealing fruit, loudly recited the *berachah* over an apple. The father instantly handed him an apple, because he wanted to save his son from having uttered a *berachah* in vain, which is a serious transgression.

"Like the little boy," the *rebbe* continued, "we too recite the *berachah* 'The King who pardons and forgives our iniquities.' Is God, our Father in heaven, different from the father of the little boy? He will surely forgive us at once, so that our *berachah* will not have been uttered in vain."

Sifran shel Tzaddikim

※※※※※※※※※※※※※※

Viduy: Confessional Prayer

The two principal themes of Yom Kippur–*teshuvah* (repentance) and *viduy* (confession)–are inextricably linked to each other; the penitent must verbally confess sin. The obligation of *viduy* is clearly spelled out in the Torah: "If a man or woman sins against his fellow man, thus being untrue to God, and becoming guilty of a crime, he must confess the sin that he has committed" (Numbers 5:6).

In compliance with this law, at the conclusion of each *Shemoneh Esrei* (*Amidah*), the *viduy* prayers of *Ashamnu* and *Al Cheit* are inserted. The sins are listed on the order of the *alef-bet,* and the offenses are formulated in the plural: "*We* have become guilty . . . *we* have spoken slander . . . *we* have rebelled . . . *we* have strayed. . . . May You forgive *us* for the sin that *we* have sinned before You under duress and willingly. . . ."

The *viduy* is said in the plural because all Jews are responsible for one another (*Shevuot* 39a). Therefore, although one is sure that he has not committed a certain misdeed, he must nevertheless confess to it (*Bamidbar Rabbah* 10). When reciting the *viduy*, one should strike the breast lightly, as if to say, "You (my heart) caused me to sin" (*Mishnah Berurah* 607:3, note 11).

The *viduy* is recited ten times on Yom Kippur, once during *Minchah* on *Erev* Yom Kippur, eight times during *Maariv, Shacharit, Mussaf,* and *Minchah* (once during the silent *Amidah* and once during the *chazzan's* repetition), and once during *Ne'ilah*. The ten confessions parallel the Ten Commandments, which we violated.

※※※※※※※※※※※※※※

According to the *Alef-Bet*

Asked the Chidushei Harym: "Why are the sins in the *viduy* listed in the order of the *alef-bet*? If a person had to enumerate all his sins, he would need all day. Arranging the sins according to the *alef-bet* assures us that there is an end to them."

Chidushei Harym

※※※※※※※※※※※※※※

We and Our Forefathers Sinned

In the preamble to the *Ashamnu* confession we say, "We and our forefathers have sinned." Why do we include our forefathers' sins in our confession?

The Talmud (*Yoma* 86b) teaches that he who repents out of love of God has his premeditated sins counted as virtues. Surely, our forefathers' *teshuvah* was motivated by love of God. Thus their sins were counted as virtues and will stand us in good stead.

Leket Yosher

※※※※※※※※※※※※※※

For Sinning with the *Yetzer Hara*

Said Rabbi Pinchas Horowitz, "In one of the *Al Cheit* confessions we ask God to pardon us 'for the sin that we have sinned before You with the Evil Inclination.'

"We recite a total of fifty-three *Al Cheit* confessions of various sins. Could it be that only one of these was prompted by the *yetzer hara*, our selfish tendency? What then provoked the other fifty-two sins?

"The truth is that most of our sins are induced by the *yetzer hatov*, our good inclination. We do not have the slightest inkling that our evil tendency is causing our sin. On the contrary, most of the time we think that our actions are virtuous and that we are motivated by noble causes. Our conscience is clear. Hardly ever do we realize that it was our *yetzer hara* that seduced us to sin."

Shemen Hatov

❋❋❋❋❋❋❋❋❋❋❋❋❋

Breast-Beating

The Chafetz Chaim was wont to say, "The main thing is not to beat our heart *after* we say *Al Cheit*, asking forgiveness for our sins. It is *before* the *Al Cheit*, *before* we commit a sin, that our heart should be beating with anxiety and prevent our doing wrong."

Iturei Torah

❋❋❋❋❋❋❋❋❋❋❋❋❋

Strict about Lifesaving

Rabbi Chaim Brisker was known to be lenient regarding feeding the sick on Yom Kippur. Once he was asked, "How can you be so lenient with the laws of Yom Kippur?" Replied Reb Chaim, "I am not lenient with the laws of Yom Kippur. It is just that I am very strict about the laws of lifesaving."

Yamim Nora'im

❋❋❋❋❋❋❋❋❋❋❋❋❋

Beyode'im uvelo Yode'im: Known and Unknown Sins

In the *Al Cheit* confession we ask God to forgive sins we committed knowingly and unknowingly. One might wonder, though, since ordinarily we confess to a moderate transgression before mentioning a more serious one, shouldn't the order be reversed to read: *belo yode'im uveyode'im*, "atone for unknown and known sins"?

When a person repeatedly commits a sin, his sensitivity to the sin becomes numbed to the point that he no longer realizes he is doing something wrong. This is the meaning of "unknown sins." Initially he knew that he was transgressing, but afterward, he sank to a level where he lost all awareness of wrongdoing. Such "unknown sins" are far worse than known sins.

Rabbi Avraham Yitzchak Kamai

Confusion of the Heart

Rabbi Simchah Zissel of Kelm remarked, "One of the offenses for which we ask forgiveness in the *Al Cheit* is 'the sin we committed through confusion of the heart' (*betimhon leivav*). What kind of sin is this?

"There are people who, on seeing a wealthy magnate living in a palatial mansion and enjoying all the luxuries and pleasures of life, think, 'This is living!' or who are envious of the big transactions a successful businessman concludes. Such people do not realize that the highest attainable goals in life are of a spiritual nature. Harboring the misguided notion that success, wealth, and fame are the aims one should strive for is sinning through confusion of the heart."

Chochmah Umussar

Torah Reading on Yom Kippur

The Torah reading for *Shacharit* is from Leviticus, chapter 16, which relates the *Kohen Gadol*'s (High Priest's) Yom Kippur service in the Tabernacle and Temple. The first verse mentions the death of Aaron's two eldest sons, Nadav and Avihu. As the *Midrash* points out, their death has a direct bearing on Yom Kippur, because "just as Yom Kippur brings atonement, so, too, does the death of the righteous bring atonement."[3]

Contemplation of the death of Aaron's righteous sons should prompt us to do *teshuvah*, for "if the fire is consuming the cedars, what can the lowly moss of the wall do?" (*Mo'ed Katan* 25b).[4] (If even great *tzaddikim* are taken from this world, then we ordinary people have reason to tremble with fear.)

For the *haftarah* we read Isaiah 57:14 to 58:14 because that text exhorts us to demonstrate the sincerity of our fast by "sharing our bread with the hungry and taking the wretched poor to our home" (Isaiah 58:7).

The reading for *Minchah* is from chapter 18 in Leviticus, which deals with incestuous and other forbidden sexual relationships. The reading of such abominations, which seems incongruent with the sanctity of Yom Kippur, comes to teach us that even if we have reached a high level of holiness and purity, we should not be complacent, for if we are not constantly on guard, we will be overcome by our passions and ensnared by temptations of the most obscene kind.

The *haftarah* for *Minchah* is from the Book of Jonah, which is a lesson in repentance. It relates Jonah's mission to the city of Nineveh, the capital of Assyria, the Iraq of today, to warn its people of its impending destruction because of their wickedness. After initially trying to avoid carrying out his mission, Jonah summoned the people of Nineveh to repent. They heeded his call, and God spared the city. The story demonstrates that sincere *teshuvah* can revoke even the harshest decree of God.

Conceit Is Worse than Sin

The Baal Shem Tov said, "I can bring scriptural proof that conceit is worse than sin. Concerning sinful acts, we read in the Torah that God dwells among the Jewish people 'even when they are unclean with transgression' (Leviticus 16:15). (This verse is in the Yom Kippur Torah reading.) By contrast, when it comes to prideful people, the Talmud states, 'God says, "I cannot endure dwelling in the world together with a haughty and proud man" ' (*Sotah* 5a).

"A sinner who is humble because he knows that he has transgressed will find that God is close to him, for it says, 'the [Divine Presence] dwells with them even when they are unclean' (Leviticus 16:15). But a conceited person, although he may be free of sin, is far removed from God, for God says, 'I cannot endure the haughty and proud man' " (Psalm 101:5).

Sefer Baal Shem Tov

❈❈❈❈❈❈❈❈❈❈❈❈❈

Vachai Bahem: Live by Keeping My Laws

The *Minchah* reading contains the following verse:

"Keep My decrees and laws, since it is only by keeping them that a person can [truly] live. I am God" (Leviticus 18:5).

The *Gemara* in *Yoma* 85b derives from this verse that you should *live* by keeping the *mitzvot* but that keeping the *mitzvot* should not result in death. This means that you may violate any commandment of the Torah in order to save a life. The only exceptions to this rule are the three cardinal sins: idolatry, murder, and forbidden sexual relationships (*Sanhedrin* 74a).

The Kotzker *rebbe* said, "*Vachai bahem*, 'live by keeping the *mitzvot*'— do the *mitzvot* with zest, fervor, and enthusiasm. Don't perform them merely out of force of habit, routinely, or as a formality."

The *Sefat Emet* expounded, "*Vachai bahem*, 'live by keeping the *mitzvot*,' implies that the fulfillment of *mitzvot* imparts life, health, and vigor to all parts of your body."

The *Degel Machaneh Efraim* notes, "The word אתם, *otam*, 'them,' in the phrase 'by keeping them' is composed of the same letters as the word אמת, *emet*, 'truth.' Thus you might translate the phrase as 'you will live by keeping (abiding by) the truth.' Therefore, being guided by honesty and sincerity and always speaking the truth are auspicious signs for a long life."

※※※※※※※※※※※※※※

Why Did Jonah Run from God?

The commentators explain the puzzling behavior of Jonah in trying to escape from God's command. Jonah was concerned that, in response to his admonition, the people of Nineveh would repent. If this were to happen, it would reflect badly on Israel, for in contrast to the Ninevites, the people of Israel consistently refused to heed their prophets' call to do *teshuvah*. Thus, Jonah's mission to Nineveh would result in a severe condemnation of Israel. Jonah refused to carry out God's will in order to protect Israel from such criticism (Rashi, Redak).

※※※※※※※※※※※※※※

Why Do We Read the Book of Jonah?

Rabbi Meir of Premyshlan explained, "The reason we read the Book of Jonah on Yom Kippur is in order to awaken the people to do *teshuvah*. In Jonah 1:6 we read that during the great storm, the captain of the ship on which Jonah was sailing cried out to him, 'How can you be sleeping so soundly! Arise, call to your God!' "

Rabbi Meir continued, "Let's take these words to heart! Let's wake up and do *teshuvah*!"

Or Hameir

A Study in Contrasts

Yom Kippur contains two contrasting elements: an ascent to the loftiest spiritual heights, which occurred when the High Priest entered the Holy of Holies, and a descent to the depths, when the scapegoat that carried the sins of the people of Israel was sent to Azazel in the wilderness, where it was pushed off a desolate high cliff to its destruction, and thereby the final pardon was obtained.

The two opposites, the pure holiness of the sanctuary in stark contrast to the desolation of Azazel, are intimately associated with one another, for the spiritual climax that is reached on Yom Kippur in the Holy of Holies can awaken thoughts of *teshuvah* even in the most hardened sinner who dwells in the spiritual desolation of ungodliness, beset by the snakes, vipers, and scorpions of callous materialism.

Hamo'adim Bahalachah

Banishing Improper Thoughts

Rabbi Moshe of Kobryn said, "In the *Selichot* prayer, we recite the verse 'I will cleanse you of all your uncleanness and all your abominations' (Ezekiel 36:25). The word *giluleichem*, 'abominations,' may be cognate to the verb *galal*, 'to roll, turn, or spin,' and thus may be rendered as 'evil thoughts that swirl up in your mind like a sudden arrow.'

"God is assuring us, 'If you cleanse yourselves of your evil deeds, I will help you to get rid of your improper thoughts.' "

Torat Avot

❋❋❋❋❋❋❋❋❋❋❋❋❋

Those Who Only Knock on the Door

Said Rabbi Mordechai of Lechovitz, "In the *Amidah* of *Mussaf* we say, '*Vechol ma'aminim*, All believe that He responds to prayer, who opens a gate to those who knock in repentance.' The Holy One, blessed is He, opens the gate wide even for those who only knock on the door."

❋❋❋❋❋❋❋❋❋❋❋❋❋

Avodah

During the *chazzan*'s repetition of the *Mussaf Amidah*, the *Avodah* is recited. The *Avodah* is the description of the service of the *Kohen Gadol* (High Priest) in the *Bet Hamikdash*. When the *Bet Hamikdash* stood, the *avodah* was the focal point of Yom Kippur, for the *Kohen Gadol*'s service brought about the atonement for all Israel, as indicated in the verse "And he shall make atonement for himself, for his family, and for the entire community of Israel" (Leviticus 16:17).

On Yom Kippur the entire service had to be performed by the *Kohen Gadol*. It consisted of the regular daily service for which he wore the eight "golden garments" (garments containing gold) and the specific Yom Kippur service for which he wore four white linen garments. He changed his garments five time and immersed himself in a *mikveh* at each change.

On Yom Kippur, the *Kohen Gadol* offered fifteen sacrifices and burned the incense three times, twice on the golden altar in the *heichal* (sanctuary) and once in the Holy of Holies. He recited the *viduy* (confession) three times: the first time, while leaning his hands on the ox, which was his own sin offering, he recited the confession for himself and his family; the second time, while leaning his hands on the same ox, he atoned for himself, his family, and his fellow priests; the third time, he leaned his hands on the head of the "goat of Azazel" and asked forgiveness for the entire nation.

During the recitation of each *viduy*, the *Kohen Gadol* would pronounce the *Shem Hameforash*, the ineffable Divine Name, three times – altogether nine times – and a tenth time when he designated the goat that had been chosen by lot as the one to be offered "Unto God."

Each time the *Kohen Gadol* pronounced the *Shem Hameforash*, the ineffable Name, the people standing in the courtyard of the Temple would kneel, prostrate themselves, fall on their faces, and say, "Blessed is the Name of His glorious Kingdom for all eternity" (*Mishnah Yoma* 6:2).

When the *chazzan* reaches this point in his recitation of the *Avodah*, it is customary to fall to the knees, the forehead touching the floor, but with paper, a mat, or a *tallit* intervening.[5]

Four times during the *Avodah* the *Kohen Gadol* entered the Holy of Holies: the first time to offer incense, two times to sprinkle the blood of the sacrifices, and a fourth time to remove the incense spoon and pan he had left in the morning.

The *Avodah* is followed by the very moving *piyut* that relates the death of the "Ten Martyrs." Opening with the words *Eileh Ezkerah*, "These I do remember," it relates the brutal murder by the Romans of ten great sages of the *Mishnah*.

✺✺✺✺✺✺✺✺✺✺✺✺✺

White Vestments for the Yom Kippur *Avodah*

Why doesn't the High Priest enter the Holy of Holies wearing his gold garments? Because gold brings to mind the Golden Calf, and we have a rule: "An accuser cannot serve as a defender" (*Rosh Hashanah* 26a). This means that when the High Priest enters the Holy of Holies to defend Israel and obtain atonement for them, he should not wear any vestment containing gold, the agent that evokes accusation against Israel. We do not want to give Satan the Accuser a pretext to charge, "Only yesterday they made for themselves an idol of gold, and today they come to ask forgiveness wearing vestments of gold" (*Vayikra Rabbah* 21).

Another reason the *Kohen Gadol* is wearing white garments is so that he may resemble the ministering angels, one of whom is described as "the man clothed in linen" (Ezekiel 9:11).

Ne'ilah Service

The concluding service of Yom Kippur is *Ne'ilah*, the Closing of the Gates. The holy day of fasting and prayer comes to a climax, and the worshipers' mood rises to a feverish pitch as they strain to get in a last fervent prayer before the Heavenly Gates close. The *Aron Hakodesh* remains open throughout *Ne'ilah*, and many remain standing during the entire service. After the *chazzan*'s repetition of the *Shemoneh Esrei*, the *Avinu Malkeinu* is said. Yom Kippur reaches its emotional zenith when the entire congregation declares its loyalty to God, crying out in unison, *Shema Yisrael*! *Hashem Elokeinu Hashem Echod*! "Hear O Israel! God is our Lord, God is One!" Then, "Blessed is the Name of His glorious Kingdom for all eternity" (three times) and "*Hashem* alone is God" (seven times).

The *shofar* is sounded–one single, long *tekiah* sound–and a palpable sense of relief and happiness pervades the congregation. Confident that God has accepted our fast, repentance, and prayers and sealed us for a good year, we feel cleansed and uplifted. Joyfully we call out, "Next year in Jerusalem!" Jews in *Eretz Yisrael* say, "Next year in Jerusalem rebuilt!"

After the *Maariv* service, if the sky is clear, the blessing over the new moon (*Kiddush Levanah*) is said. Then everyone goes home in cheerful spirits to recite *Havdalah* and eat a festive meal, for the *Midrash* says, "At the close of Yom Kippur a heavenly voice declares, 'Go and eat your bread with joy, and drink your wine in joy, for God has already accepted your efforts'" (Ecclesiates 9:7). In a moving display of love of *mitzvot*, many begin building the *sukkah* that same night, connecting the *mitzvah* of Yom Kippur with that of Sukkot, as the Psalmist says, "They go from strength to strength" (Psalm 84:8).

✖✖✖✖✖✖✖✖✖✖✖✖✖✖

Seal Us in the Book of Life

In the *Shemoneh Esrei* (*Amidah*) of *Ne'ilah*, instead of saying "*Inscribe* us in the Book of Life," we say "*Seal* us in the Book of Life." The theme of sealing is repeated throughout this service. What is the significance of sealing?

A seal is placed on an envelope to ensure that no one tampers with its contents and to guarantee that the letter reaches its addressee without outside interference.

At *Ne'ilah*, now that we have cleansed ourselves and our transgressions have been forgiven, we want to preserve this high degree of purity. We therefore ask God to place His seal on the lofty spiritual state we are in and to protect it from dissipating through outside influences. That is the reason we say "and seal us" during *Ne'ilah*.

Hamo'adim Bahalachah

✖✖✖✖✖✖✖✖✖✖✖✖✖✖

Their Needs Are Many

The Chidushei Harym said: "In the *Ne'ilah* service we say, 'The needs of Your people are many and their wisdom is lacking.' The two are

interconnected; because their wisdom is lacking, therefore their needs
are many." (Those who have the wisdom to fear God are content, even
if they lack in material possessions).

Siach Sarfei Kodesh

✳✳✳✳✳✳✳✳✳✳✳✳✳✳

Next Year in Jerusalem

Twice a year we say, "Next year in Jerusalem!" – once during the *seder*
on Pesach and once at the end of *Ne'ilah* on Yom Kippur, for there is a
difference of opinion in the *Germara* (*Rosh Hashanah* 11a) between Rabbi
Eliezer and Rabbi Yehoshua. Rabbi Eliezer says that the people of Israel
were first redeemed in *Nisan* and will ultimately be redeemed in *Nisan*,
and Rabbi Yehoshua says they were redeemed in *Nisan* and will be
redeemed in *Tishri*. Therefore, in both *Nisan* and *Tishri* we say, "Next
year in Jerusalem!"

6

SUKKOT: FESTIVAL OF REJOICING

Sukkot, the time of our gladness, is the third in the cycle of pilgrimage festivals. On Pesach we celebrate our redemption from Egypt and our freedom from physical bondage. Shavuot commemorates the Giving of the Torah, whereby we gained our spiritual freedom from the shackles of unbridled passion and unrestrained self-indulgence. With Sukkot, the cycle reaches its culmination in an exhilarating outburst of joy and a wealth of symbols that evoke memories of divine protection in the past, that lift our present to a higher spiritual plateau, and that point the way to the messianic future.

In the autumn of the year, after the harvest has been gathered, when a man's thoughts tend to focus on the rich profits he has garnered, and he dreams of acquiring mansions and estates, the Torah tells the Jew to build a *sukkah*, to exchange his solid home for a frail, makeshift dwelling. The *sukkah* is a reminder of the huts in which God made the children of Israel live during their forty-year journey through the wilderness and of the Clouds of Glory that protected them on their wanderings. As a Jew sits in the *sukkah*, under the shelter of the *s'chach*, surrounded by family and friends, he cannot help but feel God's sheltering Hand enveloping him. His spirit soars as he realizes that true happiness is found only in the eternal values of Torah and *mitzvot*, that material possessions offer no security, and that the shield of faith is the only protection he can rely on. He is aware that, like his stay in the *sukkah*, life on earth is unstable and transitory. Gazing at the stars shimmering through the greenery of the *s'chach*, he experiences a closeness to God that is almost palpable. This nearness to God is the source of his *simchah*, the exciting gladness that is the hallmark of Sukkot.

And when he takes the *Arba Minim* (the Four Species) in hand, his one-on-one relationship with God is broadened to embrace all of Israel. For symbolically, the Four Species represent all the strata that make up the Jewish people: the *etrog*, a tasty fruit with a pleasant aroma, represents the righteous people who possess both Torah and good deeds. The *lulav*, the branch of a date palm, produces a sweet fruit but has no fragrance; it stands for the scholar who is proficient in Torah but lacks good deeds. The sweet-smelling myrtle, *hadassim*, which produces no edible fruit, symbolizes the average people who perform good deeds but are deficient in Torah scholarship. Finally, the odorless and tasteless willow, *aravot*, represents the person who lacks both Torah and good deeds. Thus, the *lulav* bundle symbolizes the totality of the Jewish people, all extending a helping hand to one another, all striving toward the same goals: fulfillment of the Torah to the best of their abilities and thereby proclamation to all humankind that God is the Creator and Master of the universe.

✳✳✳✳✳✳✳✳✳✳✳✳✳✳

Selected Laws of the *Sukkot*

The *sukkah* is a temporary dwelling. Therefore, its height may not exceed twenty cubits – about thirty feet. At the same time, it must be a livable dwelling, and thus it may not be lower than ten handbreadths – about forty inches. Its walls should be strong enough to withstand a normal wind and to prevent the candles from being blown out. The *sukkah* should have four walls, but it is valid if it is built with three walls. The minimum for a kosher *sukkah* is two walls and a third wall that consists of a board over a handbreadth (four inches wide) placed at a distance from one of the two walls. The three alternatives are alluded to in the letters סכה, *sukkah*. The ס, *samach*, represents the four walls; the כ, *chaf*, represents the three-walled *sukkah*; and the ה, *hei*, represents the *sukkah* made with two walls and the third composed of a board placed away from one of the walls.

The walls may be made of any material that is available.

The most important part of the *sukkah* is the *s'chach*, the roof. We must use plant material, such as branches of trees, reeds, bamboo poles, palm boughs, or thin slats of wood. It is essential that the *s'chach* be detached from the soil; we should spread it loosely and not nail it down. We should place enough *s'chach* on the *sukkah* so that it provides more shade than sun.

If we build a *sukkah* under a tree, it is invalid, even if it has a proper *s'chach* of its own, because the branches of the tree that cover the *sukkah* are rooted in the ground.

We decorate the *sukkah* and use our finest dishes and silverware in it to demonstrate our love of the *mitzvah*.

On the first night of Sukkot, we must eat in the *sukkah*. We recite the *Kiddush*, say the *berachah Leisheiv basukkah*, "to dwell in the *sukkah*," and *Shehecheyanu*, "who has kept us alive, sustained us, and brought us to this season" (outside *Eretz Yisrael*, *Shehecheyanu* is also said on the second night). Every time we eat a meal in the *sukkah*, we say the *berachah Leisheiv basukkah*.

We take the Four Species – *lulav, etrog, hadassim,* and *aravot* – in hand every day of Sukkot, except on *Shabbat*. We take the *lulav* bundle in the right hand, then the *etrog* (with the *pitam* facing down) in the left. After reciting the *berachot*, we turn over the *etrog* and wave the Four Species in the six directions.

(For a detailed discussion of all of the laws of Sukkot, the *Shulchan Aruch, Orach Chaim* 625–669 and *Kitzur Shulchan Aruch* 134–138 are available in English translation.)

Valid and Invalid *Sukkot*

Rabbi Avraham, the *Maggid* of Trisk, told his sons to prepare for Sukkot by studying the tractate *Sukkah*. When they completed it, he told them to review it. He did this several times, and when they thought they knew the entire tractate by heart, he asked them, "Tell me, how many *sukkot* are listed as valid and how many as invalid?"

The boys did not know the answer.

Thereupon the *Maggid* told them: "In the entire tractate there are sixty-six *sukkot* listed as valid and twenty-five as invalid. It's easy to remember. In Hebrew, sixty-six is represented by the letters *samach, vav,* ו, ס, and twenty-five is represented by the letters *chaf, hei,* ה, כ. Together, *samach, vav, chaf, hei* spell *sukkah*.

Imrei Shefer

❈❈❈❈❈❈❈❈❈❈❈❈❈

Believing Is Better than Seeing

The Kotzker *rebbe* was told about a chasidic *rebbe* who actually had seen the *ushpizin* in the *sukkah*.

Replied the Kotzker, "I don't actually see the *ushpizin*, but I believe that they are present in my *sukkah*. And believing is greater than seeing." (Faith creates a reality that is far more powerful than anything that is perceived with the physical eye).

Emet Ve'emunah

❈❈❈❈❈❈❈❈❈❈❈❈❈

Ushpizin: Special Guests

It is a beautiful custom to welcome into the *sukkah* seven venerable guests (*ushpizin*): Abraham, Isaac, Jacob, Moses, Aaron, Joseph, and

David. Each day of Sukkot, another of these guests leads the others into the *sukkah*.

This custom is based on the *Zohar* (*Emor* 103b): "When a man sits in the *tzila dimehemenuta*, the "shade of faith" (meaning the *sukkah*), the *Shechinah* spreads its wings over him from above, and Abraham and five other righteous ones and David make their dwelling with him."

And so, upon entering the *sukkah*, we invite the souls of the *ushpizin* guests to join us with the words "Enter, exalted holy guests, exalted holy Patriarchs, to be seated in the shade of exalted faithfulness, in the shade of the Holy One, blessed is He."

The custom is based on the idea of extending hospitality to the needy. As the *Zohar* says, "The portions of food that would be served to the heavenly *ushpizin* should be served in the *sukkah* to poor guests here on earth" (*Zohar*, *Emor* 104a).

❊❊❊❊❊❊❊❊❊❊❊❊❊

If Dwelling in the *Sukkah* Causes Discomfort

The Kotzker *rebbe* said, "The rabbis of the Talmud rule, *hamitzta'eir patur min hasukkah*, 'If a person feels discomfort he is exempt from eating in the *sukkah*.' Why should feeling irritated relieve a person from fulfilling a *mitzvah*?

"The *sukkah* is called *tzila dimehemenuta*, the shelter of faith. It teaches you to leave behind all your worldly concerns and to dedicate yourself to God with total self-effacing faith in His mercy and compassion. If you have attained this level of self-negating faith, you feel no pain or discomfort. That is why a person who feels discomfort is exempt from the *mitzvah* of eating in the *sukkah*. Feeling discomfort proves that he has not reached the point of total self-nullification.

"Because he has not grasped the meaning of the *sukkah*, any further stay there is of no benefit to him. Therefore, he is exempt from the obligation."

Ohel Torah

❊❊❊❊❊❊❊❊❊❊❊❊❊

Why Is Sukkot in the Fall?

Sukkot commemorates that "[God] had the children of Israel live in huts when He brought them out of Egypt" (Leviticus 23:43).

But the Exodus took place in the month of *Nisan*. Why then was the date of Sukkot not fixed in *Nisan*?

If we were to move into a *sukkah* in *Nisan*, which is in the spring, it would appear as though we had built a summer cabin to provide cooling shade rather than for the purpose of performing a *mitzvah*. To preclude this misapprehension, the Torah commanded us to build a *sukkah* in the chilly autumn weather, when it is unusual to live outdoors. We leave our secure home to take up residence in the fragile *sukkah*, which symbolizes the weakness and instability of man and nature. Rabbi S. R. Hirsch[1] expounds that everyone, rich and poor alike, must abide by the requirement that the *s'chach*–the protective element of the *sukkah*–must consist of plant material. On the other hand, the walls–the isolating element of the *sukkah*–may be made of any material and constructed as solidly as you wish. The combination of the *s'chach* and the walls suggests that no matter how different we may be from one another on social and economic scales, whether our private little world is enclosed with marble walls or coarse wooden boards, we are all dependent on the same protection from above. The beggar and the rich man, both using the same *s'chach*, thereby recognize God as their protector.

❊❊❊❊❊❊❊❊❊❊❊❊❊❊

Shade of Faith

Rabbi Chanoch of Alexander: In the *Zohar* (*Emor* 130b) the *sukkah* is described as *tzila dimehemenuta*, "shade of faith," because the *mitzvah* of *sukkah* with its unstable walls and precarious roof expresses our complete dependence on and boundless trust in God's protection.

This being so, why weren't we commanded to dwell in the *sukkah* all year round?

Leaving our permanent home and dwelling in the *sukkah* for seven days has so powerful an impact on us that it makes itself felt in our life throughout the rest of the year, even while we live in our permanent, solid home.

✹✹✹✹✹✹✹✹✹✹✹✹✹

He Slept in the *Sukkah*

Rabbi Leibele Chasid of Kelm caught a cold shortly before Sukkot. Came the *Yom Tov*, and his wife pleaded with him, "Please, do me a favor, don't sleep in the *sukkah*. Your cold might get worse." Rabbi Leibele, paying no attention to his wife, slept in the *sukkah* and woke up coughing, wheezing, and gasping for breath. "I told you so," said the *rebbetzin*. "Look what you got for sleeping in the *sukkah*!"

"Women, women, they just can't understand," Rabbi Leibele grumbled. "It is a matter of simple logic. If I'm coughing and wheezing after observing the *mitzvah* of sleeping in the *sukkah*, imagine how sick I would feel if I hadn't fulfilled the *mitzvah*."

✹✹✹✹✹✹✹✹✹✹✹✹✹

Most Beautiful Ornament

On *Erev* Sukkot, Rabbi Chaim of Sanz was wont to distribute unusually large amounts of money to the needy. One year, his funds ran out, so his sons went to borrow money from the wealthy people in town. No sooner did he receive the money than he parceled it out to the poor. This he did all day long.

At night, upon entering the *sukkah*, he said, "It is customary to decorate the *sukkah* with all kinds of exquisitely beautiful ornaments.

As for me, I adorn the *sukkah* with *tzedakah*. My *sukkah* ornament is charity."

Eser Tzachtzachot

Seventy Bulls

Sukkot has a distinct element of universalism. Although it shares with the other festivals the aspect of the exclusivity of the Jewish people and their intimate bond with God, Sukkot also reaches out to the nations of the world. This idea finds expression primarily in the order of sacrifices that were brought into the *Bet Hamikdash*, notably the offering of the seventy bulls.

On the first day, thirteen bulls were offered, and on each successive day the number decreased by one, so that the total number of bulls sacrificed during the seven days of the festival came to seventy (13+12+11+10+9+8+7=70) (Numbers 29:12–34). The seventy bulls correspond to the seventy original nations who descended from Noah and who were the ancestors of all the nations of the world. Israel brought these sacrifices in order to atone for these nations and to pray for their well-being and universal peace (*Sukkah* 55b).

The *Midrash* says this about the seventy bulls: "If the nations of the world had known how valuable the *Bet Hamikdash* [where the seventy bulls were offered] was for them, they would have surrounded it with mighty legions to safeguard it" (*Bamidbar Rabbah* 1).

Four Species Symbolize the Jewish People

On the first day you are to take for yourselves the fruit of a citron tree, the branches of a date palm, twigs of a plaited tree, and brook willows, and you are to rejoice before the Lord your God for seven days (Leviticus 23:40).

The *Midrash* suggests a beautiful explanation for the symbolism of the Four Species.

The "fruit of a citron tree" is the *etrog*; it has both taste and fragrance. The "branches of a date palm" are the *lulav*; a date has taste but no fragrance. "Twigs of a plaited tree" are myrtle twigs, *hadassim*, which have fragrance but no taste. Brook willows – *aravot* – have neither taste nor fragrance.

The rabbis explain that taste represents Torah knowledge, and fragrance represents good deeds. Symbolically, the four species represent four kinds of Jews. Some, like the *etrog*, know the Torah and do good deeds; some, like the *lulav*, have Torah knowledge but lack good deeds; some, like the *hadassim*, do good deeds but are ignorant of Torah; and some, like the *aravot*, have neither Torah knowledge nor good deeds.

What does God do? He binds them all together in one bundle, so that they make up for each other's failings. The *lulav* bundle signifies the unity of the Jewish people, that all Jews, even those who are deficient in knowledge and good deeds, are needed to complete the Jewish community.

Yalkut Shim'oni, Emor

❋❋❋❋❋❋❋❋❋❋❋❋❋

Willow Twig and *Lulav*

The Gerer *rebbe* said, "The main thing is that everyone should know his place. You should realize that you cannot change a willow branch into a *lulav*. But remember that in your present state you can attach yourself to someone who is greater than you are. You thereby become united with him, just as the willow twigs are part and parcel of the *lulav* bundle.

Siach Sarfei Kodesh

❋❋❋❋❋❋❋❋❋❋❋❋❋

The *Lulav* Must Be Your Own

The Talmud says: Our rabbis derive from the phrase *ulekachtem lachem*, "you are to take for yourselves" (Leviticus 23:40), that the *lulav* must be your own, excluding a borrowed or stolen *lulav*. From this verse our sages deduced that no one can fulfill his duty on the first day of Sukkot with someone else's *lulav*, unless the latter gave it to him as a gift.

It once happened when Rabban Gamliel, Rabbi Yehoshua, Rabbi Elazar ben Azariah, and Rabbi Akiva were traveling on a ship [at Sukkot time] that only Rabban Gamliel had a *lulav*, which he had bought for one thousand *zuz*; he took it and fulfilled the *mitzvah*; then he gave it as a gift to Rabbi Yehoshua, who took it, fulfilled the *mitzvah* with it, and gave it as a gift to Rabbi Akiva, who took it, fulfilled the *mitzvah* with it, and then returned it to Rabban Gamliel. [The *Gemara* wonders:] Why does he need to mention that Rabbi Akiva returned it? [The *Gemara* answers:] He teaches us something by the way: that a gift made on condition that it be returned is a valid gift. . . . [The *Gemara* asks:] For what purpose did he need to mention that [Rabban Gamliel] had bought it for one thousand *zuz*? [The *Gemara* answers:] In order to let you know how precious the *mitzvot* are to them."

Sukkah 41b

Nothing but Happiness

Concerning Sukkot, the Torah states, *vehayita ach same'ach*, "and you shall remain only joyful" (Deuteronomy 16:14, 15).

Rabbi Samson Raphael Hirsch expounds, this means much more than "you shall rejoice." The command "you shall remain joyful" turns your rejoicing into a permanent trait of your personality, and the words "only joyful" mean that this joyfulness in your character will persist even under circumstances that would otherwise tend to cast a cloud over it. You will remain joyful in spite of everything, "only"

joyful. *Simchah*, rejoicing, is the most sublime flower and fruit to ripen
on the tree of life planted by the Law of God. In the same spirit, the
joyfulness to which the present verse refers is not restricted to festivals
and festive gatherings but extends beyond the festive seasons and
accompanies us back into everyday life, from the exuberance of the
festive assemblies into the quiet privacy of our homes, and remains
with us through all the vicissitudes of life . . . to be joyful in spite of
everything, whatever life may bring: *vehayita ach same'ach*.

❋❋❋❋❋❋❋❋❋❋❋❋❋

War of Gog and Magog

The *haftarot* of the first day of Sukkot and *Shabbat Chol Hamo'ed* deal
with the War of Gog and Magog, the prophetic vision[2] of the cata-
clysmic war of the nations of the world against Jerusalem that will
usher in the messianic age. After an initial defeat, the Jewish people
will emerge triumphant, God's greatness will be revealed to the entire
world, the final redemption will take place, and all the nations of the
world will acknowledge "God the holy One in Israel" (Ezekiel 39:7).

The connection between Gog and Magog and Sukkot is that the
final battle in which Gog and its allies will be crushed will occur on
Sukkot. Every year on the anniversary of that day, the nations will
make a pilgrimage to Jerusalem to bow down to God and to celebrate
the festival of Sukkot (Zechariah 14:16).

The rabbis teach that at the coming of the messianic age, the nations
will claim that they too would have accepted the Torah if it had been
offered to them. Thereupon God will put them to the test by offering
them an "easy *mitzvah*, namely, the *sukkah*." They will eagerly climb to
their roof and build *sukkot*, but as soon as the midday sun makes their
stay in the *sukkah* uncomfortable, they leave the *sukkah*, slamming the
door in anger (*Avodah Zarah* 3a). Sukkot is a test of man's attachment to
God, and the nations will observe Sukkot to prove their newfound
loyalty to him.

❋❋❋❋❋❋❋❋❋❋❋❋❋

Water Drawing

Every sacrifice brought into the Temple was accompanied by a pouring of wine on the altar. During the seven days of Sukkot, a libation of water was added to that of wine. The wine and the water together were poured with each of the daily morning sacrifices.

The drawing of this water, which took place on the second night of Sukkot, was an occasion for an ecstatically joyous celebration called *Simchat Bet Hasho'evah*, Celebration of the Water Drawing. All Jerusalem was lit up by giant lamps. Happy throngs filled the Temple court to listen to the orchestra of Levites playing harps, lyres, cymbals, and trumpets and to watch prominent scholars dance, perform various gymnastic feats, and juggle flaming torches in honor of the celebration. The relevant text for this celebration is "Joyfully shall you draw water, from the fountains of salvation" (Isaiah 12:3).

Rabbi Yehoshua ben Chanania said, "When we rejoiced at the *Simchat Bet Hasho'evah* we did not sleep all night. In the first hour was the morning offering [and the water libation]; then the prayer; then the *Mussaf* offering, followed by the *Mussaf* prayer; then to the *Bet Hamidrash* (House of Study) and from there to eat and drink; then to the afternoon offering and the *Minchah* prayer, and from then on (through the night) to the *Simchat Bet Hasho'evah*" (*Sukkah* 53a).

The *Mishnah* captures the euphoria and rapture of the festivities in a few words: "If you have not seen the rejoicing of *Bet Hasho'evah* you have not witnessed joy in your life" (*Sukkah* 53a).

Nowadays, in commemoration of these festivities, it is customary in many communities during the nights of Sukkot to gather in the synagogue, the *bet midrash*, or the rabbi's *sukkah* to celebrate *Simchat Bet Hasho'evah* in a convivial atmosphere, with food and drink, song and dance. The participants take turns at leading the singing of the fifteen *Shir Hamaalot* (Songs of Ascent) (Psalm 120–134), improvising at matching the unfamiliar words to popular *niggunim* (melodies), often exposing themselves to some good-natured teasing.

The *Shir Hamaalot* (Songs of Ascent), Psalms 120–134, each beginning with the words *Shir Hamaalot*, correspond to the fifteen steps in the *Bet Hamikdash* that led from the men's court to the women's court.

During the libation ceremony, the Levites played their instruments standing on these steps.

❈❈❈❈❈❈❈❈❈❈❈❈❈

Kohelet

The happiness and gaiety that are generated on Sukkot can easily lead us to immerse ourselves in worldly pleasures and cause us to lose sight of the spiritual nature of true joy. To prevent this from happening, we read the Book of Kohelet (Ecclesiastes) on the intermediate *Shabbat* of Sukkot.

Kohelet, written by King Solomon, the wisest of all men, is a sobering book that demonstrates the emptiness of mundane pursuits and comes to the conclusion that only spiritual values have lasting significance.

His immortal opening words are classic in world literature:

Futility of futilities, all is futility.
What real value is there for man
In all the gains he makes beneath the sun? (Ecclesiastes 1:2, 3)

Other well-known passages are:

Only that shall happen which has happened,
Only that occur which has occurred;
There is nothing new beneath the sun!" (Ecclesiastes 1:9)

Everything has its season, and there is a time for everything
   under the heavens.
A time to be born and a time to die;
a time to plant and a time to uproot the planted.
A time to kill and a time to heal;

a time to wreck and a time to build.
A time to weep and a time to laugh;
a time to wail and a time to dance. (Ecclesiastes 3:1–4)

Although the book seems to project a pessimistic and skeptical outlook on life, the final passage proves that it was King Solomon's intent to inspire people to greater attachment to God: "The sum of the matter, when all has been considered: Fear God and keep His commandments, for that is man's whole duty" (Ecclesiastes 12:13).

Superiority of Man over Beast

The Kotzker *rebbe* said, "It is written: 'The superiority of man over beast is nonexistent' (Ecclesiastes 3:19). You must read this phrase as follows: 'The superiority of man over beast is apparent when a man considers himself "nonexistent," when, in self-effacing humility, he thinks of himself as a nonentity. A man who considers himself as nothingness is indeed superior over beast."

Emet Ve'emunah

An Old and Foolish King

The *Maggid* of Mezritch remarked on the verse "Better is a poor wise youth than an old and foolish king" (Ecclesiastes 4:19), saying: "Rashi explains the 'old and foolish king' to be the personification of the *yetzer hara*, the evil impulse. Now, isn't it strange that King Solomon characterized the *yetzer hara* as a fool? After all, the *yetzer hara* is cunning enough to lure into its net wise men and fools alike.

"You must translate 'an old and foolish king' as 'a king [who rules even] over even old men and fools.' Unlike an ordinary king who does not have the power to induct old men and fools into his army or civil service, the evil inclination wields power even over old men and fools."

Eser Orot

Laborer's Irritant

"A worker's sleep is sweet, whether he has much or little to eat; but the rich man's abundance doesn't let him sleep" (Ecclesiastes 5:11).

Rabbi Simchah Zissel of Kelm offers a novel interpretation of this verse: "The laborer should indeed sleep well, for he put in a hard day's work, but what keeps him awake is 'the rich man's abundance,' that the rich man is living in luxury is preying on his mind."

Agadah uMachashavah beYahadut

Let Your Garments Be White

Said Rabbi Aharon of Karlin, "King Solomon says: 'Let your garments always be white' (Ecclesiastes 9:8). He is urging man to conduct his life as though he were wearing white garments and carrying a pitcher full of oil on his head. He must concentrate on keeping his balance and not come close to anything that may stain the whiteness of his garments. He must live a life of purity, for a man's soul, like a white garment, is easy to soil and hard to cleanse."

Midor Dor

Hoshana Rabbah

Hoshana Rabbah, the seventh day of Sukkot, has a solemn undertone; it is closely linked to Yom Kippur, for it is on this day that the final seal is placed on the verdict that was pronounced on Yom Kippur.[3] The service evokes the mood of the *Yamim Nora'im;* the *chazzan* who wears the white *kittel* chants the prayers with the distinctive melody of the Days of Awe. In some communities it is customary to blow the *shofar* after each *hoshana* circuit.

On *Hoshana Rabbah* we are mindful of the fact that during Sukkot, judgment is rendered concerning the rainfall for the entire world (*Rosh Hashanah* 16a). The economic fortunes of the world depend on abundant rainfall, so our prayers for rain are of crucial importance for the global economy as a whole and for *Eretz Yisrael* in particular.

This is evident in the special prayers of *Hoshana Rabbah.* During the *Shacharit* (morning) service of the first six days of Sukkot, the entire congregation makes one circuit around the *bimah* with *lulav* and *etrog* in hand while the *chazzan* leads the recitation of the *hoshana* prayer that is punctuated by the congregation's saying aloud, *Hoshana,* "Please save!" On the seventh day of Sukkot – *Hoshana Rabbah* – seven circuits are made, hence the name *Hoshana Rabbah,* which means "many *hoshanas."*

In the *hoshana* prayers we ask for rain, "to give life to the forsaken wastes, to sustain with trees, to enhance with sweet fruits, to rain on the sproutings, to elevate the thirsty earth." After the seven processions around the *bimah,* additional prayers are said, after which the *lulav* and *etrog* are laid aside and the *hoshana* bundle, consisting of five willow branches, is picked up. The *hoshana* bundle is beaten on the ground five times in accordance with an ancient custom that was instituted by the prophets Haggai, Zechariah, and Malachi (c. 350 B.C.E.).

It is the custom to stay up the night of *Hoshana Rabbah* to study Torah and read the Book of Deuteronomy.

God's Promise to Abraham

The *Midrash* says, "God told Abraham: I am one and you are one. I shall give your children a day that is uniquely suited to atone for their sins—*Hoshana Rabbah*. If Rosh Hashanah did not atone for your children, Yom Kippur will. If not, let *Hoshana Rabbah* do so."

Why was this promise given specifically to Abraham?

Just as Abraham's light began to shine twenty-one generations after Adam,[4] so will the light of Abraham's children shine brightly no later than twenty-one days after the beginning of judgment on Rosh Hashanah (*Hoshana Rabbah* falls on the twenty-first of *Tishri*).[5]

❊❊❊❊❊❊❊❊❊❊❊❊❊

Shemini Atzeret

The seven days of Sukkot which end with *Hoshana Rabbah* are followed by another holiday, Shemini Atzeret, the Eighth Day of Assembly. The Torah ordains, "The eighth day shall be an assembly for you; you may not do any mundane work" (Numbers 29:35). It is a festival in its own right, independent of Sukkot, and is observed one day in *Eretz Yisrael*; outside *Eretz Yisrael* it is observed two days. The fact that Shemini Atzeret is a separate *Yom Tov* is evident in the blessing of *Shehecheyanu* (Blessed are You, O Lord our God, King of the universe, who has kept us alive, sustained us, and brought us to this season), which is recited by women when lighting the candles and by men when reciting the *Kiddush*.

None of the special *mitzvot* associated with Sukkot are observed on Shemini Atzeret, and thus there is no requirement to take the *lulav* and *etrog*. Regarding the *mitzvah* of eating in a *sukkah* there are diverse customs. Some eat in a *sukkah* but do not say the *berachah leshev basukkah* (who has commanded us to dwell in the *sukkah*); others do not eat in a *sukkah* at all. The entire controversy is discussed in depth in tractate *Sukkah* 46b and 47a.

✳✳✳✳✳✳✳✳✳✳✳✳✳

Meaning of *Atzeret*

The word *atzeret* is derived from *atzar*, to collect, to store. The purpose of this festival is to recapitulate and to store in our memories everything we experienced and gained during the preceding *Yamim Tovim*, so that we will carry out the resolutions we have made, will retain the spiritual elevation we have reached, and will not lose them in the everyday life to which we are about to return.[6]

✳✳✳✳✳✳✳✳✳✳✳✳✳

Pure Rejoicing

Rabbi Shneur Zalman of Liadi said, Shemini Atzeret is a *Yom Tov* that is not identified with any specific symbol or *mitzvah*. It is not celebrated with either *matzah*, *shofar*, or *lulav*. The reason is that on Shemini Atzeret we reach a stage of true and pure joy, a state of happiness that requires no external symbolic stimuli. It is a joy that stems from the depth of man's inner self. Sadness and depression are the marks of a person who is distant from his inner core. A person who "is himself" and is in harmony with his inner core is filled with pure joy.

This is what the sages meant when they postulated in the Talmud, "Shemini Atzeret is a *Yom Tov* by itself"; it is a celebration and rejoicing of the essential inner self."

Likutei Amarim

✳✳✳✳✳✳✳✳✳✳✳✳✳

Prayer for Rain

The service of Shemini Atzeret reaches a peak in the *Tefilat Geshem*, the Prayer for Rain, which is recited during *Mussaf*. The *chazzan*, wearing a *kittel* (white robe), intones the repetition of the *Shemoneh Esrei* with the traditional solemn chant that evokes the mood of Yom Kippur. It is on Shemini Atzeret that the final judgment is made regarding the rainfall for the coming year.[7] *Eretz Yisrael* is a country whose agriculture and general well-being depend completely on rainfall. Hence, by praying for abundant rain for the upcoming rainy season, we demonstrate our solidarity with *Eretz Yisrael*.

❊❊❊❊❊❊❊❊❊❊❊❊❊❊

Mashiv Haruach

During *Mussaf* of Shemini Atzeret, we begin to say the words *mashiv haruach umorid hagashem*, "You cause the wind to blow and the rain to fall," in every *Shemoneh Esreih (Amidah)*. Because it does not rain during the summer in *Eretz Yisrael*, we stop saying these words in *Mussaf* of the first day of the following Pesach, in the spring.

Technically, the prayer for rain should be said at the beginning of Sukkot, rather than at its conclusion on Shemini Atzeret. The sages postponed the prayer until Sukkot is over, because rainfall on Sukkot would prevent us from eating in the *sukkah*, and it would be illogical to pray for rain at a time when we do not want it to rain.

❊❊❊❊❊❊❊❊❊❊❊❊❊❊

Rainfall and Resurrection

The words *mashiv haruach*, "You cause the wind to blow and the rain to fall," are inserted into the second prayer of the *Shemoneh Esrei*, following the words "You revive the dead with great salvation." Rainfall and the resurrection of the dead are closely associated; their common denominator is the concept of revival. Just as rain imparts life to the parched earth, making the dormant seeds sprout, so do the dead come back to life through God's abundant compassion at the time of *techiyat hemeitim,* the resuscitation of the dead.

⬚⬚⬚⬚⬚⬚⬚⬚⬚⬚⬚⬚⬚⬚

Only One Bull

During the week of Sukkot, altogether seventy bulls were brought as *Mussaf* offerings on the altar in the *Bet Hamikdash.* However, on Shemini Atzeret, only one bull was sacrificed. Why? The seventy bulls represent the seventy nations of the world; the one bull of Shemini Atzeret represents the unique nation Israel. You may compare it to a king who had held a festival for seven days and invited all of the country's inhabitants (the nations of the world) to the seven days of feasting. When the seven days of feasting were over, he said to his friend (Israel), "Let us now have a small meal together, just you and I" (*Bamidbar Rabbah* 21, *Sukkah* 55b).

⬚⬚⬚⬚⬚⬚⬚⬚⬚⬚⬚⬚⬚⬚

Union with God

Rabbi Noach of Lechowitz expounded, The theme of Shemini Atzeret may be better understood if we think of it in terms of a bride and groom. During the wedding, they are both decked out in a wardrobe of exquisite, elegant clothes and jewelry. However, when they come together in their private chamber, they remove their garments and jewelry.

It is the same with Shemini Atzeret. During the seven days of Sukkot, the Jewish people offered a profusion of seventy bulls, but on Shemini Atzeret – the moment they achieve complete unification with God – they brought only one bull (Numbers 29:36).

Torat Avot

✳✳✳✳✳✳✳✳✳✳✳✳✳

Farewell to the *Sukkah*

During the afternoon of Shemini Atzeret, before we leave the *sukkah* to return to our permanent home, we recite the following prayer: May it be Your will, Lord our God and God of our fathers, that just as I have observed [the *mitzvah*] and sat in this *sukkah*, so may I be privileged in the coming year to dwell in the *sukkah* of the hide of Leviathan.

Rabbi Aharon of Karlin said, "The name Leviathan is etymologically related to the verb *lavah*, which means 'to accompany, to escort' (as in *levayah*, funeral procession).

"When leaving the *sukkah*, we pray that the spiritual light of the *sukkah* should accompany us throughout the entire year and that the impression the *sukkah* made on us should be evident in our day-to-day conduct."

Bet Aharon

✳✳✳✳✳✳✳✳✳✳✳✳✳

Simchat Torah

The final day of Sukkot is called Simchat Torah, the Rejoicing of the Torah. In *Eretz Yisrael*, the holidays of Shemini Atzeret and Simchat Torah are celebrated on the same day. Outside *Eretz Yisrael*, an extra day is added so that Simchat Torah is observed as the second day of Shemini Atzeret, on the twenty-third of *Tishri*.

The holiday is called Simchat Torah, the Rejoicing of the Torah, because we conclude the reading of the last portion of the Torah. Although the name Simchat Torah does not occur in the Talmud, the festive character of the holiday is mentioned in the *Zohar* (*Pinechas*) and many other early writings.

Traditionally, the conclusion of the Torah or a tractate of the Talmud has been an occasion for a joyous feast. The *Midrash*[8] derives this from the Scripture, which relates that King Solomon made a feast for all his servants after he was granted wisdom (1 Kings 3:15).

※※※※※※※※※※※※※

The *Hakafot*

At night, all the Torah scrolls are taken out of the ark, and members of the congregation take turns marching around the *bimah* (reader's platform) carrying the Torah scrolls while the *chazzan* chants

> Please, God, save now!
> Please, God, bring success now!
> Please, God, answer us on the day we call.

This is followed by the text of one of the seven *hakafah* circuits. Then everyone joins in exuberant dancing and singing. Round and round they whirl, their faces radiating true happiness; young and old, strangers becoming friends, little children being showered with candy and dancing while waving little flags. Parents and grandparents dance, happily carrying their small children and grandchildren. In a spontaneous outpouring of love of God, love of the Torah, and love of the Jewish people, they sing the latest tunes proclaiming the greatness of God, dancing in the spirit of *vegilu birada*, "rejoice with trembling"

(Psalm 2:11). In *yeshivot* and chasidic synagogues, the *hakafot* last for many hours, reaching a climax when the *rosh yeshivah* (dean) or the chasidic *rebbe* dances with the Torah while thousands of entranced spectators take in the inspiring scene.

❊❊❊❊❊❊❊❊❊❊❊❊❊

Seven *Hakafot*

The number seven occupies a prominent place in Jewish thought. It symbolizes the idea of holiness. This becomes apparent in a number of Torah laws and Jewish customs:

– After six days of Creation, *Shabbat*–the **seventh** day –infusing all of Creation with holiness.

– **Seven** weeks of counting the *Omer*–the period of time from the day after the Exodus until the culmination in the giving of the Torah, fifty days later, at Sinai (Leviticus 23:15)–whereby Israel was shown the path toward holiness.

– The *shemittah*, **sabbatical** year, every **seventh** year (Leviticus 25:2–7), when the earth has its *Shabbat*.

– The *yovel*–jubilee year, the fiftieth year–after **seven** times **seven** years (Leviticus 25:8–34).

– The **seven** fruits of the Land of Israel: wheat, barley, grapes, figs, pomegranates, olives, and dates (Deuteronomy 8:8).

– The **seven** branches of the *menorah* in the Tabernacle (Exodus 25:31–40), symbol of holiness.

– The **seven** shepherds of Israel (*ushpizin*): Abraham, Isaac, Jacob, Moses, Aaron, Joseph, and David.

– **Seven** circuits of the bride under the wedding canopy, **seven** blessings, and **seven** days of celebration of groom and bride–sanctifying the marriage.

– **Seven** *hakafot* on *Hoshana Rabbah* and Simchat Torah.

❊❊❊❊❊❊❊❊❊❊❊❊❊

Torah Reading

The following morning, the *hakafot* are repeated with renewed vigor. Everyone is called up to the reading of the Torah, after which he makes *Kiddush* and is treated to the delicacies that have been prepared. After everyone has had his *aliyah*, a prominent member is called up for *kol hanearim*, "all the children." At this time, all the children under the age of *bar mitzvah* gather on the *bimah*, and a large *tallit* is held aloft over their heads. The adult who has the *aliyah* recites the *berachah* slowly and clearly, and the children say it along with him. After the second *berachah*, the familiar blessing of Jacob is said aloud, *Hamalach hago'el oti* . . . "May He bless the lads, and let them carry my name, along with the names of my fathers, Abraham and Isaac. May they increase in the land like fish" (Genesis 48:16).

The brief but exciting ceremony makes an indelible imprint on the young mind. Through the celebration of Simchat Torah, children associate Torah with joy, love, dancing, singing, and sweets. The adults see in the children's collective *berachah* a manifestation of the continuity of the eternal bond between the Torah and the Jewish people.

The *aliyah* for the final chapter of the Torah is given to the *chatan* Torah (the groom of the Torah). This honor is usually reserved for the rabbi or an outstanding member of the congregation. After the concluding Torah verses have been read, the entire congregation exclaims, *Chazak, chazak, venitchazeik!* "Be strong, be strong, and let us strengthen one another!"

No sooner has the Torah been completed than the new cycle begins with the reading of Genesis 1:1. The person called for this *aliyah* is called *chatan Bereishit*, "groom of *Bereishit*/Genesis," an honor given to one who has earned the respect of the community. The last *aliyah* is given to the *chatan Maftir*, "the groom of *Maftir*," who also reads the *haftarah* from the first chapter of the Book of Joshua.

The Torah is then replaced in the ark, accompanied by more singing and dancing, and the service concludes with a joyous *Mussaf* prayer.

Why Do We Rejoice on Simchat Torah?

Once, on the night of Simchat Torah, the Kotzker *rebbe* opened the door that led from his chamber into the *bet midrash* (study hall), where the *chasidim* were feasting and exuberantly celebrating the *Yom Tov*.

"Who can tell me," asked the *rebbe*, "the reason for the rejoicing at the completion of the Torah?"

No one replied.

The *rebbe* then answered his own question: "The reason for the happiness is that you know that you completed the Torah, and yet you realize that you have not even started. This awareness is the real source for your joyous celebration."

Emet Ve'emunah

Beginning the Torah Anew

The *Chidushei Harym* said, People think that we rejoice on Simchat Torah because on this day we conclude the Torah. They are wrong. Our happiness stems from the fact that we are beginning the Torah all over again.

Siach Sarfei Kodesh

Every Jew Rejoices on Simchat Torah

Once, during the *hakafah* circuits on Simchat Torah, Rabbi Naftali of Ropshitz observed a simple, uneducated coachman dancing and singing with all his might.

Surprised at the extraordinary fervor of the unscholarly man, Rabbi Naftali asked him, "Tell me, my good man, why are you so happy tonight? Did you study the Torah all year that you should rejoice on Simchat Torah?"

"Rabbi," replied the coachman, "if my brother makes a celebration, shouldn't I rejoice with him? Don't I have a share in his happiness?"

Agadah uMachashavah beYahadut

❋❋❋❋❋❋❋❋❋❋❋❋❋❋

The Power of Dancing

Rabbi Shalom of Belz said, "I cannot tell you the deeper meaning of the dancing on Simchat Torah. But one thing I can reveal to you: all the prayers that did not rise to heaven during the course of the year will soar upward on Simchat Torah, propelled by the fervor of your dancing."

❋❋❋❋❋❋❋❋❋❋❋❋❋❋

The Torah Must Be Happy

Rabbi Chaim Brisker said, Simchat Torah means "Rejoicing of the Torah." You see, it is not enough that a Jew rejoices with the Torah. More important is that the Torah should have reason to rejoice with the Jewish people.

❋❋❋❋❋❋❋❋❋❋❋❋❋❋

Who Wrote the Final Sentences of the Torah?

The Baal Shem Tov, commenting on the verse "So Moses, servant of God, died there . . ." (Deuteronomy 34:5), writes, "Rashi wonders how it is possible that Moses died, and yet wrote the words 'Moshe died there.' We certainly cannot say that Moses was alive when he wrote the words 'Moses died,' for that would be untrue." Rashi answers: "God dictated it to him, and Moses wrote it *bedema,* 'with tears.' "

Asks the Baal Shem Tov: How does the fact that Moses wrote it with tears solve the paradox? He answers: We know that the Torah existed 2,000 years before the world was created.[9] Now you may wonder, how could the Torah contain such stories as those of Adam and Eve, Noah, and the Patriarchs long before they actually happened? You may point to an even greater incongruity: death came into being as a result of Adam's sin. If Adam had not sinned there would be no death, yet the Torah records the death of many people. Besides, the Rambam explains at length that man was given the freedom of determination – the freedom to choose between good and evil. This being so, how could the Torah record beforehand that Adam was going to sin?

The answer is that originally the Torah existed as a mixture of letters. All the letters of the Torah from *Bereishit* until *le'eynei kol Yisrael* were not written in the order as we read them, separated into words and sentences, but as one huge jumble of letters. Whenever something occurred in the world, the appropriate letters were extracted from the mixture, placed in the proper order, and formed into words.

When Moses was about to die, the entire Torah had been written in words and sentences, for all these events had taken place already. Only the letters of the final sentences from "So Moses, servant of God, died there" until the end were still mixed up, because Moses had not yet died. However, Moses had to be the one who wrote the entire Torah, as it is written, "Be mindful of the Torah of My servant Moses" (Malachi 3:22).

What did God do? He dictated the letters to Moses in their mixed-up form, and Moses wrote them down in that jumbled order. After Moses died, Joshua decoded the letters, placing them into the proper order, and the words of the final sentences emerged. Thus, Moses did write the entire Torah until its very last word.

Now, as for Rashi's explanation that "Moses wrote it *bedema*–'with tears' "–you should know that *dema* can also be translated as "mixture," as in *Gittin* 52b, *Chagigah* 24b, and many other sources, where it denotes a mixture of *chullin* (secular fruits) and *terumah* (sacred fruits given to the priest). Hence, when Rashi says that Moshe wrote it *bedema*, he meant to say that he wrote the letters in a jumbled and unintelligible form.

Sefer Baal Shem Tov[10]

❉❉❉❉❉❉❉❉❉❉❉❉❉

Connecting the End to the Beginning

The *Chozeh* of Lublin was wont to say, "On Simchat Torah we end the Torah with the words *le'einei kol Yisrael*, "before the eyes of all Israel," and we begin with *Bereishit*, "In the beginning God created." The last letter of the Torah is a *lamed*: the first letter is a *bet*. Together they form the word *lev*, "heart." This teaches us that the most important thing is to observe the Torah with heart, with burning enthusiasm.

7

THE MINOR
FESTIVALS:
CHANUKAH AND
PURIM

Although the stories of Purim and Chanukah are separated chronolog-
ically by more than two centuries, a common thread runs through both
holidays. The theme that binds them is our grateful recognition of
God's benevolence in ensuring the survival of the Jewish people in the
face of a powerful enemy bent on their destruction.

The survival of a nation depends on two factors: the preservation of
the lives of its citizens and the continuance of the nation's cultural
heritage, beliefs, traditions, and language. The ancient Egyptians have
disappeared from the face of the earth, and today their culture and
language are dead objects on display in museums. The same is true of
the Babylonians, the Greeks, and the Romans. Their people exist no
longer and their teachings have vanished into oblivion.

The Jewish people faced a similar threat. In the days of Purim, their
physical existence was in jeopardy, as Haman sought to destroy and
exterminate all the Jews, young and old. During the time of Chanukah,
the Jews' spiritual survival was at stake, as the Greek oppressors tried to

assimilate the Jewish people by making them forget the Torah and so sever the bond that tied them to God.

Mercifully, God granted His people victory over their enemies in both cases, so that they emerged unscathed and with their Torah intact. Thus, Purim and Chanukah warn us of the twin dangers that threaten our existence as a nation and make us aware that God performed miracles for our forefathers "in those days [but also for us] at the present time."

Everyone of us can testify to this. The dreadful years of the Holocaust, when the physical extinction of the Jewish people nearly was accomplished, represented a replay of the Purim era, and the recent fall of communism, which almost succeeded in eradicating the spiritual existence of Russian Jewry, duplicates the miracle of Chanukah.

The miracles of Purim and Chanukah proclaim the invincibility of the Jewish people in both body and spirit.

Chanukah: Historical Background

The miracle of Chanukah is the culmination of a story that began 162 years earlier, with the conquest of the Middle East and Asia by Alexander the Great (356–323 B.C.E.). Leading an army of 40,000 men, Alexander crossed into Asia from his native Macedonia to defeat the mighty Persian Empire. Scoring victory after victory, the brilliant strategist swept across Syria, Egypt, and Babylonia, extending Greek power, influence, and civilization from the Nile to the borders of India. In 332 B.C.E., on one of his military campaigns, Alexander conquered *Eretz Yisrael*, which until then had been a vassal state of the Persian Empire. When he died at the young age of 32, Greek language and culture was dominating the lands of the Fertile Crescent. For the Jewish people, the encounter of Torah ethics and morality with the pagan creed of ancient Greece proved to be a traumatic shock and a clash of cultures, which threatened to undermine the very existence of Judaism.

After Alexander's death, his vast kingdom was divided into three parts: the Macedonian kingdom (now Greece), Asia (including Syria, Persia, and Mesopotamia) under the rule of the Seleucids, and Egypt, governed by the Ptolemies. After many battles between Alexander's contentious heirs, the Land of Israel became a province of Syria under the rule of the Seleucid dynasty.

Greek culture was making serious inroads among the Jews of *Eretz Yisrael*. Many of them, especially those of the wealthy aristocracy, began adopting Greek customs and beliefs. Those assimilationists are called "Hellenists," and the Greek way of life they followed is called "Hellenism," a term derived from the word *Hellas*, which means "Greece."

When a new king, Antiochus IV (also called Antiochus Epiphanes), ascended the throne in Syria in 175 B.C.E., the stage was set for a historic confrontation between Hellenist depravity and the defenders of the Torah way of life.

Under Antiochus' regime, Jerusalem began to look like a Greek city. Hellenistic Jews studied the Greek language and literature and gradually abandoned the Torah way of life, eating nonkosher food and participating in worship of the Greek gods. Some went so far as to undergo painful surgery to remove the marks of circumcision.

Gradually, the Hellenists gained greater and greater influence. By offering Antiochus a substantial bribe, they persuaded him to appoint the Hellenist Jason (real name, Yeshua) as *Kohen Gadol* (High Priest). Jason used his office to build a gymnasium very close to the Holy Temple, where Jewish youths competed in wrestling, racing, and javelin throwing. This sports stadium contained statues of Greek gods, and sacrifices were offered to Hercules at the start of the games.

After three years, Jason was replaced by Menelaus, who had offered Antiochus a larger bribe. Menelaus, the vile Hellenistic "High Priest," who was not even a *kohen*, robbed the treasury of the Holy Temple and arranged the murders of his opponents.

Returning from an unsuccessful campaign against Egypt, Antiochus, who suspected a revolt against his throne, sacked Jerusalem, killing 40,000 men, women, and children and sending an equal number into captivity. Soon after that, he decreed that Jews must abandon their belief in God and the Torah and cease offering sacrifices in the Temple.

Throughout the country, altars were erected on which pigs and other unclean animals were to be sacrificed. In addition, the Holy Temple was desecrated and images of pagan gods were placed on the holy altar, in the Temple courtyards, and in the sanctuary. In an effort to wipe out every last trace of Judaism, Antiochus outlawed the study of the Torah, the observance of *Shabbat, Rosh Chodesh*, the Festivals, *milah* (circumcision), and family purity. Jews were forced to publicly disavow their allegiance to God and the Torah. The penalty for disobedience was death. The perfidious Hellenists combed the countryside in search of violators, whom they cravenly delivered to the Greek overlords to be executed.

Many Jews fled, hiding out in the wilderness and in caves, willing to give their lives rather than break their covenant with God. Many tales of individual martyrdom and heroism dating back to this time have become part of Jewish history.

Jewish anger at the imposed Hellenization came to a head in 164 B.C.E., in Modi'in, a small town not far from Jerusalem, where Mattityahu–the Hasmonean[1] priest–and his five sons had taken refuge. When the forces of Antiochus arrived in Modi'in to erect an altar to Zeus and tried to persuade Mattityahu to offer a sacrifice to their god, Mattityahu gallantly declared his allegiance to the Almighty. As he was speaking, a Hellenistic Jew approached the altar to offer his pig. Burning with fury, Mattityahu and his five sons pulled out the short daggers they had been hiding in their robes. The aged Mattityahu mounted the altar and beheaded the Jewish traitor. Jumping down, he also killed the Syrian commander and destroyed the Greek altar, calling out, "Whoever clings to the Torah and is steadfast in the covenant, let him join me!" His five sons slew most of the soldiers in the Syrian regiment.

Mattityahu and his valiant sons (Yochanan, Shimon, Yehudah, Elazar, and Yonatan) then went into hiding in the mountains of the Judean wilderness, where they were joined by many like-minded Jews. Their act of defiance marked the beginning of a guerrilla war of Jews loyal to the Torah against the Syrian oppressors and their Hellenistic lackeys.

When Mattityahu died the following year, his son Yehudah became the next leader of the rebellion. He was known as Yehudah "the Maccabee." The title is an acronym of the initials of the verse מי כמכה באלם ה׳, *mi kamocha ba'eilim Hashem*? "Who is like You, O Lord, among the mighty?" (Exodus 15:11). The same text appeared also on Yehudah's banner in order to remind his men that any victory they won was due to God's help.

The poorly trained and ill-equipped guerrilla band attacked the superior Syrian forces and, miraculously, defeated them in every skirmish. Determined to crush the revolt once and for all, Antiochus decided to mount a massive offensive against the Torah loyalists. He assembled a huge army of 40,000 foot soldiers, 7,000 cavalrymen, and a large number of elephants – the Greek equivalent of tanks. Led by Syria's most proficient generals, this powerful force encamped at Emmaus.

Yehudah and his followers placed their faith in God. Yehudah divided his men into four groups of 1,000 each, appointing his brothers to lead them in battle. After praying to God to grant them victory, they swooped down on the unsuspecting enemy. Taken by surprise, the Syrian army panicked and took flight. The Jews set fire to the Syrian camp and pursued the fleeing Syrians, killing 3,000 troops.

But the Syrians did not give up. One year later, a powerful Syrian army of 60,000 soldiers and 5,000 cavalrymen, backed by a huge arsenal of weapons, launched an all-out attack against Yehudah's daring guerrilla band of 10,000 men at Bet Tzur. Again, God answered the Torah loyalists' fervent prayers. They routed the enemy, killing more than 5,000 Syrians. Subsequently, Yehudah and his valiant warriors captured Jerusalem and marched triumphantly toward the *Bet Hamikdash*, the Holy Temple.

They were devastated by what they saw: the sanctuary in desolation, the altar desecrated, the walls of the sanctuary breached, grass sprouting in the courtyards – a heartbreaking spectacle. Wasting no time, Yehudah issued orders to cleanse the Temple, to tear down the altar that had been defiled, and to build a new altar. The men repaired the walls of the sanctuary, purified the holy vessels, and built a new, makeshift *menorah* to replace the golden *menorah* that had been stolen.

On the twenty-fifth of *Kislev*, 165 B.C.E., three years to the day after the Syrians/Greeks had defiled the Temple and sacrificed a pig to their heathen idol, the Hasmoneans rededicated the *Bet Hamikdash* and reinstated the offering of sacrifices to God in a ceremony that lasted eight days.

When the *kohanim* searched for oil to light the *menorah*, they found only one jar of holy oil that had not been defiled. The oil in that jar was sufficient to burn for only one day, and it would take eight days until a new supply of holy oil could be produced. Miraculously, the one-day supply of oil in the jar burned in the *menorah* for eight days. The sages of that time then ordained that the eight days, beginning with the twenty-fifth of *Kislev*, should be celebrated as days of rejoicing, that *Hallel* should be recited, and that lights should be lit in all Jewish homes on each of the eight nights in order to publicize the miracle.[2]

This eight-day Festival is called Chanukah, "Dedication"; it is the Festival of Lights. The name Chanukah is also seen as a contraction of חנו כ"ה, *chanu kof hei*, "they rested on the twenty-fifth [of *Kislev*]."[3]

※※※※※※※※※※※※※※

Tales of Heroism and Martyrdom

During the dark days of religious persecution, there were many who risked their lives and observed the *mitzvot*, defying the king. Two women who had circumcised their newborn sons were denounced by the king's Hellenist agents. They were paraded through the streets with their infants tied to their necks. Then they were cast to their deaths from the city wall.

On another occasion, after offering a pig on an altar, the king's Hellenist agents seized a venerable sage named Elazar and forcibly opened his mouth to make him eat the pork. Elazar adamantly refused to eat the abomination. The Hellenists then whispered in his ear that they would give him kosher meat to eat, as long as they could publicly claim that he was eating of the offering. The ninety-year-old Elazar turned down the offer, refusing to pretend to eat of the offering and thereby lure the young people into worshiping idols. He gave his life for God and the Torah.

Chanah and her seven sons were captured and brought before the king. One after another they were told to bow down to an idol. Each one refused and was tortured and killed most barbarically. When it was the turn of the youngest son, a little boy, to bow down, he also refused. "Look, all your brothers have been killed," the king said. "I'm going to throw down my ring in front of the idol. Just pick it up. That way the people will think that you obeyed the king's order."

"I pity you, your majesty," the little boy replied. "If you are worried about your prestige that you cannot force me to do your bidding, then surely I should be concerned about God's honor."

The king ordered his execution.

"Son," Chanah cried, "go to Abraham and tell him: you erected one altar to sacrifice your son Isaac, but I erected seven altars. For you it was only a test, but for me it was reality."[4]

Chanukah in the Talmud

Although all Jewish Festivals are mentioned in the Bible and dealt with at great length in the Talmud, Chanukah is discussed only briefly in the Talmud in the following concise paragraph in *Shabbat* 21b:

Ma'i Chanukah? "What is Chanukah?" The rabbis have taught that beginning with the twenty-fifth of *Kislev*, eight days of Chanukah are observed. On these days, no eulogies should be delivered, and fasting is not permitted. For when the Greeks entered the sanctuary, they defiled all the oils. When the Hasmoneans triumphed over them, they searched and found only one remaining jar of oil that bore the seal of the *Kohen Gadol* (High Priest). Although it contained only enough oil to burn one day, a miracle occurred and it lasted eight days. A year later, the rabbis designated these days as *Yamim Tovim* on which prayers of praise and thanksgiving should be recited.

Message of the Chanukah Lights

The lights of Chanukah proclaim the survival of the Jewish people and the victory of the spirit of Torah over religious persecution and brute force. Whereas the civilizations of ancient Egypt, Babylonia, Persia, Greece, and Rome have passed into oblivion, the light of Torah continues to shine brightly and with undiminished strength. Ruins, monuments, and statues of stone and bronze, such as the pyramids of Egypt, the Acropolis of Athens, and the Colosseum of Rome, are the only remnants of those ancient civilizations. But the Torah, the *Mishnah,* and the *Gemara* – the pillars of Jewishness – are vibrantly alive, and the words of our sages are avidly studied by young and old alike, in *Eretz Yisrael* and all over the world. The endurance of the people of Israel against all odds is a supernatural phenomenon, a mystery that has baffled historians and sociologists. It can be explained only as a divine miracle, just like the lights of the *menorah* that miraculously continued to burn for eight days.

The lights of Chanukah tell us that no power in the world can sever the bond between the Jewish people and God. As it is written, "Vast floods cannot quench love, nor rivers drown it" (Song of Songs 8:7).

In the final analysis, Chanukah proclaims God's guidance of the destiny of the Jewish people and that of all mankind.

※※※※※※※※※※※※※※

Laws of Lighting the *Menorah*

All kinds of oil may be used for the Chanukah lights, but olive oil is preferred, for the miracle in the Temple also occurred using olive oil, but we may also use candles. Preferably, the wicks should be made of cotton. It is not necessary to take new wicks every night; we may light the same wicks until they are used up.

It is the custom for each member of the family to light the *menorah*: one candle on the first evening; two candles on the second, adding one candle each evening until the eighth day, when all the candles are lit.

In the days of the *Mishnah*, the *menorah* was lit in the doorway opposite the *mezuzah*, so that upon entering and leaving the house, we are surrounded by *mitzvot*. Nowadays, the *menorah* is placed in front of a window facing the street, in order to publicize the miracle.

The lights should be placed in an even row; none should be higher than any other.

The order of lighting candles is as follows: on the first night, the candle to be lit is placed at the end of the *menorah*, facing the right hand; on the second night, we add one toward the left. Likewise, on every succeeding night, we add one toward the left. We begin by kindling the light that has been added, then proceed to kindle the other lights to the right.

It is customary to light one extra light in addition to the required number of lights for the given night. The extra light is called the *shamash* (the servant). The *shamash* is used to kindle the other lights.

The lights should burn for at least one-half hour.

The time to light the *menorah* is immediately after the stars appear. We recite the *Maariv* prayer before lighting the *menorah*, having assembled the entire family for the lighting.

Women, too, are obligated to light the *menorah*, because they also benefited from the miracle of Chanukah.

The order of the *berachot* on the first night is as follows:

1. *Lehadlik ner shel Chanukah* – to kindle the Chanukah lights.

2. *She'asah nissim* – who has wrought miracles for our forefathers, in those days at this season.

3. *Shehecheyanu* – who has kept us alive, sustained us, and brought us to this season.

On all subsequent nights, the third *berachah*, *Shehecheyanu*, is omitted.

After one light has been kindled, *Haneirot Halalu*, "These lights we kindle," is recited, and during its recitation the additional lights are kindled.

After the kindling of the lights, it is customary to sing *Maoz Tzur*, "O mighty Rock of my salvation."[5]

Other Chanukah Observances

On each of the eight days of Chanukah, the full *Hallel* is recited. In addition, *Al Hanisim* is included in each *Shemoneh Esrei* (*Amidah*) and in *Birkat Hamazon* (Grace after Meals).

In the synagogue, the chapter relating the offerings brought by the heads of the twelve tribes of Israel upon the dedication of the altar in the Tabernacle is read (Numbers 7:1–8:4). Each day, the portion of one *nasi* (head of tribe) is read. On the eighth day, the Torah reading begins with the paragraph on the eighth *nasi* and continues through the entire chapter until "thus did he make the *menorah*" (Numbers 8:4).

❄❄❄❄❄❄❄❄❄❄❄❄❄

Customs of Chanukah

Chanukah is a joyous holiday, a period when relatives get together for festive meals at which the traditional *latkes* (potato pancakes) and jelly doughnuts are served. Both dishes are fried in oil, which evokes the miracle of Chanukah. Children happily receive Chanukah *gelt* (Chanukah money) and gifts, and they play the *dreidl* (a spinning top). On the *dreidl's* four sides are written the letters *nun, gimel, hei, shin*–the initials of *nes gadol hayah sham*, "a great miracle happened there." Depending on which of its sides the *dreidl* lands, the player gets all the money in the pot, half of it, or nothing or must put money into the pot. The warm feeling that is spread by the gently flickering Chanukah lights coupled with the joy of the togetherness of family and friends makes an indelible impression on children's young minds.

❄❄❄❄❄❄❄❄❄❄❄❄❄

References to Chanukah in the Torah

Although Chanukah is not mentioned in Scripture, a number of allusions to Chanukah can be found in the Torah.

1. Chanukah, the Festival of Lights, occurs on the twenty-fifth of *Kislev*. Significantly, the twenty-fifth word in the Torah is *or*, "light." It occurs in the verse *yehi or*, "Let there be light" (Genesis 1:3).

2. The twenty-fifth stop on the forty-year journey of the children of Israel through the wilderness was at a place called Chashmonah (Numbers 33:29), a name reminiscent of Chashmonaim (Hasmoneans).

3. In the portion of *Emor*, the Festivals of the entire year are enumerated in detail: *Shabbat*, Passover, Shavuot, Rosh Hashanah, Yom Kippur, and Sukkot (Leviticus 23:1–41). Immediately following the account of the Festivals, we find the command, "to bring clear illuminating oil from hand-crushed olives to keep the lamp burning constantly" (Leviticus 24:1, 2). The juxtaposition of the two passages – that of the Festivals and that of the Eternal Light – presages the emergence of a future holiday that would celebrate the kindling of the oil – the Festival of Chanukah.

Pesikta Ze'irta

❋❋❋❋❋❋❋❋❋❋❋❋❋❋

Why Eight Days?

With regard to Chanukah, a perennial question is being asked that has challenged the ingenuity of every student of the Talmud. Thousands of answers have been suggested, and every year new solutions to the problem are added. It is the famous "question of the Bet Yosef."

The Bet Yosef asks in *Shulchan Aruch, Orach Chaim* 670:6, "Since the jar that was found contained enough oil for one day, they needed a miracle for only *seven* days. Why then did the rabbis institute Chanukah for eight days?"

Following are a few of the answers:

1. At the outset, they divided the oil in the cruse into eight parts to last the eight days needed until new oil could be produced. Each night they placed in the *menorah* one-eighth of the required quantity, yet the

small quantity of oil burned the entire day. Thus the miracle took place all eight nights.

2. After they poured the oil into the lamps of the *menorah*, miraculously the jar of oil remained full.

3. On the first night, they emptied all the oil into the *menorah*, and in the morning they discovered that after burning all night, the lamps were still full. This miracle was repeated each of the eight nights.

4. The miracle of the oil actually happened only seven days. The first day of Chanukah commemorates the victory in the war against the Syrians/Greeks. The remaining seven days commemorate the miracle of the oil.

5. The fact that they discovered a jar that bore the seal of the High Priest was in itself a miracle.

6. They realized that all existence endures only by dint of divine providence, and the natural order of things is also a miracle. Thus, the lights that burned on the first day were as great a miracle as the oil's lasting seven more days.

7. The segment in the Torah that delineates the lighting of the *menorah* of the Tabernacle follows immediately after the paragraph that describes Sukkot (Leviticus, end of ch. 23 and beginning of ch. 24). The closeness in the Torah of Sukkot and the *menorah* tells us that, just as the festival of Sukkot has eight days, so too Chanukah should be celebrated for eight days.

✳✳✳✳✳✳✳✳✳✳✳✳✳✳

An Intriguing Question

Rabbi Chaim Soloveitchik offers a fascinating answer to the "question of the *Bet Yosef*."

He says: The only oil valid for lighting the *menorah* in the Temple was olive oil, that is, oil squeezed from olives that grew on an olive tree. This being so, how could they fulfill the obligation of lighting the *menorah* with miraculous oil, which did not come from olives but was produced by a miracle?

Answered Reb Chaim, We must conclude that the miracle did not cause the *quantity* of the oil to increase; no *new* oil came into being. What happened was that the *quality* of the olive oil changed miraculously, so that the original olive oil became more potent and burned more efficiently, allowing the one-day supply to burn eight days. Thus, although initially they poured the entire contents of the jar into the lamps of the *menorah*, each night only one-eighth of the oil was consumed. Consequently, the same miracle occurred on the first day as on each of the following seven days.

❈❈❈❈❈❈❈❈❈❈❈❈❈

The Lights of Chanukah

Rabbi Shneur Zalman of Liadi: The other festivals we celebrate with tangible symbols: on Pesach we eat *matzah*, on Sukkot we wave the *lulav* and dwell in the *sukkah*, on Rosh Hashanah we blow the *shofar*. Only Chanukah is marked by the spiritual symbol of light. The reason is that the war that reached its climax on Chanukah was fought for the freedom to observe the Torah, which is represented by light, as it is written, "For the *mitzvah* is a lamp, the Torah is a light" (Proverbs 6:23).

❈❈❈❈❈❈❈❈❈❈❈❈❈

Thirty-six Lights

Rabbi Pinchas of Koretz: On Chanukah we kindle a total of thirty-six lights ($1+2+3+4+5+6+7+8=36$). This number parallels the thirty-six tractates in the Talmud. Indeed, the light of Chanukah is reflected in the books of the Talmud.

❈❈❈❈❈❈❈❈❈❈❈❈❈

Chasidic Interpretation of Chanukah

Rabbi Nachman of Bratzlav sees Chanukah from a spiritual vantage point. He offers the following beautiful insight:

Chanukah, the first holiday after the *Yamim Nora'im* and Sukkot, represents the beginning of a person's education in the service of God. This is reflected in the name Chanukah, which is derived from the root *chanoch*, meaning "to educate."

Furthermore, Chanukah tells us that we cannot begin to serve God unless we first wage a war with ourselves to break the stranglehold of the power of materialism. This is the deeper meaning of the battle against Greek idolatry that led to the establishment of Chanukah.

The evil empire of the pagans wanted to alienate the people of Israel from the Torah and prevent them from fulfilling its commandments. This is symbolic of the power of corporeality – the carnal side of man, which tries to estrange man from God's Torah.

But when one is fortunate enough to subdue this evil empire and master one's base instincts, then one kindles the Chanukah lights. Its bright lights symbolize the ladder that reaches upward toward inner perfection. However, we should not remain standing on the rung we have reached. Our souls must grow and aspire to greater purity and holiness. This idea is reflected in the number of Chanukah lights, which increases from day to day.

※※※※※※※※※※※※※※※

Festival for the Family

Rabbi Samson Raphael Hirsch: "Each member of the family is obligated to kindle Chanukah lights" (*Shabbat* 21b). The lighting of the *menorah* in the synagogue is not enough. The *mitzvah* should be done at home as well by each member of the family. What good is it to praise God in the synagogue if the spirit of Torah is absent from the home? Not in the synagogue does our salvation lie. Let the rabbi preach the sermon; let the choir intone the harmonious chant; their impact is minimal. Instead, "From the mouth of infants and sucklings You have founded strength" (Psalm 8:3). We must ask ourselves this question: Does the Torah light the way for our little ones? Does the glow of Judaism warm their hearts?

Consider this: What were the factors on which depended the rescue and the survival of Judaism? Was it the light that illuminated the sanctuary of the Temple? Certainly not. The High Priests themselves betrayed it. It was the light that shone in the home of the small-town *kohen* Mattityahu that sparked the redemption.

※※※※※※※※※※※※

Miracle of the Oil

Sefat Emet: Why did the miracle happen with oil? Oil does not blend with any other liquid but will rise to the top. In that aspect, oil is symbolic of the lofty qualities of the Jewish people. Like oil, the Jewish people does not intermingle with other nations but rises to a higher plane.

※※※※※※※※※※※※

Ma'oz Tzur

The song *Ma'oz Tzur*, "O mighty Rock of my salvation," which is recited after *Hanerot Halalu*, recalls all the exiles of the Jewish people and their deliverance from their oppressors.

The first letters of the stanzas combine to form the name of the author, Mordechai, who supposedly lived in the thirteenth century.

The first stanza comprises an opening prayer for the rebuilding of the *Bet Hamikdash* and the dedication of the altar.

The second stanza alludes to the bondage in Egypt, which ended when "Pharaoh's army and all his offspring went down like a stone into the deep."

The third stanza refers to the Babylonian exile, which came to a close "when at Babylonia's demise Zerubabel came—at the end of seventy years I was saved."

The fourth stanza hints at the evil Haman, who planned to destroy the Jewish people. But God saved them, "and the enemy and all his children You hanged on the gallows."

The fifth stanza explicitly states:

> Greeks gathered against me, then in Hasmonean days.
> They breached the walls of my towers,
> and they defiled all the oils;
> And from the one remnant of the flasks
> a miracle was wrought for the roses [the Jewish people].
> Men of insight—eight days
> established for song and jubilation.

The sixth and final stanza was added later and contains a plea for divine vengeance against all enemies of the Jewish people.

※※※※※※※※※※※※※

Cleansing the Temple

Said the Rizhiner: In the *Al Hanisim* prayer, thanking God for the miracles of the past and the present, we say, "for Your people Israel You worked a great victory. . . . Then Your children cleansed Your Temple and purified Your sanctuary."

I say to you: The heart of every Jew is a temple; the mind of every Jew is a sanctuary, as it is written, "They shall make Me a sanctuary, and I shall dwell among them" (Exodus 25:8). Mind you, God does not say, "I shall dwell in *it*" but "I shall dwell among *them*" – in the heart and mind of every Jew.

Now, in the days of the Hasmoneans of old, it was God who took the initiative by granting them victory over their enemies. The people responded by "cleansing His Temple and purifying His sanctuary," purging their hearts and minds of all corrupt influences.

In our days too, may the Almighty take the first step and save the Jewish people from all trouble and distress. Being relieved of adversity and oppression, we will surely return to God as our people did in the days of Chanukah.

Irin Kadishin

❊❊ Purim: Brief Summary of ❊❊ Historical Events

The era of the first First Commonwealth of Israel was coming to a close. The spiritual decline that was sparked by the Judean king Menashe, who reigned from 533 to 478 B.C.E., had sapped the nation's moral strength. Idol worship was rampant, the people turning a deaf ear to the prophet Jeremiah's admonitions to repent and warnings of impending calamity if they failed to return to God.

Then disaster struck. On the ninth of *Av*, 423 B.C.E. (3,338 years from Creation), Nebuchadnezzar, king of Babylonia and "the rod of God's wrath," after an extended siege captured Jerusalem, burned the royal palace, and put the entire city to the torch. The Holy Temple, which had stood for 410 years, went up in flames. Jewish independence ended. Most of the Jews were led in iron chains into captivity in Babylonia, but they took a solemn oath: "If I forget you, O Jerusalem, let my right hand forget its cunning; let my tongue stick to my palate if I cease to think of you, if I do not keep Jerusalem in memory even at my happiest hour" (Psalm 137:5, 6).

Gradually, the exiles adjusted to their new environment and under a benevolent Babylonian regime, settled on the banks of the Euphrates

River. Much later, Babylonia was to become the fertile soil for the growth of Torah and the development of the great *yeshivot* of Sura and Pumbedita, the cradle of the Talmud.

Among the early exiles to Babylonia were Daniel, Chananiah, Mishael, and Azariah, who, because of their brilliance, were appointed to high posts at the court of King Nebuchadnezzar. They refused to eat the nonkosher royal delicacies they were offered but thrived on a diet of beans and water. When they refused to bow down before a large statue the king had erected in the Valley of Dura, however, he had Chanania, Mishael, and Azariah cast into a fiery furnace. Miraculously, they were saved from the flames by a protecting angel from God. Overwhelmed by the obvious divine intervention, Nebuchadnezzar praised God's power and elevated the three men to high positions in the Babylonian government.

In 397 B.C.E., Nebuchadnezzar died; his successor, Ehvil-merodach, was kind to the Jews. After Ehvil-merodach's death, his son Belshazzar ascended the Babylonian throne. During a wild orgy, the arrogant Belshazzar served wine from the holy Temple vessels that his grandfather Nebuchadnezzar had carried away from Jerusalem. Thereupon a mysterious hand appeared, writing on the wall a series of Hebrew letters that no one could read. The king called in the aged Daniel to decipher the message. The prophet read the words and interpreted their meaning:

Mene–God has counted your kingship and ended it.
Tekel–You were weighed in the scales of justice and found wanting.
Ufarsin–Your kingship is broken into pieces and given to Persia and Media. (Daniel 5:26–28).

That same night, the Medians–led by Darius I, and the Persians–under the command of Cyrus, attacked Babylonia. Belshazzar was killed, and Darius the Mede became king of the great empire. A year later, Darius was succeeded by Cyrus. Upon ascending the throne, Cyrus issued a proclamation allowing the Jews to return to Jerusalem and rebuild the Temple. The Babylonian captivity was at an end. The divine prophecy of Isaiah, predicting Cyrus' rise to power and the expansion of his empire, was fulfilled. Two hundred years before they happened, Isaiah had foretold these events with the words, "Thus said God to Cyrus, His anointed one . . . it was I who roused him [Cyrus] to victory and who leveled all roads for him. He shall rebuild My city and let My exiled people go" (Isaiah 45:1, 13). Fulfilled also was the prophecy of Jeremiah: "When Babylon's seventy years are over, I will take note of you, and I will fulfill to you my promise of favor – to bring you back to this place . . . and I will bring you back to the place from which I have exiled you" (Jeremiah 29:10, 14).

Led by the great men of that time, more than 40,000 Jews made the difficult trek through Mesopotamia, from the Persian Empire back to Jerusalem. Their celebrated leaders were Zerubavel ben She'altiel (a descendant of King David), Joshua the High Priest, Nechemia, Morde-chai, the prophets Chaggai, Zechariah, and Malachi, and the aged Daniel. It was a historic moment, an hour of great opportunity, which is referred to in the very last verse in the Bible: " . . . Any one of you of all His people, the Lord his God be with him and let him go up" (2 Chronicles 36:23).

Speaking of this crucial juncture in history, the *Midrash* says, "Had all the Jews in Babylonia/Persia heeded the call of their leaders and returned to *Eretz Yisrael*, they would have witnessed the Final Redemption, and the Second Temple would never have been destroyed" (*Shir Hashirim Rabbah* 8:9). But most of the exiles chose to remain in Persia, and a great opportunity was missed.

Under Cyrus, the Persian Empire became the dominant world power, ruling 120 countries. The Persian king had the wisdom to permit each nation under his control to retain its own language and customs.

After Cyrus' death in 369 B.C.E., Achashverosh became ruler of the Persian Empire. In the third year of his reign, Achashverosh invited all the important officials of his kingdom to an elaborate feast that lasted 180 days. At the end of the banquet, the king gave another banquet at the palace garden for the people of Shushan at which he brazenly displayed the holy vessels of the Temple.[6] Regrettably, many in the Jewish community, unable to resist the temptation, joined the festivities, drank forbidden wine, and ate forbidden food. Our sages say that the decree mandating the annihilation of the Jews came as the result of their participation in Achashverosh's feast.[7]

Achashverosh, the foolish king, ordered Queen Vashti to display her beauty in front of his guests, which she refused to do. Queen Vashti was deposed, and Esther was chosen to replace her.

Haman, a descendant of Israel's nemesis Amalek, became the king's prime minister. His innate hatred of the Jewish people was fanned when Mordechai, Esther's cousin, "would not kneel or bow down [to him]" (Esther 3:2). Haman persuaded the king to issue an edict to exterminate all the Jews in his realm. At Esther's request, the Jews fasted three days, repented, and prayed to God for deliverance. Risking her life for the sake of her people, Esther approached the king without his prior invitation—a trespass punishable by death. Charmed by the lovely Esther, however, the king smiled. "What troubles you, Queen Esther?" the king said. "Even to half the kingdom, it shall be granted you" (Esther 5:3). Demurely, Esther invited the king and Haman to come to a party she had prepared for them. At the feast, she requested only that the king and Haman come back for another party on the following day.

The king was having a sleepless night. To pass the time, he asked that the Book of Chronicles be read to him. The book was opened to the page recording the attempt on the king's life by Bigtan and Seresh, and Mordechai's saving of the king's life by discovering the planned assassination.

Then and there, the king decided to reward Mordechai. He issued orders that Mordechai be paraded through the city, dressed in royal regalia, riding on horseback, and that Haman was to lead the horse and announce, "This is what is done to the man whom the king wants to honor!" (Esther 6:11). The event marked the beginning of Haman's downfall.

At the party for the king and Haman on the following day, Esther revealed that she was Jewish and had been secretly observing her religion. She continued, "For I and my nation have been sold to be destroyed, massacred, and exterminated" (Esther 7:4).

"Who is he?" the king angrily shouted. "Where is the one that dared do this?"

"The adversary and enemy is this evil Haman!" Esther replied, pointing at Haman.

Haman was hanged, and the evil decree rescinded. A new proclamation was issued whereby the Jews were permitted to fight against their enemies. Many non-Jews, impressed by the Jewish victory, converted to Judaism. To commemorate the miracle, Esther and Mordechai established a festival they called Purim, for *pur*, which means "the lot." Haman had made a *pur*–had cast lots–to determine the day on which to destroy the Jews.

Esther and Mordechai ordained that Purim should be observed "as a day of feasting and merrymaking and as an occasion of sending food to one another and gifts to the poor . . . and Purim shall never cease among the Jews, and the memory of them shall never end among their descendants" (Esther 9:22, 28).

❈❈❈❈❈❈❈❈❈❈❈❈❈

Meaning of Purim

On the surface, Purim is nothing more than a joyous day of feasting, drinking, singing, masquerading, boisterous laughing, and exchanging of gifts of food and delicacies. It is a festival on which noisemaking during the reading of the *Megillah* is encouraged, a day when even the rabbi may be subjected to good-natured ribbing.

But there is more to Purim than feasting and fun. At first glance, the story of Purim has the appearance of a tale of palace intrigue and political infighting, a power struggle in which God plays no part at all. The fact that neither the name of God nor the word *miracle* is mentioned in the Book of Esther seems to lend credence to the assumption. However, on closer examination it becomes clear that implicitly God is present on every page of the book. It is He who guides the destiny of kings and nations. When things looked bleak, and the doom of the Jewish people seemed to be sealed, a man like Mordechai did not bow to the demands of the tyrant but found strength in his faith in the

Almighty. A valiant woman like Esther was ready to give her life to save her people. And the people repented and prayed to God. In response, God, performing a *nes nistar*, a "hidden miracle," turned things around, *venahafoch hu*, "and the opposite happened." All Haman's plans boomeranged. The gallows he prepared for Mordechai was used for him; the day he designated for the destruction of the Jews became the day on which they overpowered their enemies. Haman wanted to kill all Jewish children, but his own children were hanged from the gallows he built for Mordechai.

The message of Purim is that the entire spectrum of what we call nature and all the events of history are hidden manifestations of God. Purim tells us to recognize God's hand in our everyday life, to ascribe our successes and failures in business, the state of our health, our joys and sorrows to *Hashgachah*, divine providence. As in the days of Mordechai and Esther, circumstances may appear to be hopeless, but we can remove evil decrees and change the course of history through repentance, prayer, and good deeds.

❋❋❋❋❋❋❋❋❋❋❋❋

Selected Laws of Purim

The moment *Adar* arrives, our happiness increases.

On the *Shabbat* before Purim, after the reading of the weekly portion, the paragraph in the Torah dealing with the villainous attack of Amalek—*parashat Zachor*—is read (Deuteronomy 26:17–19). It ends with the words *lo tishkach!* "do not forget!" enjoining us always to remember what Amalek and all the enemies of our people, including Nazi Germany—the latter-day incarnation of Amalek—have done.

Purim is on the fourteenth of *Adar*, and the day before Purim is the Fast of Esther. In the evening and in the morning of Purim, the *Megillah* is read in the synagogue; both men and women are obligated to hear the *Megillah*. The reader folds the *Megillah* like a letter because the *Megillah* is described as an *iggeret*, "a letter of Purim" (Esther 9:29).

The reader recites three *berachot* before the reading: *Al mikra megillah*, "regarding the reading of the *Megillah*"; *She'asah nissim*, "who has wrought miracles for our forefathers, in those days at this season"; and *Shehecheyanu*, "who has kept us alive, sustained us, and brought us to this season." After the reading, the *berachah Harav et rivenu*, "who takes up our grievance," is said.

In the *Shemoneh Esrei* and in *Birkat Hamazon* (Grace after Meals), *Al Hanissim* is inserted.

On Purim it is a *mitzvah* to send gifts of food to friends, *mishlo'ach manot*, and to give charity to the needy, *matanot la'evyonim*.

It is a *mitzvah* to eat, drink, and be merry on Purim. The Purim meal, *seudat Purim*, should begin in daytime. We should set a festive table, light candles, and drink wine abundantly. The rabbis said that on Purim we should drink until we are unable to tell the difference between "Cursed is Haman" and "Blessed is Mordechai."[8] Of course, if drunkenness would cause problems, we should not become intoxicated.

In the *Megillah* we read that the Jews of Shushan fought their enemies for an additional day, on the fifteenth of *Adar*. Because Shushan was a walled city, the rabbis decreed that all cities with walls dating back to the days of Joshua[9] (who inflicted the defeat on Amalek, as it says, "Joshua weakened Amalek and his allies with the sword" [Exodus 17:13]) observe Purim on the fifteenth of *Adar*. Accordingly, in Jerusalem, Purim is celebrated on the fifteenth of *Adar* rather than on the fourteenth.

Customs of Purim

Purim is a special day for children. During the reading of the *Megillah*, every time the name of Haman is read – fifty-four times in all – children sound their *gragger*, "noisemaker." The reader is exasperated by the incessant interruptions but patiently waits for the noise to subside. The little ones wear delightful costumes and masks as they make the rounds delivering *mishlo'ach manot*, "gifts of food," to relatives and friends. The costumes run the gamut from reproductions of the vestments of the High Priest to cowboy's or policeman's outfits; boys dress up like Mordechai with beard and *peyot*; Queen Esther is the favorite among girls.

Traditional Purim treats that are enjoyed by everyone are *kreplach*–triangle-shaped pieces of dough filled with chopped meat–and *hamantashen*–triangular pastries filled with poppy seeds or prune marmalade.

(For a detailed discussion of all the laws of Purim, *Shulchan Aruch* 686–697 and *Kitzur Shulchan Aruch* 141–142 are available in English translation.)

✳✳✳✳✳✳✳✳✳✳✳✳✳

Purim–Yom Kippur

The Arizal notes that in Hebrew, *Yom Kippurim* can also be read as *Yom kePurim*, "a day like Purim." At first glance, this sounds like a pun, but it is a pun that has a deeper meaning.

Rabbi Simchah Bunam of Pshis'cha comments: I am telling you, Purim is even greater than Yom Kippur. The reason is this: on Yom Kippur it is a *mitzvah* to afflict yourself, and on Purim it is a *mitzvah* to drink until you cannot tell the difference between blessed is Mordechai and cursed is Haman. Now, I'm asking you, is there a greater affliction than losing your capacity to think?

✳✳✳✳✳✳✳✳✳✳✳✳✳

Fear and Love of God

Rabbi Eliyahu Eliezer Dessler: There are two ways of serving God: you can serve Him with *yirat Hashem* (fear of God) and with *ahavat Hashem* (love of God), and love of God is the loftier of the two. On Yom Kippur your sins are washed away through your fear of God, but on Purim your failings are forgiven through your love of God.

❋❋❋❋❋❋❋❋❋❋❋❋❋

Purim in the Warsaw Ghetto

In the dark days of Purim 1941, in the Warsaw ghetto, Rabbi Kalonymos Kalman of Piasetzna sat at the head of the table, surrounded by a group of gaunt and despondent *chasidim*, who were staring forlornly into nothingness. With death hanging over their heads, how could anyone rejoice? Said the *rebbe*: In the *Zohar* it is written that *Yom Kippurim* means *Yom kePurim*, "a day just like Purim." That is to say, just as on Yom Kippur – whether you like it or not – you must fast on orders of the Holy One, blessed is He; so must you rejoice on Purim. Even if Satan runs amok in the streets, you have to be happy; it is the will of God.

❋❋❋❋❋❋❋❋❋❋❋❋❋

Until You Cannot Tell the Difference

The *Gemara* states that on Purim you should drink until you cannot tell the difference between "Cursed is Haman" and "Blessed is Mordechai."[10]

The Rambam explains this to mean that you should drink to the point of becoming drowsy. Before long, you will fall asleep, and then you will be oblivious of both Haman and Mordechai.

Abudraham offers a striking insight in this regard, noting that the numeric value of ארור המן, *arur Haman*, "Cursed is Haman," is exactly the same as that of ברוך מרדכי, *baruch Mordechai*, "Blessed is Mordechai," both amounting to 502. Now, when you are a little drunk, you are unable to make this kind of calculation.

※※※※※※※※※※※※※※※

They Enjoyed It

The *Gemara* in *Megillah* 14a writes that the reason the Jews under the reign of Achashverosh deserved to be destroyed was that they enjoyed partaking of the banquet of that evil king.

Comments the *Yaarot Devash*: It was bad enough that they were not brokenhearted over being forced to eat forbidden food. But to make things worse, they enjoyed it! A person who transgresses and enjoys doing so deserves grave punishment.

※※※※※※※※※※※※※※※

Reading Backward

If you read the *Megillah* backward, you have not fulfilled your obligation (*Megillah* 17).

Rabbi Yitzchak of Volozhin: Metaphorically, this refers to someone who reads the *Megillah* as a tale that happened in days gone by, as miracles that took place in ancient times but that have no bearing on the present. A person who reads the *Megillah* without understanding and believing that the message of Purim is relevant today has not discharged his obligation.

※※※※※※※※※※※※※※※

Haman in the Torah?

The *Gemara* in *Chullin* 139b asks an astonishing question: "Where do we find an allusion to Haman in the Torah?" The answer: his name can be found in the passage *hamin ha'etz asher tziviticha* [God, speaking to Adam], "Did you eat from the tree which I commanded you not to eat?" (Genesis 3:11). Evidently, the *Gemara* has in mind the identical spelling of Haman and *hamin—hei, mem, nun.*

Surely this is more than a play on words. There must be a deeper meaning behind it. Rabbi Aharon Kotler, illustrious founder of the Lakewood *Yeshivah,* offers the following striking insight:

The root of Haman's vile character becomes evident in *Megillat Esther.* As the king's prime minister, Haman enjoyed everything a man could want: wealth, power, and prestige. In spite of that, the failure on the part of one single Jew to bow down to him led him to exclaim, "Yet all this [wealth, children, prominence] means nothing to me as long as I see that Jew Mordechai sitting in the palace gate" (Esther 5:13).

Haman's wickedness stems from the fact that although he possessed everything, he desperately wanted the one thing that was beyond his reach: Mordechai's subservience.

There is a striking parallel to this in the story of Adam's sin. In the Garden of Eden, Adam had everything his heart desired. He conversed with God, he had everlasting life, and he had all the food he could eat. He lacked only one thing: permission to eat the fruit of the Tree of Knowledge. The desire for this one insignificant forbidden fruit so overwhelmed him as to cause him to transgress his Creator's will.

The root of all evil is man's dissatisfaction with his lot in life and his constant drive to acquire things that are beyond his reach. Though he may be wealthy, his chase after unattainable goals makes all his riches seem worthless to him.

No'am Siach, p. 138

Esther in the Torah?

Where is there a hint for Esther in the Torah? It can be found in the verse *ve'anochi hasteir astir panai meihem,* "Yet I will keep My countenance hidden" (Deuteronomy 31:18).[11]

At first sight, this seems to be a pun based on the similarity of the name Esther and *hasteir astir.* However, the underlying thought is that in the story of Purim, "God's countenance was hidden," and His providential guidance of events was clothed in a mantle of causality, of things seeming to happen by chance. To the casual observer, the story reads like drama in which good triumphs over evil without an assist by God. But the discerning reader recognizes God's involvement every step of the way in bringing about the rescue of the Jewish people.

****

He Will Not Bow

All the king's courtiers at the palace gate knelt and bowed low to Haman . . . but Mordechai would not kneel or bow low (Esther 3:2).

. . . but Mordechai would not kneel or bow low. The literal translation of the phrase is, "but Mordechai **will** not kneel and **will** not bow low."

By using the future tense, the verse indicates that in every generation there will arise a spiritual leader who will not kneel and bow to the tyrant of his time. Haman knew that even if he killed Mordechai, another intrepid leader would emerge to take Mordechai's place. That is why Haman wanted to destroy all the Jews in the kingdom.

Sefat Emet

****

An Astounding Omen

An order was given in Shushan, and they hanged Haman's ten sons (Esther 9:13).

The names of the ten sons are listed in chapter 9, verses 7, 8, and 9. It is odd that in three of the names, one letter is written smaller than the others: the *tav* of Parshandata, the *mem* of Parmashta, and the *zayin* of Vayzata. There is an astounding prophecy in this anomaly.

The combination of the three odd-sized letters—*tav, shin, zayin*—is the designation of the Jewish year 5707, which coincides with the secular year 1946-47. Amazingly, it was in 1946 that the Nuremberg trials took place, at which the eleven top German war criminals were sentenced to death by hanging. Göring committed suicide, and on October 16, 1946, which fell on 16 *Tishri*, 5707—it was the Festival of *Hoshana Rabbah*—the ten Nazi chiefs were hanged. One of the condemned war criminals was the demented Julius Streicher, a vicious Jew-hater and publisher of *Der Stürmer*, the notorious Nazi hate sheet. Staring at the witnesses facing the gallows, he shouted, "Purimfest 1946!"

The hanging of these "ten sons of Haman" was the literal fulfillment of the prophecy hidden in the Book of Esther.

Their execution on *Hoshana Rabbah* was predicted in the *Zohar*: "On the seventh day of Sukkot (i.e., *Hoshana Rabbah*), the judgment of the nations of the world is finalized. Sentences are issued from the residence of the King. Judgments are aroused and executed on that day" (*Zohar Vayikra Rabbah* 316).[12]

❊❊❊❊❊❊❊❊❊❊❊❊❊❊❊

Amalek and Balaam

Haman was a descendant of Amalek, the nation that attacked the children of Israel shortly after the Exodus. The *Midrash*[13] says that Amalek mounted its attack at the advice of Balaam, the evil prophet.

The close kinship of these two arch enemies of the Jewish people, along with their implacable hatred that has endured over the ages, becomes apparent in their names.

Placing the name בלעם, Balaam, directly above the name, עמלק, Amalek, like this: בלעם

עמלק,

a combination of the first two letters of both names, yields בלעם, Balaam; the union of the last two letters of both names forms עמלק, Amalek. This suggests that all foes of the Jewish people are linked by the same blind hatred, regardless of whether they attack by the sword, as Amalek did, or whether they spew their venom by oratory, emulating Balaam.

✣✣✣✣✣✣✣✣✣✣✣✣✣

Chanukah and Purim

Rabbi Levi Yitzchak of Berditchev asked: Why is it that the sages ordained to celebrate Purim with "feasting and merriment," whereas Chanukah is to be remembered with "expressions of thanks and praise"?

Haman's aim was the physical extermination of the Jewish people, and therefore the downfall of Haman is commemorated through the physical enjoyment of food and drink. The peril of Chanukah was assimilation and the threat to the spiritual survival of the Jewish people, as the Syrian/Greek enemies "tried to make them forget the Torah and compel them to stray from God's laws." The miracle of Chanukah meant the preservation of the Jewish soul. This requires a spiritual kind of celebration through giving thanks and praise and the kindling of lights – the symbol of Torah.

✣✣✣✣✣✣✣✣✣✣✣✣✣

Why is *Hallel* Not Said on Purim?

Unlike Chanukah, on Purim we do not recite *Hallel*, which comprises psalms in praise of God. The reason is that the reading of the *Megillah* constitutes *Hallel* (*Arachin* 10b). Another reason is that *Hallel* is not said for a miracle that occurred outside of *Eretz Yisrael* (*Megillah* 14a).

※※※※※※※※※※※※※※

Why No *Megillah* for Chanukah?

Rabbi Meir Yechiel of Ostrowtza asked: Why was there no *Megillah* written for Chanukah?

The Torah has a body and a soul. The written words are the body; their study and comprehension are the soul of the Torah. For Purim, a *Megillah* was written, because Haman wanted to destroy the body of the Jewish people; not so for Chanukah, for on Chanukah, our enemies wanted to uproot the soul of the Jewish people.

Or Torah

※※※※※※※※※※※※※※

The Power of Torah

[In the battle against Amalek], as long as Moses held his hands up, Israel would be winning, but as soon as he let his hands down, the battle would go in Amalek's favor (Exodus 17:11).

Chafetz Chaim: The Hebrew text in the Torah reads *yarim Moshe*, "as long as Moses will hold his hand up." This carries a message that is valid for all time: As long as the principles of Torah are held aloft, studied, and observed, then Israel will win, but if not, then, God forbid, Amalek will gain the upper hand.

※※※※※※※※※※※※※※

Strength in Unity

Remember what Amalek did to you on your journey, after you left Egypt (Deuteronomy 26:17).

Rabbi Simchah Bunam of Pshis'cha: *Zachor,* "remember," is written in the singular, addressing one individual. Indeed, the entire paragraph recounting Amalek's attack is in the singular. Why does it not say *zichru,* "remember," in the plural?

Amalek could overwhelm only those who lived in isolation and could defeat only people who had broken away from the community. Those who were united and were attached to the body of the Jewish nation were protected by the Clouds of Glory. This was a portent of things to come: As long as Jews are united, Amalek has no power over them.

Kol Simchah

8

PASSOVER

Passover, the festival of our freedom, is the first in the cycle of the three pilgrimage holidays. On this holiday we relive the agony of Egyptian bondage and the glorious events of the Exodus that led to the emergence of the Jewish people.

✠✠✠✠✠✠✠✠✠✠✠✠✠✠

Season of Rebirth

The *Yom Tov* is celebrated in the month of *Nisan*, which falls in the spring, the season when the dormant earth begins to blossom, and nature, released from winter's grip, is born anew. Like every birth, the genesis of the Jewish nation was accompanied by harrowing birth pangs.

For 210 years, the people of Israel toiled under the Egyptian task-masters' whips, performing backbreaking, mind-numbing labor. Broken in body and spirit, they descended to the depths of despair, to a spiritual nadir, where only physical survival occupied their mind and where spiritual values were all but forgotten. The sages tell us that they passed through the "forty-ninth gate of spiritual impurity." Had they passed the fiftieth gate, they would have been irretrievably lost. The metaphor implies that the people of Israel adopted the cultural mores of Egypt and became virtually indistinguishable from their overlords.

It was at that crucial juncture that God intervened, arousing the people of Israel from their spiritual stupor by giving them their first commandment as a nation, the *mitzvah* that was to usher in the Exodus: "This renewal of the moon shall be the first of the months to you" (Exodus 12:2). In the words of Rabbi Samson Raphael Hirsch, "God showed them the sickle of the moon struggling to emerge from darkness into renewed light, and said, 'This is to be the model for your own conduct! Just as the moon renews itself by the laws of nature, so you, too, should renew yourselves, but of your own free will.' "

Hirsch, *Commentary on the Pentateuch*

✳✳✳✳✳✳✳✳✳✳✳✳✳✳✳

Sanctification of the Month

It is significant that the story of the birth of *B'nei Yisrael* begins with the commandment of *kiddush hachodesh*, the sanctification of the month at the moon's renewal. The Torah states, "This month shall mark for you the beginning of the months; it shall be the first month of the year for you" (Exodus 12:1).

Rabbi Ovadiah Seforno, the great Torah commentator, notes that the verse seems to stress the words "for you." God seems to say, "While you were slaves, your time belonged to your Egyptian masters. From now on, you will be masters of your time, to use at your own discretion."

✳✳✳✳✳✳✳✳✳✳✳✳✳✳✳

The Jewish Calendar

This month shall be the head month to you. It shall be the first month of the year (Exodus 12:2). This verse mandates that *Nisan* is to be the first month of a year that is composed of twelve months.

There exists a fundamental difference between the Jewish and the secular calendars. The Jewish months are measured by the time that passes from one new moon until the next. The secular calendar calculates a month by dividing the 365 days and 6 hours of the solar year – the length of time of the rotation of the earth around the sun – into twelve parts, without regard to the appearance of the moon.

We must remember that a lunar month has approximately 29.5 days, and a lunar year 12 × 29.5, or 354 days. Because the solar year has 365 days, we find that the lunar year is about 11 days shorter than the solar year. Now, if the Jewish year were based solely on the rotation of the moon, Passover would occur some 11 days earlier each successive solar year, and the months of the years would retrograde through the seasons.

However, the Torah requires that Passover be celebrated in the month of "standing grain," namely, the spring.

"Safeguard the month of standing grain so that you will be able to keep the Passover to God, since it was in the month of standing grain that God your Lord brought you out of Egypt at night" (Deuteronomy 16:1).

Accordingly, the commandment to "safeguard the month of standing grain" must be understood as mandating that the cycle of the lunar months be adjusted parallel to the seasons of the solar year. The necessary adjustment is accomplished by adding an extra month in some years (*Sanhedrin* 11a), a method called intercalation. The added month, *Adar Sheini*, is added in seven out of every nineteen years.

The calculation of the calendar was transmitted to the sages in an unbroken chain, going back to Moses. In 361 c.e., Hillel II established the calendar system we have today and that is valid for all future generations.

According to the ancient calculations, the exact time between one new moon and the next is 29 days, 12 hours, and 793 *chalakim* "parts of an hour" (the hour is divided into 1080 parts). In other words, one lunar month has 29.53059 days.

It is interesting to note that according to NASA (National Aeronautics and Space Administration), the time between one new moon and the next is 29.530588 days. Of course, NASA has at its disposal the most advanced and sophisticated telescopes and computers. Nevertheless, the difference between NASA's figure and that used by Hillel II, which originated more than 3,000 years ago, is .000002, or two millionths of a day, calculated for the period of one month.[1]

※※※※※※※※※※※※※※

The Creation of Time

These are the times appointed by God, the sacred Festivals, which you must proclaim each at its appointed time (Leviticus 23:4). Rabbi Avraham Yehoshua Heshel of Apta: These are the times appointed by God. In reality, the concept of time does not apply to God, as He transcends nature and time. However, prompted by His great love of His people Israel, God created the universe for their sake. This necessitated the creation of time. Thus, the opening word of Torah reads, *Bereishit*, "In the beginning," which denotes the creation of time. Of course, God Himself remains above the confines of time and space. Now, on the three *Yamim Tovim* – Pesach, Shavuot, and Sukkot – God allows His Presence to be drawn into the realm of time, and His spiritual Light is then revealed to Israel. But we must take the initial step. And how do we induce God's holiness to enter the limitations of time? We do it on *Yom Tov* by focusing our thoughts on the moment when God created time out of love of Israel, as it is expressed in the verse "Israel is holy to God, the *beginning* of His harvest" (Jeremiah 2:3). We thereby attach ourselves to a higher, timeless world and arouse the erstwhile love that caused God to bring time into being. In so doing we draw down – if we may say so – God's Presence to dwell among us on earth.

This, then, is the meaning of the present verse, "These are the times appointed by God." On these three Festivals, God reveals Himself within the strictures of time, "which you must proclaim." You, the Jewish people, must invite Almighty God and draw down His Presence into the physical world and the limitations of time.

Oheiv Yisrael

Seven *Yamim Tovim*

There are times appointed by God, which you must proclaim as sacred Festivals. These are My appointed times: on six days, work may be done, but the seventh day is a Sabbath of Sabbaths, a sacred Festival. You shall do no work; it shall be a Sabbath to God wherever you may live (Leviticus 23:1–3).

These verses present a strange anomaly. The first verse opens by announcing the Festivals, but instead of a description of the *Yamim Tovim*, what follows is the prohibition of work on *Shabbat*. The *Vilna Gaon* offers an ingenious solution to this problem. He points out that the Torah gave us seven *Yamim Tovim* (Festivals): The first and last day of Pesach,[2] one day of Shavuot, one day of Rosh Hashanah, Yom Kippur, the first day of Sukkot, and one day of Shemini Atzeret. It is these seven days that the present verse has in mind when it states, "On six days, work may be done, but [on] the seventh day . . you shall do no work." For on six of the *Yamim Tovim*, all labor related to the preparation of food, such as cooking and baking, is permitted, but "the seventh day"–Yom Kippur–"is a Sabbath of Sabbaths," a day on which no work whatsoever may be done, not even labor related to the preparation of food.

The Life-Giving Spirit of *Yom Tov*

We note that the Torah established six Festivals in the Jewish year–analogous with the six days of Creation. Two of the Festivals–Pesach and Sukkot – last seven days; each of the other four – Shavuot, Shemini Atzeret, Rosh Hashanah, and Yom Kippur – are one-day Festivals. Thus, the total number of *Yamim Tovim* (as instituted by the Torah) amounts to eighteen – the equivalent of *chai*, "life." Indeed, the *Yamim Tovim* infuse Jews with life, giving them the vitality and tenacity to grapple with the problems facing them on the weekdays of the year.

※※※※※※※※※※※※※

Symmetry of the *Yamim Tovim*

The six biblical *Yamim Tovim* of the year are arranged in a pattern of three strikingly similar pairs:

1. Pesach and Sukkot: Both of these Festivals begin on the fifteenth of the month: the fifteenth of *Nisan* and the fifteenth of *Tishri*, the day when the moon reaches its fullness. Both Festivals end on the twenty-first day of the month. The interval between Pesach and Sukkot is exactly the same as that separating Sukkot from Pesach – six months.

2. Shavuot and Shemini Atzeret: Each of these festivals is closely linked to one of the seven-day *Yamim Tovim*. Shavuot is tied to Pesach by means of *sefirat ha'omer*, the counting of the *Omer*. We count the *Omer* every night for forty-nine days, beginning with the second night of Pesach – the sixteenth of *Nisan* – until the evening before Shavuot. Shemini Atzeret, being the closing day of Sukkot, is intimately connected to that *Yom Tov*. Unlike the other Festivals, neither Shavuot nor Shemini Atzeret is marked by any specific *mitzvot* peculiar to that day.

3. Rosh Hashanah and Yom Kippur: These Festivals fall into the separate category of *Yamim Nora'im*, Days of Awe. Rosh Hashanah opens the *Aseret Yemei Teshuvah*, Ten Days of Penitence, which culminate in Yom Kippur, the Day of Atonement.

※※※※※※※※※※※※※

Miracle of the Exodus

Renewal, in essence, negates the dictates of time. The sun, the moon, and the heavenly bodies, whirling in their immutable orbits, measure time in a senseless, monotonous, interminable cycle of hours, days, months, and years. The passage of time says, "You are getting older," but the story of the Exodus says, "You can break the chains of an empty, time-bound life of physical existence. Spiritually, you can be young again. You can rise above the inexorable march of time by attaching yourself to the Creator, who transcends time and space." *Mitzvot* are the cables that bind us to God, and the first *mitzvah* was the mandate to sanctify time.

In addition, the Exodus saga of redemption tells us that the Creator is not a remote deity who is uninvolved in worldly affairs but a God who is concerned, who oversees the flow of events, and who deals with each of us according to our deeds. He is the God who delivered His people and gave them a code of laws and ethics to transform and ennoble them, entrusting them with the mission to serve as "a light of nations" (Isaiah 42:6). The miraculous Exodus from Egyptian slavery to freedom is, in fact, the cornerstone of the Jewish faith.

※※※※※※※※※※※※※※

Commemorating the Exodus

Lofty ideas must represent more than the abstract musings of a few starry-eyed visionaries. The concepts of liberty and divine supervision inherent in the Exodus must be anchored in the consciousness of the entire Jewish people so as to become a tangible part of a Jew's every waking moment. Jews must be able to experience the Exodus with all five senses, bite into it, taste it, touch it. It is for this reason that Jews are reminded of *yetziat Mitzrayim* (the Exodus) in every step of their daily routine: in the *Shema*, which is recited twice each day, and by biblical verses recalling the Exodus, which are contained in the parchments inside the *tefillin* (phylacteries).

The Exodus from Egypt is mentioned in the Torah in connection with the commandments to wear *tzitzit* (ritual fringes) and to love one's neighbor and with many other *mitzvot*. Furthermore, the *Shabbat* was given as a remembrance of the Exodus from Egypt: "You must remember that you were slaves in Egypt, when God your Lord brought you out with a strong hand and an outstretched arm. It is for this reason that God your Lord has commanded you to keep the *Shabbat*" (Deuteronomy 5:15). We also recall the Exodus in *Birkat Hamazon* (Grace after Meals) and in the *Kiddush* of *Shabbat* and *Yom Tov*.

On Passover, the commemoration of the departure from Egypt reaches a climax when the entire journey from slavery to freedom is reenacted during the *seder*, on the actual night of deliverance, in fulfillment of the dictum "In every generation it is one's duty to regard himself as though he personally had gone out of Egypt" (from the *Haggadah*).

The continual retelling of the miracles of the Exodus impresses on our mind the awareness that God dominates and guides the forces that shape history and that He Himself "brought you out of the iron crucible that was Egypt, so that you would be His heritage nation, as you are today" (Deuteronomy 4:20).

✖✖✖✖✖✖✖✖✖✖✖✖✖

Israel Is Like the Moon

The Sefat Emet said: The Torah commands us to measure the year by the revolutions of the moon around the earth. By contrast, the non-Jewish nations use a solar calendar, whereby the length of the year is determined by the duration of the earth's orbit around the sun.

The Talmud states it succinctly: "Israel counts according to the moon; the gentile nations count according to the sun" (*Sukkah* 29a).

Whereas the moon is symbolic of the Jewish people, the sun represents the other nations. The non-Jewish nations continue to flourish as long as the sun of fortune shines brightly on them. But when their sun wanes and their political and economic power declines, they fade from the scene. On one hand, the pages of history offer countless examples of the rise and fall of great civilizations. The Jewish people, on the other hand, continue to illuminate the world even during periods of darkness and dreadful oppression, like the moon that lights up the world during the darkest night.

❈❈❈❈❈❈❈❈❈❈❈❈❈❈❈

Removing the *Chametz*

Preparations for Passover begin with a thorough cleaning of the entire house, well before the onset of the *Yom Tov*, for the purpose of removing all *chametz*. By *chametz* (leaven) is meant any dough prepared from flour (of the "five species": wheat, rye, spelt, barley, and oats) mixed with water, which is allowed to ferment for eighteen minutes before being baked.

The Torah forbids eating *chametz*: "Whoever eats leaven from the first day until the seventh day will have his soul cut off from Israel" (Exodus 12:15). Torah law not only forbids eating *chametz* but also prohibits its presence during Passover. It may not be seen (*bal yeira'eh*) or found (*bal yimatzeh*) during the entire festival (Exodus 13:7 and 12:19).

These prohibitions are observed meticulously and with great stringency. Even the minutest particle of *chametz* is forbidden on Passover, and even the tiniest quantity of *chametz* mixed with a non-*chametz* food one thousand times its bulk renders the food unusable. Care is taken, therefore, to eat only foods that are certified as kosher for Passover so as to avoid both eating products that contain ingredients that are *chametz* and drinking beverages such as whiskey and beer, which are made of grain.

(For a comprehensive treatment of all the laws of Passover, the *Shulchan Aruch, Orach Chaim* 429–491 and *Kitzur Shulchan Aruch* 107–120 are available in English translation.)

❈❈❈❈❈❈❈❈❈❈❈❈❈❈❈

No Smugglers of *Chametz*

Rabbi Levi Yitzchak of Berditchev, the great advocate of the Jewish people, went out into the street in the afternoon of the day before Passover. There he came upon one of the local black marketeers.

"Tell me," the *rebbe* asked him, "do you have any contraband silks for sale?"

"Certainly," replied the smuggler, "I can get you as much as you want."

Rabbi Levi Yitzchak, continuing on his way, met a Jew. "Do you have any *chametz*?" the *rebbe* asked.

"God forbid," answered the Jew with a horrified look on his face. "How can you ask such a question! It's two in the afternoon!"

Meeting another Jew, the *rebbe* asked, "Do you have any *chametz*?"

"Rebbe," the man replied, "*chametz* at this hour? Do you think I abandoned the Jewish faith, *chas veshalom* [God forbid]?"

The *rebbe* then exclaimed, "*Ribbono shel Olam*, look what a good nation are Your people of Israel and how careful they are to observe Your commandments. The czar has many inspectors, border guards, judges, and prisons, and yet he cannot stop the flow of contraband across the border. You wrote in Your Torah, 'No leaven may be found in your homes' (Exodus 12:19). You have no border guards or inspectors, but You will find not one crumb of *chametz* smuggled into any Jewish home on Passover."

Eser Orot

✺✺✺✺✺✺✺✺✺✺✺✺✺✺

Chametz–Matzah

The words *chametz*, חמץ, and *matzah*, מצה, have two letters in common, the *mem* and the *tzadi*. They differ only in the third letter. *Chametz* has a *chet*, ח, , whereas *matzah* has a *hei*, ה, two letters that are almost identical.

Indeed, *chametz* and *matzah* bear many similarities. Both are made of

flour and water and baked in an oven. The difference is seen when we
wait and do nothing. The dough of *chametz* begins to rise, and its taste
becomes sour. However, producing *matzah* is very hard work, requiring
constant kneading of the dough.

Matzah symbolizes diligence and zealousness; *chametz* stands for
idleness and sloth.

�֍✖✖✖✖✖✖✖✖✖✖✖✖✖✖

Chametz: The Evil Tendency

Chametz is a metaphor for the *yetzer hara*, the evil tendency, which is
rooted in pride. The leavened dough has the bloated shape of pompous
self-importance and arrogance. Like the rising dough, pride grows
continually. The search for *chametz*, in a figurative sense, is the self-
examination we should undertake to pinpoint our evil tendencies. The
burning of the *chametz* symbolizes the heartfelt elimination of our
negative inclination.

✖✖✖✖✖✖✖✖✖✖✖✖✖✖

The Difference between *Chametz* and *Matzah*

The Chatam Sofer calculated that the numeric value of the word
chametz, חמץ, amounts to 138 (*chet* = 8, *mem* = 40, *tzadi* = 90), whereas
the numeric value of *matzah*, מצה, is 135 (*mem* = 40, *tzadi* = 90, *hei* = 5).
The difference of 3 represents the three base instincts that are the root
cause of all sin: envy, lust, and glory. The *Mishnah* in *Avot* 5:28
identifies these three characteristics as the factors that remove a man
from the world. Like the *chametz*, these bad traits must be eliminated.

Torat Moshe

✖✖✖✖✖✖✖✖✖✖✖✖✖✖

Matzah: The Bread of Freedom

The Maharal observes: "*Matzah*, the symbol of Passover, is called *lechem oni*, 'the bread of poverty' (Deuteronomy 16:3). Now you may wonder, how can poverty be a metaphor for freedom? The two seem to be opposites rather than synonyms.

"Incongruous as it may sound, the fact is that poverty is the underlying idea of freedom. Redemption means gaining independence. Unlike a slave who is bound to a master, a free and independent man has no ties to anyone or anything. A rich man is wealthy by dint of his possessions. Because his wealth is an inherent part of his existence and he is inseparably bound to it, he is not really free. Only a poor man who owns nothing at all can be considered absolutely free. *Matzah*, made of flour and water, without any enriching ingredients such as yeast and shortening, is the bread of poverty and therefore the perfect symbol of freedom and independence.

"This explains also why the redemption took place specifically in the first month. Freedom means being completely detached from any outside force or influence. The first month, being first in time, has no linkage to any moment that preceded it. The second month is not really independent; it is second because it follows the first month. Thus, the first month is the ideal month for the deliverance. To sum it up, liberation means divesting oneself from all outside factors and influences."

Gevurot Hashem, ch. 51

❈❈❈❈❈❈❈❈❈❈❈❈❈❈

Timeless *Matzah*

The Maharal continues to expound on the same subject: "Why do we eat *matzah* on Passover? The Torah relates, '[The Israelites] baked the dough that they had taken out of Egypt into unleavened (*matzah*) cakes, for it had not risen. They had been driven out of Egypt and could not delay . . .' (Exodus 13:39), and 'they left Egypt in a rush' (Deuteronomy 16:3). That hasty departure indicates that their liberation was instantaneous; it did not require any time. The timelessness is inherent in the *matzah*, a bread that comes into being virtually in an instant, without undergoing the time-consuming process of leavening."

Gevurot Hashem

✳✳✳✳✳✳✳✳✳✳✳✳✳✳

Shabbat Hagadol

The *Shabbat* before Passover is *Shabbat Hagadol*, the Great *Shabbat*. Traditionally, on this *Shabbat*, the rabbi delivers a major sermon consisting of a talmudic lecture and a homiletic discourse on a Passover theme. Also included in the sermon is a discussion of the laws of Passover.

Why is this *Shabbat* called "the Great *Shabbat*"? A variety of answers are given.

According to *Seder Olam*, the Exodus took place on Thursday, the fifteenth of *Nisan*. The Torah states that on the tenth of that month, which fell on the previous *Shabbat*, the people of Israel were to take a lamb for each family (Exodus 12:3). Each Israelite took a lamb – the animal that was worshiped by the Egyptians – and tied it to his bedpost. When the Egyptians asked, "Why are you doing this?" the Israelites replied, "We will offer this lamb as a sacrifice to God as we were told to do." Horrorstricken, the Egyptians were rendered powerless to lift a finger against the Israelites, who were about to sacrifice the object of Egyptian worship. Because of this miracle, which occurred on that *Shabbat*, the *Shabbat* before Passover is known as *Shabbat Hagadol*.

Tur Orach Chaim, par. 430

✳✳✳✳✳✳✳✳✳✳✳✳✳✳

A Long Sermon

The *Shibbolei Haleket*, in what may be a tongue-in-cheek comment, attributes the name *Shabbat Hagadol*, the Great *Shabbat*, to the fact that the people are obliged to listen to a protracted sermon by the rabbi, so that the *Shabbat* seems to them to last very long. They feel it is a great, seemingly interminable *Shabbat*. Hence the name *Shabbat Hagadol*.

Like a *Bar Mitzvah*

Abudraham suggests: A boy who becomes thirteen years old and takes on the obligation to fulfill the *mitzvot* is called a *gadol*, an adult.

By the same token, the day on which the entire people of Israel were given their first *mitzvah*–"on the tenth of this month, every man must take a lamb for each family" (Exodus 12:3)–is called *Shabbat Hagadol*.

The Search for *Chametz*

On the night of the fourteenth of *Nisan*, the evening before the *seder*, the house undergoes a final inspection, *bedikat chametz*, by the light of a candle. Preferably, it should be done as soon as the stars appear, and every room where *chametz* may have been brought during the year should be searched. Before the search is begun, a blessing is said praising God, "who has . . . commanded us concerning the removal of *chametz*."

After the search, the *chametz* is wrapped to be burned in the morning. Then a declaration is made by which any *chametz* that may still be in the house is nullified, to become "like dust of the earth."

In the morning, all *chametz* is burned, and the declaration renouncing ownership and nullifying any unfound *chamtez* is repeated. However, a question arises (*Tosafot Pesachim* 2a, s.v. *Or*): Since we renounce ownership of the *chametz* and nullify it, why is it necessary to search the entire house for *chametz*?

Tosafot's answer: Because we are used to eating *chametz* throughout the year, we may forget the prohibition if we find it in the house on Passover. It is therefore required that we search for it and remove it before the time the prohibition goes into effect.

✹✹✹✹✹✹✹✹✹✹✹✹✹

The Fourteenth of *Nisan*

It is a universally accepted custom for firstborn sons to fast on the day before Passover. This fast, called *Taanit Bechorim*, commemorates the miracle that the firstborn Jews were spared from the tenth plague that killed every firstborn Egyptian. It is customary to arrange for someone in the community to make a *siyum* (completion of a tractate of the Talmud) after *Shacharit* (the morning service). This *mitzvah* is cause for a celebration in which the firstborn are allowed to participate. Once the firstborn have broken the fast for a *mitzvah*, they are permitted to eat the rest of the day.

We may eat *chametz* until the fourth hour (about 9:30 A.M.). *Matzah* should not be eaten the entire day, in order that we will enjoy the *matzah* at night with greater appetite. Of course, we may eat fish, meat, soup, fruit, and vegetables, but we should not overeat; we want to be able to eat *matzah* at the *seder* with relish.

In compliance with the Scripture, "Be careful regarding the *matzahs*" (Exodus 12:17), many people go to great lengths to eat only handmade *matzah shemurah* (*matzah* that has been watched carefully from the time of the cutting of the wheat). These *matzot* are round, to signify that we believe in the Creator, Who has neither a beginning nor an end (Responsa Mahari Assad, No. 157). Handmade *matzot* are very thin and crispy and have a delectable taste. Their color, texture, and irregular shape summon up the time of our ancestors' liberation, whose "bread of affliction" must have had the same appearance and taste.

Don't Deal Harshly with the Widow

Rabbi Yisrael Salanter was in the habit of personally supervising the baking of *matzot*. He made sure that the kneading, rolling, and baking all were done meticulously in accordance with the most stringent requirements of the law. One year, Rabbi Yisrael did not feel well and he sent his disciples to the bakery to oversee the baking of the *matzot*. Before setting out on their assignment, the students asked Rabbi Yisrael, "Please, Rabbi, tell us what phase of the baking process we should watch with the greatest vigilance?"

"The one thing that you should be concerned about primarily," replied Rabbi Yisrael, "is to be kind to the woman kneading the dough. Make sure you don't rush her, hurt her feelings, or speak harshly to her; you see, she is a widow."

Agadah uMachashavzh beYahadut

The *Seder*

On the night of the fifteenth of *Nisan*, the Exodus becomes a tangible reality for every Jew. In a heartwarming outpouring of joy and love of God, family and friends gather around the sparkling, festive *seder* table to recall the miraculous events that happened 3,300 years ago, in the year 2448 of Creation (1313 B.C.E.), and to thank God both for redeeming us and our ancestors from Egypt and for the greatest miracle of all, the survival of the Jewish people.

The *seder* – the word means order – is structured around a program of fifteen points, which indicate the step-by-step sequence of the night:

1. *kadeish* – reciting the *Kiddush*;
2. *urechatz* – washing the hands without reciting a *berachah*;
3. *karpas* – eating a vegetable dipped in salt water;
4. *yachatz* – breaking the middle *matzah*, hiding the larger part for the *afikomen*;
5. *maggid* – reciting the *Haggadah*, telling the story of Passover;
6. *rochtzah* – washing the hands for the meal; the *berachah* is said;
7. *motzi* – reciting the *berachah Hamotzi* and *al achilat matzah* over the *matzah*;
8. *matzah* – performing the *mitzvah* of eating the *matzah*;
9. *maror* – eating the bitter herbs;
10. *korech* – eating bitter herbs with *matzah*;
11. *shulchan orech* – eating the *Yom Tov* meal;
12. *tzafun* – eating the *afikomen* the piece of *matzah* that was hidden under *tzafun* (see item 4);
13. *bareich* – reciting *Birkat Hamazon* (Grace after Meals);
14. *hallel* – reciting the psalms praising God;
15. *nirtzah* – singing additional songs of praise, ending with *Chad Gadya*, "A kid, a kid."

❊❊❊❊❊❊❊❊❊❊❊❊

The *Haggadah*

The *Haggadah* (from the verb *lehaggid*, to tell) tells the story of the Exodus, and the symbols on the *seder* plate bring back to life the events of the past. The symbols are:

– the three *matzot* – called *Kohen* (priest), *Levi*, and *Yisrael* – which symbolize the unity of the Jewish people in times of both adversity and good fortune

—the *zeroa* (roasted shankbone), which recalls the Paschal lamb, the *korban Pesach*, because "God passed over the houses of our fathers in Egypt" (Exodus 12:27), hence the name Passover

—the *matzah*, "because the dough of our fathers did not have time to get leavened before God redeemed them" (Exodus 12:39)

—the bitter herbs, *maror* (romaine lettuce and horseradish), because "the Egyptians embittered the lives of our fathers in Egypt" (Exodus 1:14)

—the *charoset*, a mixture of chopped apples, nuts, spices, and wine, which resembles the clay that the Israelite slaves were forced to use to make bricks in Egypt—a dish with salt water and a hard-boiled, roasted egg, as a remembrance of the *chagigah*, the regular festival sacrifice in the Temple.

✳✳✳✳✳✳✳✳✳✳✳✳✳✳

The Five Organs of Speech

The Gerer *rebbe*, commenting on the significance of the Four Cups, said: "We read in the *Zohar* that when the people of Israel were in Egypt, the power of speech was also in bondage. At the Exodus, the power of speech was redeemed together with the people.

"We all know that the spoken word comes into being by virtue of the five instruments of speech: the lips, the teeth, the tongue, the palate, and the throat. After having been in bondage, these five organs of speech were set free at the first Passover. Therefore, to celebrate the redemption of the teeth, we eat the *matzah*, and for the deliverance of the other four parts of the mouth, we drink the Four Cups, using our lips, tongue, palate, and throat."

Sefat Emet

✳✳✳✳✳✳✳✳✳✳✳✳✳✳

Passover: The Holiday of Free Speech

The Arizal says that Pesach (Passover) is a composite of the words *peh*, mouth, and *sach*, speaking; it is the holiday we celebrate by speaking about it and relating its wonders.

In Egypt, the Jews had no freedom of speech. That is why Scripture says, "The Israelites were groaning and they cried out," rather than "they prayed"; they were unable to pray.

When they were liberated, they gained their freedom of speech and could sing the praises of God, hence the name Pesach, *peh sach*, the Festival of "the mouth that is able to speak freely." Therefore, it is a *mitzvah* to tell about the Exodus on the night of Passover, and "the more you tell about the Exodus, the more you are praiseworthy."

※※※※※※※※※※※※※※※

The Number Four

As the *seder* progresses, we cannot help but notice that many of the things mentioned come in sets of four: the Four Cups, the four expressions of redemption, the four questions of the *Mah Nishtanah*, and the 'four sons' of the *Haggadah*.

What can be the connection between Passover and the number four?

The *dalet*, ד, which is the fourth letter in the *alef-bet* and represents the number four, is shaped like a man bent over in total submission. It symbolizes the quality of self-effacing humility. It was such complete self-nullification that the people of Israel exhibited at the time of the Exodus, when, with unquestioning faith in God, they left their homes to follow God "into the uncharted wilderness" (Jeremiah 2:2), without preparing any provisions for the long journey (Exodus 12:39).

The sets of four at the *seder* hint at this *dalet*-like character trait of self-negating meekness.

The Sochatchover *rebbe* suggests a novel reason for the Four Cups.

He says that we drink four cups of wine—a beverage that goes to our head and confuses our mind—in order to demonstrate our willingness to give up our intellect and act on blind faith only, just as our forefathers did at the time of the Exodus.

Shem Mishmuel

✺✺✺✺✺✺✺✺✺✺✺✺✺

Not a Moment to Spare

Rabbi Simchah Bunam of Pshis'cha commented on the verse "I will take you away from your forced labor in Egypt" (Exodus 6:6). The word *sivlot*, "forced labor," is related to the term *savlanut*, "patience." Although their labor was backbreaking, the Israelites had accustomed themselves to it and accepted their fate. They began to see their condition of servitude as natural and adopted a slave mentality. When God observed that the people of Israel were reconciled with their lot and did not perceive their hard labor as an injustice, He knew that He could not delay their redemption any longer.

Siach Sarfei Kodesh, Va'eira

✺✺✺✺✺✺✺✺✺✺✺✺✺

The Egg on the *Seder* Plate

The Chatam Sofer offered the following rationale for displaying an egg on the *seder* plate:

The egg differs from all other foods; the more you cook it, the harder it becomes. With the Jewish people, too, the more severely they are persecuted and oppressed, the more unbending and steadfast they become in their faith. The Torah attests to this phenomenon: "The more [the Egyptians] oppressed them, the more [the Israelites] proliferated and spread" (Exodus 1:12).

Torat Moshe

❈❈❈❈❈❈❈❈❈❈❈❈❈

The Four Cups

An essential part of the *seder* consists of the *arba kosot*, the four cups of wine, which correspond to the four stages in which the redemption took place:

I will **take you away** from your forced labor in Egypt,

I will **free you** from their slavery,

I will **liberate you** with an outstretched arm,

I will **take you to Myself** as a nation (Exodus 6:6, 7).

The fifth cup, Elijah's cup, corresponds to the fifth expression: "I will bring you to the land regarding which I raised My hand, [swearing] that I would give it to Abraham, Isaac, and Jacob. I will give it to you as an inheritance; I am God" (Exodus 6:8). The fifth cup is called Elijah's cup as an expression of our belief that the prophet Elijah will appear in the near future to herald the coming of *Mashiach*.

(Those who cannot drink wine may dilute it or substitute grape juice.)

❈❈❈❈❈❈❈❈❈❈❈❈❈

The Symbols of Passover

The sages of the *Midrash* state that the three primary symbols of Passover—*pesach* (the Paschal lamb), *matzah*, and *maror* (bitter herbs)—correspond to the three Patriarchs—Abraham, Isaac, and Jacob. Thus it may also be said that the Four Cups correspond to the four matriarchs—

Sarah, Rebeccah, Rachel, and Leah. Indeed, the people of Israel were redeemed in the merit of the Patriarchs and the Matriarchs.

It is fitting that the four cups of wine recall the four Matriarchs because an accomplished wife is compared to a vine: "Your wife shall be like a fruitful vine" (Psalm 128:3).

Gevurot Hashem

9

THE *OMER*

On the second night of Passover, we begin counting the *Omer* (*Sefirat Ha'omer*). We count forty-nine days, until the first day of Shavuot, which is celebrated on the fiftieth day.

The *mitzvah* of counting the *Omer* is written in the Torah: "You are to count seven complete weeks after the day following the [Passover] holiday from the day you brought the *Omer* offering that is waved, until the day after the seventh week, when there will be a total of fifty days" (Leviticus 23:15, 16). In the time of the Temple, the *Omer* – a measure of new barley – was offered in the Temple on the second day of Passover as a token of gratitude for the ripening fruit and as a prayer for a bountiful harvest in the future.

We count the *Omer* every night after the stars appear. We should stand during the counting, before which we recite the *berachah*, "Blessed are You . . . who has sanctified us with His commandments and has commanded us regarding the counting of the *Omer*." Then we recite the appropriate day's count. If we forget to count at night, we do so during the following day but without a *berachah*. We may continue to say the *berachah* on the succeeding nights. If we forgot to count even on the next day, we should omit the *berachah* on all succeeding nights.

In the count, we must mention both days and weeks. Thus, for example, on the twelfth day of counting, we say, "Today is twelve days, which are one week and five days, of the *Omer*."

❋❋❋❋❋❋❋❋❋❋❋❋❋❋

Counting the *Omer*

For a deeper understanding of the counting of the *Omer*, we must realize that the world is endowed with fifty Levels of Wisdom. Moses, the greatest man who ever lived, attained forty-nine of those levels. The ultimate wisdom contained in the fiftieth level was beyond his reach. The forty-nine levels of wisdom are represented by the forty-nine days of the Counting of the *Omer*. The fiftieth day, Shavuot, the day of the Giving of the Torah, parallels the fiftieth Level of Wisdom.

As a counterpart to the fifty Levels of Wisdom and Holiness, there are fifty Levels of Spiritual Contamination, because God created the world in perfect balance, making "the one opposite the other" (Ecclesiastes 7:14): the good and the evil inclination, the forces of holiness opposite the forces of impurity.

In Egypt, the people of Israel degenerated, declining morally to the forty-ninth Level of Spiritual Contamination. They needed to be extricated from that state. God wanted to lift Israel gradually from these forty-nine Levels of Immorality by illuminating on each of the days between Pesach and Shavuot the Level of Holiness corresponding to the Gate of Spiritual Contamination on the opposite side of the scale. We relive this *tikkun*, correction or restoration, of gradual ascent to *kedushah*, holiness, each year in the Counting of the *Omer* on the forty-nine days between Pesach and Shavuot. Shavuot thus represents the illumination of the fiftieth Gate of *Binah*, Understanding, and *Kedushah*, Holiness.

Choker Umekabel

❋❋❋❋❋❋❋❋❋❋❋❋❋❋

Interdependence of Torah and Sustenance

You shall then count seven complete weeks after the day following the [Passover] festival when you brought the *Omer* as a wave offering (Leviticus 23:14).

Maharal: "You shall then count" – Why do we count the forty-nine days from the bringing of the *Omer* offering [consisting of new barley] until Shavuot, the day of the Receiving of the Torah? By counting these days, we demonstrate the interdependence of nourishment and Torah. As the sages put it, "If there is no flour there is no Torah; if there is no Torah there is no flour" (*Avot* 3:21).

Be'er Hagolah

❄❄❄❄❄❄❄❄❄❄❄❄❄❄

Significance of the *Omer* Count

Rabbeinu Nissim explains the significance of the *Omer* count from a historical perspective. "When Moses announced to the people of Israel that after their liberation they would become God's servants on Mount Sinai (Exodus 3:12), they asked, 'Moses, when will that service take place?' Moses replied, 'After fifty days.' Thereupon, each person counted the days in eager anticipation of this great event."[1]

In reenacting the events of Passover, we, like our ancestors, begin to count the days as we are looking forward to Shavuot, the day that commemorates the Giving of the Torah.

The Rambam (Maimonides) suggests the following rationale for this *mitzvah*:

"Shavuot is the day on which the Torah was given. To accentuate the importance of that day, we count the days from Passover until Shavuot. You can compare it with a man who is waiting for his best friend to arrive. He will count the days, yes, even the hours, until their reunion. The same applies to the counting of the *Omer* from Passover until Shavuot. By linking the two festivals through the act of counting, we declare that receiving the Torah was the purpose and fulfillment of the Exodus."

Guide of the Perplexed 3:43

✳✳✳✳✳✳✳✳✳✳✳✳✳✳✳

Bring the *Omer* on Pesach

Why has the Torah commanded us to bring an *Omer* on Pesach? Pesach is the season when the crops ripen. Therefore, God ordained that an *Omer* be brought on Pesach so that the produce of the field will be blessed (*Rosh Hashanah* 16).

✳✳✳✳✳✳✳✳✳✳✳✳✳✳✳

Reasons for Counting the *Omer*

1. Rabbeinu Nissim: When Moses told the people of Israel in Egypt, "You shall serve God at this mountain [Mount Sinai]," they asked him, "When will this service take place?" He replied, "At the end of fifty days." Then each person began to count the days in eager anticipation of this great event.

2. Abudraham[2] suggests as a rational reason for counting the *Omer* that everyone was busy working in the fields, and the people were broadly scattered about the countryside, unable to communicate with one another. Therefore, it was important to count the days leading to the next pilgrim festival so as to make certain that no one forgot to come to Jerusalem to celebrate the *Yom Tov* there.

3. The *Zohar*,[3] noting the state of spiritual impurity of the people of Israel in Egyptian bondage, compares them with a woman awaiting the end of menstruation. When they attached themselves to God, their impurity ended. Just as a woman whose menstrual period has ended

"must count seven days" (Leviticus 15:28), so too the people Israel, when their impurity terminated, were told by God, "Count your days of purification" [by counting the *Omer*]. Counting for what purpose? To become pure in the holy waters from Above and thereby to be united with the King and receive His Torah.

❋❋❋❋❋❋❋❋❋❋❋❋❋

The Forty-nine Gates

Rabbi Moshe Chaim Luzzatto explains the counting of the *Omer* from a kabbalistic viewpoint: "The wisdom of the world is contained in the fifty Gates of Wisdom. Moses attained forty-nine of these gates, but the fiftieth gate—that of quintessential wisdom—he did not attain. Analogously, there are forty-nine days of counting the *Omer*, and on the fiftieth day [which is the festival of Shavuot] the Torah was given. Just as there are fifty Gates of Wisdom and Holiness, so there are fifty Gates of *Tum'ah*, Impurity.

When the Israelites were in Egypt, they sank to the depth of the forty-ninth Gate of Impurity. God wanted to extract Israel from the forty-nine gates in stages, by illuminating on each day between Passover and Shavuot the Gate of Holiness that is the counterpart of its opposite Gate of Impurity. This *tikkun*, correction or restoration, comes to life each year in the counting of the *Omer*, on the forty-nine days between Passover—the day of the Exodus—and Shavuot—the day of the Giving of the Torah. Shavuot represents the illumination of the fiftieth gate of *Binah*, Understanding, and *Kedushah*, Holiness.

Choker Umekabel, ch. 18

❋❋❋❋❋❋❋❋❋❋❋❋❋

Counting the Days

Rabbi Samson Raphael Hirsch offers a profound insight on the Counting of the *Omer*. He notes that we know the seven-day periods in the laws of uncleanness and purity as periods during which the individual strives to bring uncleanness to a close in order to enter a state of purity on the eighth day.

Thus, a sevenfold counting of seven-day periods, that is, a counting of forty-nine days, would symbolize the complete elimination of uncleanness, namely, of bondage to our senses. The fiftieth day would mark our final entry into purity, that is, into the realm of moral freedom. The *Omer* count thus symbolizes the idea that we can acquire moral freedom only through sevenfold intensive work on ourselves.[4]

※※※※※※※※※※※※※※※

The Commandment of Counting the *Omer*

You shall then count seven complete weeks from the day after the Passover Festival–when you bring the *Omer* as a wave offering–until the day after the seventh week. You must count fifty days, and you shall bring an offering of new grain to God (Leviticus 23:9, 10).

We are commanded to count forty-nine days from the second day of Pesach–the day the *Omer* was brought into the Temple–until Shavuot, which is celebrated on the fiftieth day. The *Omer* should be counted after nightfall and by each person individually.

The expression *sefirat ha'omer*, "Counting the *Omer*," is derived from the offering of the *Omer*, which took place on the second day of Pesach–the sixteenth of Nisan. On that day, an offering of an *Omer*, a measure of one half gallon of barley of the new crop, was brought to the Temple. New produce was never eaten until after the offering of the *Omer*. The *Omer* count reaches its climax on Shavuot, when another offering of new grain was brought. This was the offering of the Two Loaves made of the wheat of the new crop and marked the beginning of the bringing of the First Fruits, the *Bikkurim*.

※※※※※※※※※※※※※※※

The Mournful Period of *Sefirat Ha'omer*

Historically, the days of Counting of the *Omer* have been regarded as a time of mourning, a period during which no weddings are celebrated and other signs of mourning are observed in commemoration of the death of the 24,000 students of Rabbi Akiva, who perished during that time (*Yevamot* 62b). Because the plague ceased on the thirty-third day of the *Omer – Lag Ba'omer –* that day is celebrated as a day of rejoicing.

The weeks of *Sefirat Ha'omer* are darkened by other tragic events in Jewish history. It was during that season in the years 1096 and 1146 that the Crusaders spread death and terror throughout the Jewish communities of the Rhineland in Germany, decimating the Jewish populations of Cologne, Worms, and Speyer. And it was also during the time of the Counting of the *Omer*, in the spring of 1648, that Chmielnicki and his horde of cossacks unleashed their fire and fury on the Jews of the Ukraine and Poland, destroying 300 communities and murdering more than 200,000 Jews in a massacre unequaled in ferocity until the horrors of the Holocaust.

※※※※※※※※※※※※※※※

The Cycle of Seven

The cycle of seven is a recurring theme in Jewish law and tradition. Basically, the number seven stands for completion and perfection, and groups in series of seven have become the pattern for a rhythm that is evident in all of Creation. And so we observe how the cycle of seven is repeated in a series of widening spirals of days, weeks, months, years, and millennia.

To cite a few examples:

– The six days of Creation culminate in *Shabbat*, the seventh day, on which God rested after completing His work and thereby introduced spirituality into the corporeality of the universe.

– The seven weeks of Counting the *Omer* link the second day of Passover to the Giving of the Torah, fifty days later, on Shavuot.

– The three Festivals of the Torah – Passover, Shavuot, and Sukkot – all occur within the seven months that separate *Nisan* (the New Year of months) from *Tishri* (the New Year of years).

– The *Shemitah* year (sabbatical year) is the final year of the seven-year cycle during which the land had to rest: "Six years you may plant your field, prune your vineyards, and harvest your crops. But the seventh year is a sabbath of sabbaths for the land. It is God's sabbath during which you may not plant your fields, nor prune your vineyards" (Leviticus 25:3, 4).

– At the end of seven *Shemitah* cycles, namely, after seven times seven years, the *Yovel* year (jubilee) is celebrated in the fiftieth year, the year in which land returns to its original owner.

– The association of seven and holiness is evident in the fact that Noah was commanded to take into the ark seven pairs of each clean animal and only two pairs of each unclean animal.

– There are seven Noachide commandments – the universal code of moral law that is applicable to all humankind:[5]

1. the obligation to institute courts of law for the administration of justice
2. the prohibition against blasphemy and against cursing God's name
3. the prohibition against idol worship
4. against murder
5. against incest and adultery
6. against robbery
7. against eating flesh torn from a living animal

– Under the wedding canopy, a bride and groom receive seven blessings. They celebrate their wedding for seven days, known as the week of *Sheva Berachot*, "Seven Blessings."

– The Tabernacle was inaugurated in a ceremony that lasted seven days (Leviticus 8:33–35).

– *Eretz Yisrael* is praised for seven fruits it produces: wheat, barley, grapes, figs, pomegranates, olives, and dates (Deuteronomy 8:8).

—According to Kabbalah, the seven weeks of the *Omer* correspond to the seven *sefirot*, spheres or emanations. The *sefirot*, the vessels through which God guides the world, are:

1. *chesed*, kindness
2. *gevurah*, strength (in the sense of restraint)
3. *tiferet*, beauty (in the sense of harmony)
4. *netzach*, triumph
5. *hod*, splendor
6. *yesod*, foundation
7. *malchut*, kingship

Other examples demonstrating the prevalence of the number seven in Jewish thought are the seven *hakafot* (circuits) around the *bimah* (reader's platform) on *Hoshana Rabbah* and on Simchat Torah, the seven branches of the *menorah* in the Temple, and the seven heavens.

※※※※※※※※※※※※※

The Song of Songs

On the *Shabbat* of Chol Hamoed (the Intermediate Days of Passover), *Shir Hashirim* (the Song of Songs) is read before the Torah reading. This literary masterpiece of unexcelled beauty, written by King Solomon, is an allegorical poem. It is an exquisite love song declaring the passionate ardor that binds God and Israel, whereby the Beloved represents God, and the "rose among the thorns" symbolizes Israel among the nations.

Shir Hashirim is a dialogue between two lovers in which Israel expresses its intense yearning to be close to its Creator, and God declares His fervent wish to bestow His love on His "perfect dove," Israel.

The song comes to a climactic close, with Israel's saying to God, "Hurry, my Beloved, rescue us from our Exile, quick as a gazelle or a young stag in Your swiftness to redeem us, and rest Your Presence on the hills of spice, Mount Moriah, site of Your Temple" (8:14, interpretation according to Rashi).

Holy of Holies

Rabbi Akiva, one of the foremost *Tanna'im* (sages of the *Mishnah*), states, "All the songs of the Bible are holy, but *Shir Hashirim* (Song of Songs) is holy of holies" (*Yadayim* 3:5).

Rabbi Yisrael Salanter, founder of the *Mussar* movement, wonders in what respect *Shir Hashirim* is holier than any other song in the Bible.

Rabbi Yisrael answers: All other songs have a hidden metaphoric and mystical meaning, while on the surface they can also be read as a simple song or poem. In other words, they can be interpreted both allegorically and literally. Their mystical, symbolic dimension imparts to them an aspect of holiness, while their plain meaning gives them a secular character.

Shir Hashirim is unlike any other song. It may not be translated literally, for that would completely distort its meaning. It can be interpreted only allegorically, as alluding to spiritual, holy concepts. Since *Shir Hashirim* has no secular aspect at all, it is endowed with twofold holiness: both internally and externally. Therefore, all songs of the Bible are holy, but *Shir Hashirim* is holy of holies.

Two Ways of Looking

My Beloved is like a gazelle or like a young stag. There He stands behind our wall, gazing through the window, peering through the lattice (Song of Songs 2:9).

Rabbi Yisrael Salanter: "gazing through the window, peering through the lattice" – what is the meaning of this seemingly redundant phrase? The meaning becomes clear if we bear in mind the saying "Ever since the destruction of the Holy Temple, a steel wall has separated the Jewish people from their Father in Heaven" (*Berachot* 32).

Before the destruction of the Temple, we lived in a state that might be termed "gazing through the window." We were like a son whose father was watching him through the window. The father could observe the son, and the son could see the father. After the destruction, however, when a steel wall formed a barrier between us and our Father, we became like the son whose father peers at us "through the lattice." The father sees the son and watches over him, but the son, unable to see the father, is dismayed, confused, and in despair, believing his father has abandoned him.

✼ The Final Days of Passover ✼

The Seventh Day

The sages of the Talmud (*Sotah* 36b) tell us that the parting of the Red Sea took place on the seventh day of Passover. To commemorate this momentous event, its biblical account forms the Torah reading of the seventh day. The story of the miraculous rescue of the children of Israel from the pursuing Egyptians culminates in the *Shirah*, the Song at the Sea (Exodus 15:1–18).

The First to Enter the Red Sea

The Talmud (*Sotah* 36a, 37b) relates that when the children of Israel, pursued by Pharaoh's mighty legions, were facing the raging waters of the Red Sea, a fight broke out among the heads of the various tribes. One said, "I won't be the first one to enter the water!" Another said, "I won't go in either! Let someone else go first!" While they argued, Nachshon ben Aminadav, leader of the tribe of Judah, boldly jumped into the sea, whereupon the waters parted.

As a reward for Nachshon's courageous act, the tribe of Judah brought forth King David, patriarch of the royal dynasty of the Jewish people and the progenitor of *Mashiach*.

✺✺✺✺✺✺✺✺✺✺✺✺✺✺

Rejoicing at the Egyptians' Downfall

Shelah: The Talmud (*Megillah* 12) relates that when the Red Sea parted and the children of Israel were saved, the angels wanted to sing God's praises. The Holy One, blessed is He, chided them, saying, "My handiwork [the Egyptians] are drowning in the sea and you utter a song of praise!"

Now you may ask, if it was improper for the angels to sing, why did Moshe lead the children of Israel in the Song at the Sea?

The answer is this: During the long years of Egyptian bondage, the children of Israel suffered bitterly, toiling ceaselessly at building Egyptian cities and seeing their children killed by cruel taskmasters. Their song and elation at their oppressors' downfall was wholly justified.

Unlike the children of Israel, the angels were not enslaved and tormented by the Egyptians. They could view the Egyptians dispassionately, not as enemies but as creatures of God–human beings who were drowning. Therefore, it was not fitting for the angels to raise their voices in a victory chant.

In that connection, we should take note of a law in the *Shulchan Aruch*, which poignantly reflects the noble spirit of our sages. In the *Shulchan Aruch, Orach Chaim* 490:3, it is stated that on Passover the entire *Hallel* (Psalms 113–118) is recited only on the first two days, and on the last six days of Passover, a shortened version is recited. In this abbreviated version, the first eleven verses of Psalm 115 and Psalm 116 are omitted. The *Mishnah Berurah* explains that the reason for reciting only the shortened version of *Hallel* on the last six days is that because so many Egyptians drowned on the seventh day of Passover, we want to tone down our expression of joy – even though they were our enemies and we had every right to vent our unbridled jubilation.

✺✺✺✺✺✺✺✺✺✺✺✺✺✺

The Song at the Sea

Sefat Emet: The Song at the Sea begins with the words, "Moses and the children of Israel then sang this song:" (Exodus 15:1). Although the verse is translated in the past tense – "Israel then *sang*" – the Torah uses the future tense, *yashir*, – "Israel *will sing* this song." What is the reason for this anomaly?

When the children of Israel saw their Egyptian oppressors dead on the seashore, they suddenly realized that divine justice had been meted out. The Egyptians who had drowned their children had themselves been swallowed up by the sea. They recognized that their long years of hard labor and suffering had been God's design.

The lesson to be derived from this is that we must give thanks and praise to God even if times are bad, in the firm belief that whatever happens is God's way of preparing good things for us.

The children of Israel embedded this sense of trust in divine justice into the collective consciousness of the Jewish people. You might say that it became part of the genetic code of the Jewish people. Therefore, Scripture says, *yashir*, "Israel *will sing*," they *will* proclaim this faith for all time to come. And it is for this reason that we recite the *Shirah* every day in our morning prayers.

✺✺✺✺✺✺✺✺✺✺✺✺✺✺

Song without an Ending

Maharal: The *Shirah* (Song at the Sea) begins with the verse "Then Moses and the Israelites sang this song to God. They said: 'I will sing to

God for He has triumphed gloriously; horse and driver He has hurled into the sea' " (Exodus 15:1).

The song concludes: "For the horses of Pharaoh, with his chariots and horsemen, went into the sea; God turned back the waters of the sea; but the Israelites marched on dry ground in the midst of the sea" (Exodus 15:19).

Significantly, the last verse of the song is closely linked to its first verse. Ending and beginning can be read as one unbroken verse: " . . . God turned back the waters of the sea, but the Israelites marched on dry ground in the midst of the sea; then Moses and the Israelites sang this song . . ."

So we see that the Song at the Sea is a closed circle, a cycle of eternal return, a song without a beginning or an ending, a never-ending hymn. This continuum is indicative of the song's absolute perfection. Things that have an ending are finite, and things that are finite are limited and restricted; thus they are not perfect. God is absolute perfection; His goodness is infinite and His praises are endless; He is "without beginning, without conclusion."[6] Therefore, the Song at the Sea, having no ending, is the ideal vehicle for expressing the limitless praises of God's boundless benevolence.

Conclusion of Passover

Each year on the last day of Passover, the *Chozeh* of Lublin was wont to sing with great fervor the hymn *Chasal Siddur Pesach*, "Ended is the Passover *Seder*." Once, as he was chanting the last line, *Leshanah Habaah Birushalayim*, "Next year in Jerusalem," he was so moved by the words that he broke down and cried. A hush fell over the *chasidim* thronging around the festive *Yom Tov tish* (table), their mood plunging from elation to gloom. It was at that moment of crisis that Mordechai Rackover, a jovial fellow who often lifted the *rebbe's* spirits with a well-chosen wisecrack, approached the *rebbe* and said:

"Rebbe, let me tell you something. It is you who is delaying the *ge'ulah* [redemption]. It is because of you that *Mashiach* isn't coming. You see, at the close of Yom Kippur, when you exclaim, 'Next year in Jerusalem,' your plea is answered in heaven, and the coming of *Mashiach* is postponed until the next year. Then when Passover comes, and again you pray, 'Next year in Jerusalem,' *Mashiach*'s arrival is put off for yet another year. This keeps on going year after year, and there's no end in sight. It's only because of you, *Rebbe*, that *Mashiach* hasn't come yet!"

The joke had the desired effect. The *rebbe's* face lit up in a broad smile. The assemblage of *chasidim* was relieved, and the lively *Yom Tov* mood resumed with joyous singing and happy laughter.

Sifran shel Tzaddikim

❋❋❋❋❋❋❋❋❋❋❋❋

The *Neshamah Yeteirah*, the Additional Soul

In the *Havdalah* ceremony at the departure of *Yom Tov*, the blessing over *besamim* (aromatic spices) is not recited. This blessing is said only in the *Havdalah* at the conclusion of *Shabbat*. Why is this so?

The Ramban offers this explanation: the reason for smelling the pleasant aroma of spices in the *Havdalah* at the close of *Shabbat* is in order to alleviate the trauma caused by the departure of the *neshamah yeteirah* (additional soul), which we are granted every *Shabbat* and which leaves us at the close of *Shabbat*.

By contrast, the *neshamah yeteirah* we attain on *Yom Tov* does not depart at the close of the festival but remains with us at undiminished strength. Thus, there is no need for fragrant spices at the close of *Yom Tov*.

Commenting on the above commentary, the Avnei Nezer expounds: a gift from heaven that is one-sided—one that is bestowed on us from God without any effort on our part—does not endure. *Shabbat* is such a unilateral divine gift. Ever since the days of Creation, at the end of the six weekdays, the sanctity of *Shabbat* descends on the universe, automatically and with unfailing regularity. Since we make no contribution to the process, the *neshamah yeterah*, the additional soul we receive on *Shabbat*, does not endure but departs at the close of *Shabbat*. By contrast, the Festivals are a divine gift that requires the cooperation of man, since the days on which the *Yamim Tovim* fall are fixed by the *Bet Din*,[7] the rabbinical court of justice. Thus, unlike *Shabbat*, which is immutably appointed by God, the Jewish people do play a part in establishing the Festivals; you might say, *Yom Tov* is a joint effort by God and the Jewish people. This being so, the *neshamah yeterah* of *Yom Tov* endures even after the departure of the festival.

✳ *Sefirah* and *Lag Ba'omer* ✳

Sefirah, a Time of Mourning

Beginning in talmudic times, the days of *Sefirah*, the period between Passover and Shavuot, became a time of sadness and mourning. The Talmud (*Yevamot* 62b) mentions the death of the 24,000 students of Rabbi Akiva, all of whom perished during this period.

In the course of Jewish history, tragic events of major proportions have occurred during the *Sefirah* period, adding further to the traditions of sadness and mourning. Notably, the first Crusade in 1096 was a time of intense anguish for the Jewish people when the Crusaders' mob massacred the Jews of Speyer, Worms, Mainz, and many other communities during the *Sefirah* period. Again in the *Sefirah* period, during the second Crusade in 1147, the crusaders decimated the Jewish communities of Wurzburg, Cologne, and Bachrach as well as many others on their way to capture Jerusalem from the Moslems.

In 1648, the *Sefirah* period was marred by one of the greatest disasters in Jewish history, when the Ukrainian cossacks, led by Bogdan

Chmielnicki, went on a savage rampage, destroying 300 Jewish communities in eastern Europe and killing more than 200,000 Jews. It was a bloodbath that was surpassed in fiendish barbarity only by the German Holocaust (1933–1945).

In commemoration of these tragic events, traditions of mourning are observed during the *Sefirah*: no marriages are performed, no music is played, and people do not get haircuts.

Lag Ba'omer

The exception to this period of mourning is the day of *Lag Ba'omer*, the thirty-third day of the *Omer* (the numeric value of *Lag* is 33: *lamed* = 30, *gimel* = 3). It is a festive day on which all restrictions of mourning are lifted. According to tradition, it was on this day that the plague that ravaged Rabbi Akiva's students stopped.

Today in Israel, the anniversary of Rabbon Shimon bar Yochai's death, which occurred on *Lag Ba'omer*, is celebrated with joyous festivities and the lighting of torches and bonfires at his tomb in Meron. The celebration is attended by tens of thousands, who camp out overnight. Rabbi Shimon bar Yochai, a prominent *Tanna* (sage of the *Mishnah*) who lived during the second century C.E., was condemned to death by the Romans for criticizing their regime. He and his son Rabbi Elazar escaped and spent twelve years hiding in a cave. A miracle occurred whereby a carob tree and a well of water were created for them. When the emperor, Antoninus Pius, died, the two left the cave (*Shabbat* 33b). During his twelve-year banishment in the cave, Rabbi Shimon bar Yochai wrote the *Zohar* (Book of Splendor), the basic work of Kabbalah, which deals with the profound mystical concepts hidden in the Torah.

Why is the day of the passing of this great sage a source of ecstatic celebration? Because on that day he revealed the mysteries of the *Zohar* to his disciples (*Zohar* 3:291, 296).

Among *chasidim* and *Sephardim* it is the custom not to cut a boy's hair until he is three years old. On *Lag Ba'omer*, many parents take their three-year-old sons to Rabbi Shimon bar Yochai's gravesite for the first haircut in a ceremony called *chalakah*.

※※※※※※※※※※※※※※※

Hallel

The *Hallel*, the inspiring hymn of praise and prayer, is comprised of Psalms 113 through 118. It is recited on the Festivals of Passover, Shavuot, and Sukkot, as well as on Chanukah and *Rosh Chodesh* (New Moon). However, it is not said on Rosh Hashanah, Yom Kippur, or Purim. The sages chose these psalms because they express five basic beliefs of Judaism: the Exodus, the Parting of the Red Sea, the Giving of the Torah, *techiyat hameitim* (resurrection of the dead), and the coming of *Mashiach*.[8]

The origin of *Hallel* reaches back to the dawn of Jewish history. The *Gemara*[9] relates that Moses and the people of Israel chanted the *Hallel* after the miraculous parting of the Red Sea; Joshua, after defeating the kings of Canaan; Deborah and Barak, after vanquishing Sisera; King Hezekiah, after defeating King Sennacherib of Assyria; Chananiah, Mishael, and Azariah, after being saved from King Nebuchadnezzar; and Mordechai and Esther, after defeating the wicked Haman.

On *Rosh Chodesh* and the last six days of Pesach, a shortened version of the *Hallel* ("half-*Hallel*") is recited, in which the first eleven verses of Psalms 115 and 116 – the segments "*Lo lanu*" and "*Ahavti*" – are omitted. *Hallel* is not said on Rosh Hashanah and Yom Kippur because on those days God sits in judgment and decides our fate. Thus it would be improper for us to raise our voices in songs of praise.[10] *Hallel* is not recited on Purim, because we do not say *Hallel* for a miracle that occurred outside *Eretz Yisrael*, and the miracle of Purim took place in Persia. Another reason is that the reading of the *Megillah* is Purim's *Hallel*.[11]

Psalm 113

From the rising of the sun to its setting, God's Name is praised (Psalm 113:3). – Look up to the sky and contemplate the magnificent radiance of the sun from its rise until its setting. You will then realize the greatness of the Creator and praise His Name (*Tanna debei Eliyahu*). (Metaphorically, this verse urges us to praise God in times of both abundance and adversity [*Kehillat Moshe*].)

He raises the poor from the dust; lifts up the needy from the refuse heaps, to set them with the great, with the great men of his people (Psalm 113:7). – In a spiritual sense, "the needy" refers to one who is spiritually poor and devoid of *mitzvot*; God will lift him from the dust of his earthiness. And he who is stained with sin and wants to cleanse himself, God will raise him from the refuse heap of his degradation (*Gaon* of Vilna).

Psalm 114

When Israel went forth from Egypt, the house of Jacob from a people of strange speech, Judah became His sanctuary, and Israel, His dominion (Psalm 114:1). – This verse alludes to two of the factors that preserved Israel's national identity during the sojourn in Egypt and earned Israel the merit to be redeemed: the Israelites did not change their Hebrew names; neither did they abandon their Hebrew language.

"When *Israel* went forth from Egypt," they retained their name, Israel, and did not adopt Egyptian names; "the house of Jacob from a people of strange speech." Although they lived among Egyptians, the Egyptian language remained a foreign tongue to them; they clung to Hebrew, the holy tongue of their ancestors.

Etz Hadaat Tov

Tremble, O earth, at the presence of the Lord, at the presence of the God of Jacob, who turned the rock into a pool of water, the flinty rock into a flowing fountain (Psalm 114:7, 8). In the previous verse, the earth asked the sea and the Jordan, "What alarmed you, O sea, that you fled, Jordan that you ran backward?" Their reply to the earth was,

"You, too, should should be in awe of our Creator. Just as He turned the sea into dry land, so can He transform the earth into water, a flinty rock into a fountain."

Torat Chesed

Psalm 115

Those who make [idols], all who trust in them, shall become like them (Psalm 115:8). – After they die, they will not be resurrected. Thus, they will return to the inanimate and vegetative state, becoming like their idols, mere pieces of wood and stone.

Tehillot Hashem

O Israel! Trust in the Lord! He is their help and shield (Psalm 115:9). – Unlike the idol worshipers, Israel places its trust in the Rock of their salvation. Therefore, trust in the Lord, even if your rescue is long in coming. Remember that He has been your help and shield in the past, and He will be so again in the future.

Rabbi Yaakov Emden

As for the heavens, the heavens belong to God, but the earth He has given to mankind (Psalm 115:17). – Although the heavens are more precious than the earth, the angels and heavenly bodies are inferior to man because they have no free choice. The earth is given to man, who is endowed with freedom of choice and the ability to surmount his earthly temptations.

Tzofnat Pane'ach

An explanation in the chasidic tradition: In the heavens, perfection reigns. They are filled with God's glorious majesty. But earth was turned over to man. He was given the task to elevate the earth's material nature to a spiritual level.

Be'er Mayim Chayim

Another interpretation: The heavens belong to God—people who ponder the marvels of the heavenly expanse with its myriad stars and galaxies come to recognize God as the Creator. "But the earth He has given to man"—if people's thoughts are focused only on earthly, material things, that is where they will end up—in an earthly grave.

Me'iri

But we will bless God, now and forever. Halleluyah! (Psalm 115:18). —Do not say, "I am steeped in sin. How can I presume to approach God in prayer?" Such thoughts stem from your evil inclination, which is trying to discourage you and make you despondent. What you should say is, "*Now* and forever praise God!" The *now*, the present, is the only thing that matters. Set aside the sins of the past. If you adopt this attitude, you will praise God forever.

Rabbi Avraham of Slonim

Psalm 116

I have believed [in God], although out of great suffering I spoke and said rashly, "All men are deceitful" (Psalm 116:10, 11). —Even though I made rebellious comments such as "All men are false," deep in my heart my faith never wavered. I really should not be penalized for saying such things, for "I spoke out of great suffering," and a person cannot be held accountable for things he says in anguish.

Rabbi Moshe Yosef Mercado[12]

I will raise my cup of salvations and invoke the name of God (Psalm 116:13). —"Salvations" in the plural refers to the salvation of the soul and the body.

Siddur

I will offer a thank offering to You and invoke the name of God (Psalm 116:17). —What is the connection between the two segments of this verse? The Psalmist teaches us that whenever we thank God for kindnesses He bestowed in the past, we should immediately pray for

His kindness in the future. The Psalmist says, "I will offer a thank offering" for kindness in the past, following this up with "I will invoke the name of God," asking Him for kindness in the future. In keeping with this rule, we recite in *Birkat Hamazon* (Grace after Meals), "He did good, He does good, and He will do good to us."

Rabbi Y. Chayun[13]

Psalm 117

Praise the Lord, all you nations; extol Him, all you peoples. For His kindness has overwhelmed us, and the truth of God endures forever. Halleluyah! (Psalm 117:1, 2). – This psalm contains only two verses and is the shortest chapter in all the Scriptures. It describes the messianic era, when Israel and the non-Jewish nations will stand face-to-face and praise God: Israel in perfect observance of the Torah, the Gentile nations abiding by the seven *Noachide* laws,[14] which were given to all mankind.

Redak

"His kindness has overwhelmed us." – Both Israel and the nations to whom Israel is appealing have experienced God's kindness. God in His kindness has led the nations out of their estrangement and restored them as His servants.

Hirsch, *Commentary on Psalms*

Taking a different approach to the same verse, we may ask, Why should the Gentile nations praise God for all the kindness He has bestowed on Israel? The answer is this: the non-Jewish nations, far better than the Jews, recognize the kindness that God has shown to His people. Only the Gentile nations know the countless evil designs they hatched against us that were frustrated through God's intervention. We don't even know how many of their sinister schemes were foiled through God's kindness. They have tangible proof of God's overwhelming benevolence toward the Jewish people. The Gentiles are the ones who should praise God.

Brisker *Rav*

Psalm 118

You [the enemy] pushed me hard to make me fall, but God helped me (Psalm 118:13). – The *Zohar* says that the enemy in this verse refers to the evil inclination, which was tempting David. But God helped him to resist its seductive enchantment. If a person has the will to battle the evil impulse but cannot overcome it, God will assist him.

Zohar, Vayishlach

Open for me the gates of righteousness that I may enter them and thank God. This is the gate of God; the righteous shall enter through it (Psalm 118:19). – The more intensely a righteous man serves God, the more he realizes that he cannot attain Godlike perfection. For God is infinite, and His goodness is endless. In fact, reaching the awareness that perfection is beyond man's grasp is in itself the aim of serving God. The righteous man says, "Open for me the gates of serving God so that I can enter to serve my Creator." Noting how distant he still is from achieving his goal of nearness to God, he imagines that until now his entire *avodah* (service) amounted to nothing. The answer he receives is, "This is the gate of God," the recognition that our service of God is incomplete and that Godlike perfection, by its very nature, is unattainable, that in itself is the main objective of *avodah*, serving the Almighty.

No'am Elimelech

I thank You for You have answered me and have become my deliverance (Psalm 118:21). *Ki anitani*, "for You have answered me," can also be translated "for You have afflicted me," giving rise to the following interpretation: the Psalmist says, "Although you have caused me pain, I do not murmur; instead, I thank You, for I know that all Your actions are for the best, even though this may not be immediately apparent."

This brings to mind the story of Rabbi Akiva, who once attempted to board a ship but was refused passage. The ship sailed, leaving him stranded, but during the voyage it sank. Thereupon Rabbi Akiva thanked and praised God.

Shaarei Chaim

10

SHAVUOT

The children of Israel were released from bondage, the waters of the Red Sea parted before them, and their hated oppressors were dead on the shore of the Red Sea. They saw God's great power, beholding it with their own eyes. Nourished by the *manna* from heaven, their thirst slaked by the water from Miriam's well, a throng of 600,000 marched into the wilderness at God's behest. In a spectacular display of pure faith, casting aside all doubt and fear, they advanced toward an unknown destination.

How long could the euphoria last? How long before liberty would be confused with license, before freedom would degenerate into anarchy?

Once before, God had revealed Himself to humankind. When He created the universe, He revealed Himself through His works, through nature. The magnificent sun, the myriad galaxies, the earth in full bloom, and the mighty oceans would proclaim to mankind the existence of the Creator. But man, seeking only possessions and pleasure, failed to recognize the Master of the universe; arrogantly man established himself as master of the earth. Beginning with Adam and for 2,000 years, generations came and went, and God was completely eliminated from life and from nature.

Since contemplation of nature had not led people to recognize the Creator, how was God's design for the world to be realized? It became necessary that a people be introduced into the ranks of nations, which through its history and its life should declare God as the cause of existence and should serve as a model and an instruction to humanity.

On the sixth of *Sivan*, in the year 2448 of Creation, God revealed Himself to the nation of Israel. In the wilderness, Israel received the Torah and its mission to be "a kingdom of priests and a holy nation." It was through Israel that God's master plan for the universe would be implemented. Israel was to be "a light unto the nations," and its mission was to show the peoples of the earth that God is the Source of all blessing and that fulfillment of His will means the attainment of all happiness.

And throughout its agonizing history, the Jewish people has remained faithful to the covenant of Sinai, and in spite of pain and torment it has been remarkably successful in fulfilling its mission. Through Christianity and Islam—religions that consider themselves extensions of Judaism—much of the paganism that existed throughout the world has been destroyed, and monotheism has spread to the far reaches of the earth. Speaking of these religions, the Rambam (Maimonides, 1135–1204) states in *Hilchot Melachim* 11:4 (ch. 11 and 12 of *Mishneh Torah* have been expunged by the censor and do not appear in most standard texts but are included in full in later editions), "Ultimately, all the deeds of the Nazarene and that Ishmaelite [Mohammed] who arose after him will only serve to prepare the way for *Mashiach*'s coming and the improvement of the entire world, motivating the nations to serve God together, as stated by Zephania, 'I will make the peoples pure of speech that they will all call upon the name of God and serve Him with one purpose' (*Zepanaia* 3:9). How will this come about? The whole world has already become filled with mention of *Mashiach*, Torah, and *mitzvot*. These matters have been spread to the farthest islands and to many stubborn-hearted nations, and they discuss the matters and the *mitzvot* of the Torah. . . . When the true *Mashiach* arises and proves successful, they [the Christians and Moslems] will all return and realize that their ancestors endowed them with a false heritage and their prophets caused them to err."

And so, every year, in a reenactment of the *Ma'amad Har Sinai*, the Stand at Mount Sinai, we celebrate Shavuot and commit ourselves anew to the sacred task our ancestors received and accepted with the words *naaseh venishma*, "we shall do and we shall listen." That task will be completed with the coming of *Mashiach*, when "the glory of God will be revealed and all flesh – as one – shall see that the mouth of God has spoken" (Isaiah 40:5).

Seeing and Hearing

All the people saw the sounds, the lightning, the blast of the ram's horn, and the mountain's smoking. The people trembled when they saw it, standing at a distance (Exodus 20:18).

"All the people saw the sounds." This phrase gives rise to a perplexing question: How could the people *see* the sounds? Sound is heard, not seen. Rabbi Chaim Sanzer offers this penetrating insight: of the five senses, vision is the preferred one, as it affords the most accurate perception of the subject matter and makes the deepest impression on our soul. By contrast, in the case of hearing, although we believe what we hear, hearing does not have as strong an impact as seeing. Indeed, Moses broke the tablets only after *seeing* the people worshiping the Golden Calf; being told about it by God – hearing of the perfidy – did not affect him to the same extent. However, the sense of vision has the drawback that we cannot always see clearly. In the dark, we cannot see at all.

Candlelight, dim light, atmospheric conditions, and poor eyesight distort our view, but our hearing is not affected by any of these factors. Strange as it may seem, there exists also a combined form of hearing and seeing. It occurs in an individual who is capable of rising above the limitations of the senses. Such a person can see sound and hear a vision.

A prophet can do this. When receiving divine prophecy, the prophet divests himself of his corporeality, and his sense of hearing and vision blend into one. At Mount Sinai, after undergoing fifty days[1] of spiritual refinement, the children of Israel attained the level of prophecy. They "saw the sounds," and thereby the belief in God was anchored in their hearts.

Divrei Chaim

❋❋❋❋❋❋❋❋❋❋❋❋❋

The Ten Commandments

If we consider the order in which the Ten Commandments were given, an important fact emerges that sheds new light on this divine set of laws. The first group, five commandments, begins with *Anochi*, "I am the Lord your God," and ends with *Kabeid*, "Honor your father and your mother." The second half begins with *Lo tirtzach*, "Do not commit murder," and ends with *Lo tachmod*, "Do not be envious." Thus, the demand that we acknowledge God opens with a challenge to our intellect: "I am the Lord your God" and "You shall have no other gods." However, it is not enough to recognize God in theory; we must acknowledge Him also in practice by exercising control over our words ("Do not take the name of God in vain"), our deeds ("Remember the *Shabbat* to keep it holy"), and our family lives ("Honor your father and your mother").

The social legislation contained in the second half of the Ten Commandments begins with demands on both our actions and words ("Do not commit murder; do not commit adultery; do not steal; do not testify as a false witness"). But controlling our words and deeds is not enough; the Law demands that we also exercise control over our thoughts and feelings ("Do not be envious").

The underlying truth is that all so-called religious adoration is worthless if belief in a Supreme Being does not translate into control of words and actions toward our family and our social life. Only our deeds prove that our glorification of God is genuine. Conversely, all social virtues are trivial if their only aim is to gain acceptance or if they are not rooted in a pure belief in God. Indeed, the two tablets, both "the religious one" and "the social one," form one indivisible union.

Rabbi Samson Raphael Hirsch

✳✳✳✳✳✳✳✳✳✳✳✳✳

The Fourth Commandment

Remember the *Shabbat* to keep it holy (Exodus 20:8).

Notice how closely the number seven is linked to *Shabbat*: *Shabbat* is the seventh day of the week. The commandment to observe *Shabbat* begins with the letter *zayin* of *zachor*, "remember" (Exodus 20:8), and *zayin* is the seventh letter of the *alef-bet*. The commandment of *Shabbat* begins with the seventh verse of the Ten Commandments. The words "Do not do any work" are addressed to seven: "you, your son, your daughter, your slave, your maid, your animal, and the stranger in your gates."

Baal Haturim

✳✳✳✳✳✳✳✳✳✳✳✳✳

The Torah and the Nations of the World

The *Midrash* (*Pesikta* 21) relates that God offered the Torah to all the nations of the world but they rejected it. Then He came to Israel, and they accepted it. First, He approached the children of Esau and said to them, "Will you accept the Torah?"

They asked, "Master of the universe, what is written in it?"

He answered, "Do not commit murder" (the sixth commandment).

They replied, "This is the legacy our father left us; as it says [in the blessing Isaac gave to Esau], 'And upon your sword shall you live' [Genesis 27:40]; we cannot accept the Torah."

Thereupon He appeared to the children of Ishmael and asked them, "Will you accept the Torah?"

They asked, "What is written in it?"

He told them, "Do not steal" (the eighth commandment).

They responded, "Our very livelihood depends on robbing and stealing; as it says, 'And he [Ishmael] shall be a wild man; his hand shall be against every man and every man against him' [Genesis 16:12]; we cannot accept the Torah."

He heard a similar reply from the children of Ammon. God went from one nation to the other, offering the Torah to all. When he finally came to the children of Israel, they called out in unison, *Naaseh venishma!* "We will do and we will hear!" (Exodus 24:7).

※※※※※※※※※※※※※※※

The Right and the Left Tablets

How were the Ten Commandments inscribed on the tablets? Five commandments were on one tablet, five on the other:

I am the Lord your God	Do not commit murder
You shall have no other gods	Do not commit adultery
Do not take the name of God in vain	Do not steal
Remember the *Shabbat*	Do not bear false witness
Honor your father and your mother	Do not covet

The *Midrash* (*Pesikta Rabbati* 21) finds deep significance in the juxtaposition of the commandments:

Opposite "I am the Lord your God" is written, "Do not commit murder." By placing these commandments side by side, the Torah comes to teach us that whoever sheds innocent blood diminishes the image of God, for "man is made in the image of God" (Genesis 9:6).

Opposite "You shall have no other gods" is written, "Do not commit adultery." The Torah teaches us that whoever worships idols is regarded as though he committed adultery against God.

Opposite "Do not take the name of God in vain" is written, "Do not steal." The Torah teaches us that whoever steals will eventually swear falsely.

Opposite "Remember the *Shabbat*" is written, "Do not bear false witness." The Torah tells us thereby that whoever desecrates the *Shabbat* is regarded as though he testified that God did not create the world in six days and that He did not rest on the seventh day.

Opposite "Honor your father and your mother" is written, "Do not covet your neighbor's wife." The Torah teaches that whoever covets his neighbor's wife will father a son by her, who will honor a stranger as his father and curse his real father.

Receiving the Torah

Said the Kotzker *rebbe*: Shavuot is also called *Zeman Mattan Torateinu*, "The Time of the Giving of our Torah." Why isn't this *Yom Tov* called "The Time of the *Receiving* of our Torah?" The reason is that on that momentous day at Mount Sinai, only the giving of the Torah occurred, whereas our receiving of the Torah is taking place each and every day. In addition, the Torah was given to all Jews alike, without distinction between one person and another. On the other hand, the Torah has been received by each person differently, each according to his perception and level of understanding.

Agreement without Involvement

The Kotzker *rebbe* commented on the verse "All the people saw the sounds and the lightning, the blare of the ram's horn and the mountain's smoking; and when the people saw it they trembled and stood at a distance" (Exodus 20:15). He said, "There are people who see and nod their head in agreement, but in spite of that they keep their distance."

❈❈❈❈❈❈❈❈❈❈❈❈❈❈❈

The Torah and Israel Are Identical

Rabbi Levi Yitzchak of Berditchev said: God gave the Torah to Israel. The souls of Israel are the body of the Torah. How is this to be understood? There are 600,000 souls in Israel, and there are 600,000 letters in the Torah. Thus we can say that the Torah and Israel are one and the same, each Jew representing one letter of the Torah.

Kedushat Levi, Bamidbar

❈❈❈❈❈❈❈❈❈❈❈❈❈❈❈

The Fifth Commandment

Honor your father and your mother. You will then live long on the land that God is giving you (Exodus 20:12).

This commandment follows immediately after the commandment to remember Shabbat. The two *mitzvot* are interrelated, as is evident also from the verse "Every person must respect his mother and father and keep My *Shabbat*" (Leviticus 19:3).

What is the factor that links these two commandments? During the six days of Creation, God brought into being the prototype of each species, including man. If God had not stopped the process of Creation but continued to fashion living things, then the system of procreation – of parents begetting offspring – would not exist. God Himself would create each individual. When God ceased the process of Creation on *Shabbat*, He ensured the continuance of life on earth by means of reproduction – parents begetting children. Thus, we may say that parents are partners of God. They beget the child's body, and God endows it with a soul and breathes life into it. Consequently, that we are born of a father and a mother is the direct result of God's resting on *Shabbat*. This is the key to understanding the connection between "honor your mother and your father" and "keep the *Shabbat*."

Malbim, commentary on the Torah

✶✶✶✶✶✶✶✶✶✶✶✶✶✶

Alef before *Bet*

I am the Lord your God . . . (Exodus 20:2).

The *Midrash* asks: Why do the Ten Commandments begin with the word *Anochi*, "I am"? *Anochi* teaches us that the Holy One, blessed is He, rates the Giving of the Torah more highly than the creation of the world, for the story of Creation begins with the letter *bet* of *Bereishit*, "In the beginning," whereas the Ten Commandments begin with the *alef* of *Anochi*, "I am."

Rabbi Elazar said: During the twenty-six generations that came before the Giving of the Torah, the letter *alef* protested to God, "Master of the universe, I am the first of all letters. Why didn't You create the world with me instead of with the *bet*!" Replied the Holy One, blessed is He, "You must understand; the entire world was created only for the sake of the Torah. I assure you, when the time comes that I give the Torah to My children, I will begin the Ten Commandments with you, the *alef*."

✶✶✶✶✶✶✶✶✶✶✶✶✶✶

Moses Receiving the Torah

Rabbi (Don) Yitzchak Abarbanel: Tractate *Avot* opens with the words, "Moses received the Torah from Sinai." Why was his acceptance not linked to God, who gave the Torah? It should have stated that Moses accepted the Torah from *God*; instead it says that he received it from Sinai! What's more, if the *Mishnah* intended to indicate merely the place where the Giving occurred, the expression should have been *at* Sinai and not *from* Sinai!

The answer is this: Our teacher Moses was not taught by man. It was God who filled him with the spirit of higher wisdom and prophecy to an extraordinary degree. And all this was attained from Sinai! The meaning is that it was attained as a result of his lonely stay there – at Sinai – without food or drink throughout the days of spiritual communion with God. Adam was the beginning for all mankind; so too was Moses in his prophecy, when the divine spirit descended on him, the first of all the prophets. The prerequisite for this perfection was Sinai, the mountain that God chose for His Divine Presence and Revelation. Moses' lonely sojourn at Sinai enabled him to achieve all this. This is the explanation for the statement by our sages that "Moses received the Torah *from* Sinai." It was Moses' remarkable stay at Sinai that caused him to reach the highest degree attainable in order to receive the Godly Torah. The Written Law was inscribed by Moses on scrolls, but the commentary on it and all that is to be derived logically from it Moses taught to Israel orally.

Abarbanel, Commentary on *Avot*

Complete Silence

When God gave the Torah, not a bird chirped, no fowl flew, no ox lowed, angels did not fly, seraphim did not say "Holy, holy, holy," the sea did not stir, no creature spoke. The world was utterly silent, when a voice was heard: "I am the Lord" (*Shemot Rabbah* 29).

The Ten Commandments Addressed to Mankind

Rabbi Yochanan said, Each word that was uttered by the Almighty was divided into seventy languages. Rabbi Yishmael expounded, it was "like a hammer that shatters a rock" (Jeremiah 23:29). Just as a hammer striking a rock produces many sparks, so was each divine word divided into the seventy major languages of mankind (*Shabbat* 88b).

❋❋❋❋❋❋❋❋❋❋❋❋❋❋

The World Hinges on "the Sixth Day"

Resh Lakish expounded on the verse "And there was evening and there was morning, the sixth day." He asked, "Why is it that the story of the sixth day of Creation concludes with the words '*the* sixth day,' whereas the other days end with the phrase 'a second day, a third day. . . .' "

The definite article, "the," comes to teach us that God created the world with a stipulation: "If the people of Israel accept the Torah, which will be given on *the sixth day* of *Sivan*, the universe will remain intact; but if they do not, I return the entire cosmos back to *tohu vabohu*, to its primordial formlessness and emptiness" (*Shabbat* 88b).

❋❋❋❋❋❋❋❋❋❋❋❋❋❋

The Factor of Three

The *Gemara* in *Shabbat* 88 establishes a close link between Shavuot and the number three. It expounds: Blessed is our God, who gave us a Torah, which has *three* parts: Torah, Nevi'im (The Prophets), and Ketuvim (The Writings).[2] He gave the Torah to a people that is divided into

three groups: *Kohanim*, Levites, and Israelites. It was given through one
who was the third (Moses was his mother's third child), on the third
day (of the final day of the Three Days of Abstinence, which preceded
the Giving of the Torah), in the third month (the month of *Sivan*).

✼✼✼✼✼✼✼✼✼✼✼✼✼✼✼

We Will Do and Hear

Rabbi Yisrael of Rizhin explained the age-old question concerning the
Giving of the Torah: The people accepted the Torah with the immortal words *naaseh venishma*, "We will do and we will hear all that
God has declared" (Exodus 24:7). They said "do" before "hear." But
how can you do something before hearing what it is you are asked to
do?

Said the Rizhiner: They said it correctly. Look at it this way. For
example, if you want to open a door, you certainly don't have to tell
your hand, "Turn the knob." Your head and your mind encompass all
your limbs, and if your mind wants to take a certain action, your hand
instinctively senses this without being told specifically.

At the Giving of the Torah, there existed a perfect union between
the Holy One, blessed is He, and the people of Israel. God was the Head
of the nation. Consequently, when God wanted Israel to accept the
Torah, the entire nation sensed what was asked of them. There was no
need to teach them the specific details of the Torah. Like the hand,
which instantly obeys the head, they had apprehended the Torah in its
entirety. Thus they readily declared, "We will do and hear"–"do"
before "hear."

Irin Kadishin

✼✼✼✼✼✼✼✼✼✼✼✼✼✼

Man's Ups and Downs

Moses led the people out of the camp toward God, and they stood at
the foot of the mountain (Exodus 19:17).

Rabbi Eliyahu Lapian: "And they stood at the foot of the mountain" – the literal translation of this phrase reads, "they stood *underneath* the mountain." This leads the *Gemara* in *Shabbat* 88 to expound that God, in a threatening gesture, lifted up the mountain and, holding it over the heads of the people of Israel, warned, "If you accept the Torah, all is well, but if you don't, this will be your grave."

This is strange indeed. Just a short while before, the people of Israel had willingly accepted the Torah, solemnly declaring, *Naaseh venishma,* "We will do and we will listen" (Exodus 24:7). Why the need to threaten them with a mountain hanging over them?

Rabbi Eliyahu Lapian answers: God knows human nature. He knows the lofty heights of spirituality a soul can reach, but He also is aware that man is made of the dust of the earth and possesses a carnal nature. Man is a fusion of two antithetical forces – the spiritual and the material.

At the Giving of the Torah, the people of Israel were on a most exalted spiritual plateau, resembling celestial angels. Having reached that close an attachment to God, it is not surprising that they unequivocally accepted the Torah. But no man can remain at such a level forever. Eventually, his pure heart will become ensnared by his natural tendencies. His passions will impel him to satisfy his lust, and the only thing that can control his craving for forbidden things is the fear of punishment. Mindful of the weakness in human nature, God provided – at the moment of highest spiritual elevation – this admonition: "If you don't, this will be your burial place."

Lev Eliyahu

❈❈❈❈❈❈❈❈❈❈❈❈❈❈

The Tenth Commandment

"Do not be envious of your neighbor's house. Do not be envious of your neighbor's wife, his slave, his maid, his ox, his donkey, or anything that belongs to your neighbor" (Exodus 20:14).

Said Rabbi Yitzchak of Radvil: Why is the commandment "Do not be envious" placed at the end of the Ten Commandments? Because if you have observed this commandment, you surely have observed all those that precede it. But he who does not have sufficient self-control to fulfill the prohibition against being envious must begin again from the first commandment: believe that God rules the world. For had he sincerely believed in God, he would not be envious of that which God had apportioned to others.

Or Yitzchak

Thoughts on Envy

Rabbi Nachman of Bratzlav said:
When jealousy ceases, the Redemption will arrive.
Often envy is the cause of destruction and murder.
Envy of someone else's property may drive a person insane.

Likutei Moharan

Better than Gold and Honey

[The Torah] is more desirable than gold, than much fine gold; sweeter than honey, than drippings of the comb (Psalm 19:11).

Baal Shem Tov: "More desirable than gold . . . sweeter than honey"–gold is very desirable but it does not satisfy, since no man is ever content with the amount of gold he possesses. Honey is very sweet but unpleasant to a person who is satiated. But the Torah is both satisfying and pleasant.

The Talmud, the Oral Law

He has made me dwell in darkness, like those long dead (Lamentations 3:6).

Rabbi Simchah Bunam of Pshis'cha: The *Gemara* (*Sanhedrin* 27) comments that the expression "He has made me dwell in darkness" means, "He gave me the Babylonian Talmud." Why is the Talmud compared to darkness? Rabbi Bunam explains that the expression "He has made me dwell" also means "He has refreshed and restored me." Thus, the prophet tells us that even in the darkness and degradation of the Exile, God gave us one way to refresh and restore our soul. He gave us the Talmud, which has inspired and stimulated the Jewish people throughout the night of the *galut*.

Kol Simchah

✳✳✳✳✳✳✳✳✳✳✳✳✳✳

Outward Appearance

All the people saw the sounds, the lightning, the blast of the ram's horn, and the mountain's smoking. The people trembled when they saw it, and stood at a distance . . . but Moses entered the thick mist where God was (Exodus 20:18–21).

"The people . . . stood at a distance . . but Moses entered the thick mist" – some people, when visiting a holy man, observe carefully his outward actions, believing that these show his greatness. This is wrong. To know a man's greatness, one must take note of the creative powers of his soul. And so we read in the Torah that the people saw the thunder and the lightning, and they stood at a distance. They saw only the outward manifestations of God's majesty; therefore, they were far from knowing God. Moses, however, entered the inner region, and there he found God.

Likutei Maharil

✳✳✳✳✳✳✳✳✳✳✳✳✳✳

Dairy Food on Shavuot

It is customary to eat dairy dishes on Shavuot. Some of the reasons suggested for this practice are as follows:

1. The infant Moses was drawn out of the Nile on the sixth of *Sivan*. He was willing to be nursed only by a Hebrew mother. By eating dairy dishes on Shavuot, we recall this merit of Moses.[3]

2. Before receiving the Torah, the people of Israel were permitted to eat the meat of animals that were not kosher. At Mount Sinai they were given the laws of forbidden foods and those of *shechitah*, ritual slaughter. When they returned home, they found that they had no kosher cooking utensils. Thus, they were forced to eat only dairy foods that do not require cooking.

3. The numeric value of *chalav*, milk, equals forty, corresponding to the forty days of Moses' sojourn on Mount Sinai (*chet, lamed, bet* = $8 + 30 + 2 = 40$).

The *Shelah* adds a word of caution: "It is the custom to eat dairy food followed by meat dishes, because the rabbis stated, "without meat on the table there can be no real festive joy." We should take great care to rinse our mouths thoroughly and to recite *Birkat Hamazon* (Grace after Meals) after the dairy meal, to wait an hour, to cover the table with a different tablecloth, and then to set the table for a meat meal.

Rabbi Pinchas of Koretz said: It is the custom to eat dairy foods on Shavuot as a sign of humility in welcoming the Day of the Giving of the Torah. By eating dairy foods, we regard ourselves as young children who are still too young to eat meat.

✖✖✖✖✖✖✖✖✖✖✖✖✖

The Names of Shavuot

The Festival of Shavuot is known by several other names, each highlighting a specific aspect of the *Yom Tov*:

1. Festival of the Harvest – *Chag Hakatzir*: "Also keep the Festival of

the Harvest of the first fruits of your produce that you planted in the field" (Exodus 23:16). We thank God for bringing forth a bountiful crop.

2. Festival of Shavuot – *Chag Shavuot*: "You shall then celebrate the Festival of Shavuot (the Festival of Weeks) to God your Lord" (Deuteronomy 16:10). After counting the seven weeks of the *Omer*, we observe Shavuot.

3. The Festival of the First Fruits – *Yom Habikkurim*: "On the day of the first fruits when you bring a new grain offering to God on your Shavuot Festival" (Numbers 28:26). On Shavuot, a special offering of two loaves was made. These loaves came from the new wheat crop, "the first fruits of the wheat harvest" (Exodus 34:22).

4. In the Talmud, Shavuot is known by the name *Atzeret*, the Last Assembly Day, implying that the festival is the closing day of a continuous religious observance that starts with Pesach, in the same way that Shemini Atzeret is the closing day of Sukkot. Indeed, Shavuot is closely linked to Pesach, as it is the fiftieth day of the *Omer* count, which begins on the second night of Pesach (*Pesikta* 30:193). It is for this reason that the Jews of Greece called Shavuot by the name Pentecost, which means "Festival of Fifty Days."

5. The Time of the Giving of our Torah – *Zeman Mattan Torateinu*: Although the Torah gives no specific date for the revelation at Sinai, the rabbis calculated, by analyzing the biblical text, that it occurred on the sixth day of *Sivan*, the day of Shavuot.

※※※※※※※※※※※※※※

Floral Decorations

An old Shavuot tradition consists of decorating the synagogue and the home with flowers and branches, as a reminder of Mount Sinai, which was covered with vegetation. Evidence of this verdancy is seen in the warning "Let no sheep and cattle graze before this mountain" (Exodus 34:5).

※※※※※※※※※※※※※※

Staying Awake

Another widespread custom is to stay awake the entire first night of
Shavuot, studying Torah. The *Midrash* relates that at Sinai, before
receiving the Torah, the people of Israel slept all through that night.
When God appeared amid thunder and lightning, Moses had to rouse
them from their sleep, as it says, "And Moses led the people out of the
camp to meet God" (Exodus 20:17). By staying awake all night, we
will not make the same mistake.

※※※※※※※※※※※※※※※

Akdamut and *Azharot*

In Ashkenazic communities, it is customary to recite aloud the *Akdamut*
before the Torah reading of the first day of Shavuot. This sets the tone
for the reading from the portion of *Yitro*, which contains the Ten
Commandments. An inspiring hymn praising God, and written in
Aramaic, it was composed by Rabbi Meir ben Yitzchak, who lived in
Worms, Germany, during the eleventh century. In Sephardic communities, *Akdamut* is omitted. Instead, in the afternoon the *Azharot* is
recited, which is a liturgical poem based on the 613 commandments of
the Torah and composed by the highly acclaimed Rabbi Shlomoh ibn
Gabirol (Spain, c. 1021–c. 1058).

※※※※※※※※※※※※※※※

For the Sake of the One Rose

It is customary to decorate both the synagogue and the home with
greenery and flowers as a remembrance of the Giving of the Torah[4]. At
that time, Mount Sinai was covered with vegetation. Floral decora-

tions bring to mind the following poignant parable from the *Midrash*:[5] ". . . A king, examining his garden, found it to be full of thorny weeds. He brought in gardeners to cut down the noxious growth. Suddenly he noticed one single rose. Thereupon the king commanded, 'For the sake of the one rose, let the entire garden be spared.' . . . For the sake of the Torah the entire world shall be saved."

✸✸✸✸✸✸✸✸✸✸✸✸✸

The Final Words of the *Ger Tzedek*

In the days of the Vilna *Gaon*, 1720–1779, the prominent Count Pototzky of Vilna, recognizing the truth of Torah, converted to Judaism, much to the chagrin of the Catholic clergy. The count was given the Hebrew name Avraham ben Avraham (Abraham being the father of all converts), and he immersed himself in the study of Torah, becoming an eminent scholar. The church desperately searched for him, wanting to bring him back into the fold. He was betrayed and brought before a church tribunal, where he was given the choice of embracing Catholicism or being burned at the stake. He offered his life *al Kiddush Hashem*, for the sanctification of God's name, and died a martyr's death on the second day of Shavuot, the twenty-fourth of May, 1749. His remains were buried in the mausoleum of the *Gaon* of Vilna.

Rabbi M. M. Yasher[6] relates the following moving anecdote:

On the day before Shavuot, all tables and benches in the large *bet midrash* (study hall) of the *yeshivah* were removed. This was done in order to make room for the *bachurim* (students) to dance and enjoy the *Yom Tov*. At the height of the dancing, the *rosh yeshivah* (dean) Rabbi Hirsch Levinson would silence the cheerful crowd. With deep emotion he would begin to tell the story of the *Ger Tzedek* (righteous convert) Rabbi Avraham ben Avraham and to explain how he was able to reach such a lofty stage that he died a martyr's death, giving his life for *Kiddush Hashem*, the sanctification of God's Name, on the *Yom Tov* of

Shavuot. The rabbi described how the *Ger Tzedek* had given up a life of affluence and chosen to live in exile, dedicating himself to the study of Torah, and how in the end he was betrayed. Then the rabbi would quote the words that Rabbi Avraham ben Avraham spoke before going to his death:

"Where do converts to Judaism come from? When God approached all the nations and asked them whether they would be willing to accept the Torah, they all declined. There were, however, among each of those nations a few lone exceptional individuals who did want to receive the Torah, but they were outvoted by the majority. These individuals are the progenitors of all *gerim* (converts), whose souls were also present at the Giving of the Torah. If I have merit in the eyes of our Father in heaven, I will bring to everlasting life even the person who betrayed me and informed against me to the authorities. For this person brought about a great merit for me, for through his deed I was given the opportunity to pass the test and offer my life for *Kiddush Hashem*."

※※※※※※※※※※※※※

Why No *Mitzvot* to Commemorate Shavuot?

Rabbi Aharon Kotler: We note that the Torah did not designate any tangible symbols to commemorate the Giving of the Torah at Mount Sinai. Moreover, the Torah does not even mention the fact that Shavuot is the day on which the Torah was given. By contrast, the Torah does institute a great number of rituals to remind us of our redemption from Egypt.

On reflection, we can distinguish a distinct difference between the two events. The signs and wonders of the Exodus are miracles that happened *in the past*. On one hand, we need symbolic reminders to help us relive these glorious events. On the other hand, the idea of the Stand of Sinai requires no memorial. It is inherent in the Torah itself. The Giving of the Torah is described as "a loud and never-ending voice" (Deuteronomy 5:19), as Onkelos[7] translates it. Indeed, the loud voice of the Giving of the Torah is manifest continuously in the Torah itself. By being close to Torah, as are the sages who engross themselves in the Torah, we earn the reward of having studied Torah, and our life will be filled with the radiance of Torah.

Mishnat Rabbi Aharon

❈❈❈❈❈❈❈❈❈❈❈❈

The Number Seven

On your Shavuot festival, the Apter *rav* remarks, "The Holy One, blessed is He, loves the number seven. The seventh day of the week is *Shabbat*; every seventh year is *shemittah*, the sabbatical year. Between Pesach and Shavuot we count the *Omer* for seven weeks. The seventh of the Thirteen Divine Qualities (Exodus 34:6, 7) is *emet*, truth, and *emet* is the "seal of God."

Oheiv Yisrael

❈❈❈❈❈❈❈❈❈❈❈❈

In a Thick Cloud

[Announcing the Giving of the Ten Commandments] God said to Moses, "I will come to you in a thick cloud so that all the people will hear when I speak to you" (Exodus 19:9).

Rabbi Chanoch of Alexander asks: How will God's coming in a cloud be conducive in making the people hear His words? He offers the following original insight.

We all know from personal experience that our senses interfere with one another and disrupt each other's function. Our sense of vision inhibits our ability to use our hearing to the fullest. When you are listening to a speech or a musical composition, your mind is diverted by images or scenes that appear before you. If you want to listen attentively, you close your eyes. This, then, was the reason God came "in a thick cloud." He wanted to shut out any visual distraction, so that all Israel would listen with undivided attention and total concentration. They would be "all ears."

Accepting the Torah by Acclamation

All the people answered as one, saying, "All that God has spoken we will do!" And Moses brought back the people's words to God (Exodus 19:8).

Meshech Chochmah: "All the people answered as one." It is impossible for one Jew to fulfill all the *mitzvot* of the Torah, for there are many *mitzvot* that do not apply universally. Certain *mitzvot* relate specifically to *kohanim*, others only to a king, to a landowner, a homeowner, to women, and so on. Therefore, it is written, "All the people answered as one," because only the people of Israel in its entirety can declare, "*All* that God has spoken we will do." No single individual can make this statement.

Spiritual Climb

God said to him, "Go down and come back up together with Aaron, but let not the priests and the people break through to come up to God, lest He will send destruction among them" (Exodus 19:24).

Rabbi Moshe Chaifetz: "Go down and come back up." Metaphorically, this verse teaches us that the climb to holiness does not proceed

along a straight upward line. It is an ascent in which progress alternates
with relapse; we can anticipate many ups and downs before we reach
the summit. Therefore, the place a *baal teshuvah* (returnee to Torah
observance) occupies is so lofty that it is beyond the reach of even a
perfect *tzaddik*. The circuitous route to this lofty plateau is best described as "Go down—and come back up."

※※※※※※※※※※※※※※

The Torah Is not in Heaven

When Moses ascended to heaven, the angels said to the Almighty,
"Master of the universe, what is one born of a woman doing here
among us?"

God replied, "He came to receive the Torah."

The angels protested, "Are You going to give this cherished treasure
to a man who is merely flesh and blood?"

Said God to Moses, "You answer them."

Moses responded, "I am afraid that they will burn me with the
breath of their mouths."

God reassured Moses, "Hold on to My throne, and give them an
answer."

Moses then said to the angels, "In the Torah it is written, 'I am the
Lord who has taken you out of the land of Egypt.' Have you gone
down to Egypt? Have you been slaves to Pharaoh? Why should the
Torah belong to you?

"What else is written in it? 'Do not have any other gods.' Do you
live among nations who worship idols?

"What else is written in it? 'Remember the *Shabbat* to keep it holy.'
Do you do work that you should need rest?

"What else is written in it? 'Honor your father and your mother.'
Do you have fathers and mothers?

"What is further written in it? 'Do not commit murder. Do not
commit adultery. Do not steal. Do not be envious.' Is there envy
among you? Do you have the impulse to do evil?"

All the angels agreed. They all became dear friends of Moses and gave him a gift. Even the Angel of Death gave him a gift. He taught Moses the secret that the *ketoret* (incense) atones for death (*Shabbat* 89a).

✳✳✳✳✳✳✳✳✳✳✳✳✳

Yom Habikkurim: The Festival of the First Fruits

In the Torah, the Shavuot holiday is also named *Yom Habikkurim*, the Day of the First Fruits (Numbers 28:26), since from the time of Shavuot on, the farmers of *Eretz Yisrael* brought their *bikkurim* (first fruits) as an offering to the Temple. Only the seven fruits for which *Eretz Yisrael* is known were brought: wheat, barley, grapes, figs, pomegranates, olives, and dates.

How were the first fruits separated? When a farmer noticed figs, clusters of grapes, or a pomegranate that had begun to ripen, he tied a reed rope around the fruits and said, "Let these be *bikkurim*" (*Bikkurim* 3:1). The *bikkurim* were taken to Jerusalem in a festive procession. The *Mishnah* (*Bikkurim* 3:2–8) describes the ceremony: "When they arose in the morning, the district leader would proclaim, 'Let us rise to go up to Zion to the House of God.' An ox, its horns bedecked with gold, led the way. Flutists were playing rousing melodies while the marchers were singing, 'I rejoiced when they said to me, "Let us go to the House of God"' (Psalm 122:1). When the marchers approached Jerusalem they were met by a delegation of *Kohanim* (priests) and *Levi'im* (Levites). When they reached the Temple Mount, each person placed his basket on his shoulders and together they sang, 'Halleluyah, praise God in His Sanctuary' until the completion of the psalm, 'Let everything that has breath praise God, Halleluyah' (Psalm 150). All the while, they wound their way up the Temple Mount until they reached the Temple Court. With their appearance, the *Levi'im* choir burst forth in jubilant song."

✳✳✳✳✳✳✳✳✳✳✳✳✳

Releasing the Holy Spark

On the day of the first fruits, your Shavuot Festival, when you bring an offering of new grain to God, it shall be a sacred holiday to you when you may not do any mundane labor (Numbers 28:26).

Rabbi Levi Yitzchak of Berditchev offers this kabbalistic interpretation of the offering of the first fruits on Shavuot:

The *Zohar* teaches that all of existence contains sparks of holiness, *nitzotzot hakedoshim*. Whenever a Jew performs a *mitzvah*, recites a *berachah* over a fruit, clothes the needy, eats a *Shabbat* meal, or performs any other *mitzvah*, he releases the holy spark that is trapped in the article he uses for the *mitzvah*, returning that spark to its source of sanctity. It is Israel's mission in the world – by doing *mitzvot* – to free all the captive sparks, thereby bringing about the ultimate Restoration and the advent of *Mashiach*.

Says Rabbi Yitzchak: Those fruits that possess the strongest and purest spark are the first to ripen. Therefore, God commanded that these fruits should be the ones to be offered in the *Bet Hamikdash* (Holy Temple) as *bikkurim*.

※※※※※※※※※※※※※※※

The Book of Ruth

It is an ancient custom, dating back to the Geonic Period (589–1038 C.E.), that on Shavuot the Book of Ruth is read. Various reasons are offered for this reading of Ruth.

1. Ibn Yarchi, in his work *Hamanhig* suggests as a reason that the story of Ruth took place "at the beginning of the barley harvest" (Ruth 1:22), which coincides with Shavuot, the *Chag Hakatzir*, Feast of the Harvest (Exodus 23:16).

2. Abudraham advances the reason that before receiving the Torah, our forefathers became converts by undergoing *milah* (circumcision) and *tevilah* (immersion). Similarly, Ruth was a convert to Judaism,

placing herself under the protective wings of the *Shechinah* (Divine Presence), saying, "For wherever you go, I will go . . . your people are my people, and your God is my God" (Ruth 1:16).

3. Another reason, advanced by *Tvuat Shor* is that Ruth was the ancestress of King David, who was born and died on Shavuot.

4. *Sefer Matamim* suggests as a reason that the numeric value of the name Ruth equals 606 (*resh + vav + tav*; 200+6+400=606. Adding 606 *mitzvot* in addition to the seven *Noachide mitzvot* yields 613, the total number of *mitzvot* that were given at Sinai.

Perhaps the most touching passage in the Book of Ruth contains Ruth's declaration of kindness toward Naomi and loyalty toward God and the people of Israel: "But Ruth said, 'Do not urge me to leave you, to turn back and not follow you. For wherever you go, I will go; where you lodge, I will lodge; your people are my people, and your God is my God; where you die, I will die, and there I will be buried. Thus may God do to me – and more – if anything but death separates me from you" (Ruth 1:16, 17).

11

ROSH CHODESH

Perhaps the discussion of *Rosh Chodesh*, "first day of the month," should have appeared as the first chapter of this book, for the commandment to proclaim the new month was the first *mitzvah* given to the Jewish nation as a whole: "This month shall mark for you the beginning of the months; it shall be the first of the months of the year for you" (Exodus 12:2). Nevertheless, *Rosh Chodesh* is not a full-fledged *Yom Tov*, because labor is not prohibited, and it does not commemorate a specific event in Jewish history. Its importance lies in the fact that the Jewish people – through their rabbinic courts – were given the authority to determine the first day of the new month and thereby fix the days on which the Jewish Festivals would occur. This salient feature makes *Rosh Chodesh* a common denominator of all holidays, and therefore this chapter forms a fitting conclusion to the story of the *Yamim Tovim*.

The Jewish calendar is built on lunar months, the period during which the moon makes a complete revolution around the earth. The moon reflects the light of the sun, so only the area of the moon that faces the sun is fully or partially illuminated, depending on the position of the moon relative to the sun. This is the cause of the changing phases of the moon. On the fifteenth of a Jewish month, when the earth is in line between the sun and the moon, we see the moon's fully illuminated side, called a full moon. From that point on, the moon wanes as the bright side gradually shrinks, and we see more and more of its dark side. Finally, at the end of the lunar month, when the moon passes a point between the sun and the earth – the point of conjunction – the moon appears completely dark and is invisible to us. Shortly after that, it reemerges as a thin, crescent-shaped line. That moment is called *molad halevanah*, "birth of the new moon," and *Rosh Chodesh* is the day on which the new moon appears. The calculation of the precise moment of the appearance of the new moon was transmitted to the sages in an unbroken tradition that goes back to Sinai. It was called *sod ha'ibur*, "principle of intercalation" (*Rosh Hashanah* 20b). Although the exact time of its reemergence was known, the new moon was sanctified by the *Bet Din* in Jerusalem on the testimony of two witnesses who had sighted its appearance. In fact, a large part of tractate *Rosh Hashanah* is devoted to the subject of *Kiddush Hachodesh*, "sanctification of the month."

The period between two new moons is 29.53 days. To be exact, it is 29 days, 12 hours, and 793 *chalakim* (parts of an hour). The hour is divided into 1080 parts, or 3⅓ seconds each. The reason for dividing the hour into 1080 parts is that the number 1080 can be divided by 2, 3, 4, 5, 6, 8, 10, and many other divisors.

When the *Bet Din* proclaimed the new month on the thirtieth day, a string of torches was lit on the following evening – the eve of the thirty-first – to inform the people in the Diaspora that the new month had begun on the thirtieth. But if *Rosh Chodesh* were being proclaimed on the thirty-first day, no torches were lit. By this method, the people in the Diaspora would know the correct day of the beginning of the month. The Samaritans, a sect opposed to traditional Judaism, sabotaged this system by lighting torches on the wrong day in an attempt to mislead the Jews in the Diaspora. It was then decided, rather than rely on torches, to send messengers to notify the people in the distant communities of the day of *Rosh Chodesh*. In communities where the messengers did not arrive in time to announce which day the new month was being proclaimed on, *Rosh Chodesh* was observed for two days – on the thirtieth and thirty-first.

After the destruction of the Temple, no messengers could be dispatched to notify the far-off communities when *Rosh Chodesh* had been declared. Without the information, people did not know the days on which Festivals should be observed. Because of the doubt, the Jews of the Diaspora observed two days of *Yom Tov* (*Yom Tov Sheni shel Galuyot*, "Second *Yom Tov* Day of the Diaspora"). And although the accurate date of *Rosh Chodesh* was known by calculation, the tradition of the second-day *Yom Tov* was strictly adhered to outside *Eretz Yisrael* (*Pesachim* 52a). In *Eretz Yisrael*, where the people could be notified in time, only one day of *Yom Tov* is observed on the first and last days of Passover and Sukkot and one day on Shavuot. However, since Rosh Hashanah begins on the first of the month, it is observed for two days even in *Eretz Yisrael* because of the uncertainty as to whether witnesses sighting the moon would arrive on the thirtieth or the thirty-first day.

With the dispersion of the Jewish people, the danger arose that Jewish communities in distant places would not know the day on which the new month was proclaimed and would therefore be uncertain on what days to celebrate Festivals. This would lead to disastrous division and total chaos. To avoid such a calamity, a universally accepted calendar was established at the end of the talmudic era by the Nasi Hillel (c. 358–359 C.E.) on the basis of the Sinaitic tradition. This is the calendar that we are using today and that forms the bond uniting the entire spectrum of the Jewish people.

Accordingly, in countries outside *Eretz Yisrael*, on Passover, the first, second, seventh, and eighth days are observed as *Yom Tov*. Shavuot is two days, and on Sukkot, the first, second, eighth, and ninth days are observed as *Yom Tov*, days on which all labor is forbidden, except the preparation of food and carrying.

(For a comprehensive discussion of the laws of *Yom Tov*, *Shulchan Aruch*, *Orach Chaim* 495 and *Kitzur Shulchan Aruch* 98 are available in English translation.)

※※※※※※※※※※※※※※※

Interrogation of Witnesses

The first pair of witnesses who had sighted the new moon were interrogated separately in order to determine whether their testimonies agreed. The judges asked each witness, "Tell, how did you see the moon? Which way were the horns of the crescent pointing? Was the dark side of the moon facing the setting sun or was it away from the setting sun? How high was it? Which way was it leaning? How wide was it?"

Of course, if a witness said that the dark side of the new moon were facing the setting sun, the testimony was invalid, because this is impossible, for the moon's crescent is the surface that is facing the sun.

If the answers of the two witnesses coincided, their testimony was accepted. All the other pairs of witnesses were asked a few perfunctory questions, so that they should not feel disappointed. As a sign of appreciation, feasts were prepared for the many witnesses who had sighted the new moon and had come to testify (*Rosh Hashanah* 23b).

After the head of the *Bet Din* (the *Nasi*) determined that the witnesses' testimony was valid, he declared the day as *Rosh Chodesh*, the first day of the new month, proclaiming, "*Mekudash!*" "It is sanctified!" And all the people present responded, "*Mekudash, mekudash!*"

※※※※※※※※※※※※※※※

Peace among the Heavenly Bodies

The astronomical phenomenon of the sun's illumination of the moon inspired a moving lesson. Said Rabbi Yochanan, "It is written, 'He makes peace in His heights' (Job 25:2). This means to say that God maintains the peace among His creations by making certain that the sun never sees the deficiency (the dark side) of the moon, for the moon would feel embarrassed if its weakness were exposed" (*Rosh Hashanah* 23b).

The implication is that we can all keep the peace if we overlook other people's shortcomings and concentrate instead on their good qualities.

※※※※※※※※※※※※※※※

New Moon, Festivals, and *Shabbat*

There exists a fundamental difference between the fixing of the dates of the Festivals and the establishment of *Shabbat*.

God empowered the Jewish people to set the dates of *Rosh Chodesh* and *Yom Tov* and sanctify them when He said, "These are God's Festivals that *you* must declare as sacred holidays at their appropriate times" (Leviticus 23:4). The Talmud states that they become Festivals only by virtue of *your* [the *Bet Din*'s] proclamation, "even if you erroneously or intentionally appointed the wrong day."[1]

This is reflected also in the *Kiddush* of *Yom Tov* in which we say, "Who sanctifies Israel and the festive seasons," mentioning "Israel" before "the festive seasons," because it is Israel that sanctifies the holidays in accordance with the fixing of *Rosh Chodesh*. By contrast, in the *Kiddush* of *Shabbat*, we say, "Who sanctifies the *Shabbat*," without mentioning Israel, because *Shabbat* has been sanctified from Creation; its sanctity is independent and absolute (*Beitzah* 17a).

The *Midrash*[2] strikingly illustrates this idea: "The angels gather before God and ask him, "Master of the universe, when is Rosh Hashanah?' God answers, 'Why do you ask Me? Let us both ask the *Bet Din* below.' " In other words, God is bowing to the decision of the court.

🞕🞕🞕🞕🞕🞕🞕🞕🞕🞕🞕🞕

Second Day of *Yom Tov*

The question has been raised as to why we still today observe a second day *Yom Tov*. After all, so the argument goes, the precise moment of the appearance of the new moon is known to within a fraction of a second, and even if we once again sanctified the new month on the basis of visual sighting, we would not need messengers to notify the Diaspora, because modern communications would instantly broadcast the news to even the most remote Jewish community, precluding any doubt.

The question misses the point. By instituting the *Yom Tov Sheini shel Galuyot*, "Second *Yom Tov* of the Diaspora," our sages wanted to anchor in the Jewish consciousness the awareness that the Torah intended for the new month to be proclaimed on the basis of visual sighting. We thus become mindful of the significant principle that the months are not automatically fixed and consecrated simply by the astronomical conjunction of the sun and the moon. Rather, God empowered the Jewish people–represented by the rabbis of the *Bet Din*–to sanctify the months and the Festivals. We are made aware that as Jews we are dominated not by the limitations of the physical world and the strictures of time but by our sanctification of the beginning of each new month, when we accentuate our spiritual nature, which transcends the bounds of physicality and the strictures of time.

※❈❈❈❈❈❈❈❈❈❈❈❈❈❈❈❈※

Intercalation

The duration of a lunar month is about 29½ days, and the lunar year, of twelve lunar months, is 12 × 29.5, or about 354 days. The solar year–the period of time in which the Earth completes one revolution around the sun–comprises 365 days. Consequently, the lunar year is about eleven days shorter than the solar year. This means that if in a given year Passover falls in April, then the next year, it would fall eleven days earlier, and so on. If nothing were done to correct the situation, then Passover and all the other holidays would be moving through the four seasons of the year. Such is indeed the case in Islam, which uses a strictly lunar calendar, and Moslem festivals do indeed retrogress through the seasons, making a complete cycle every 32½ years.

The Torah demands that Passover be in the spring: "Safeguard the month of standing grain so that you will be able to keep the Passover to God your Lord" (Deuteronomy 16:1). Therefore, the lunar calendar is adjusted to the solar year so that *Nisan* remains in the spring, making the Jewish year a lunisolar year. The correction is achieved by periodically inserting a thirteenth lunar month, *Adar* II, as a "leap month," a procedure called intercalation. During nineteen years, the annual discrepancy between the solar and lunar years grows to 209 (19 × 11) days, roughly equivalent to seven lunar months. Therefore, in a cycle of nineteen years, seven years are intercalated as leap years of thirteen months. This is done in the third, sixth, eighth, eleventh, fourteenth, seventeenth, and nineteenth years of the cycle.

Months of the Year

1. *Nisan*–Aries–the fifteenth of *Nisan* is the first day of Passover.

2. *Iyar*–Taurus–there is no *Yom Tov* in *Iyar*; the eighteenth of *Iyar* is *Lag Ba'omer*.

3. *Sivan*–Gemini–the sixth of *Sivan* is Shavuot.

4. *Tamuz*–Cancer–the seventeenth of *Tamuz* is the fast of *Shivah Asar BeTamuz*.

5. *Av*–Leo–the ninth of *Av* is the fast of *Tishah Be'av*.

6. *Elul*–Virgo–there is no holiday in *Elul*; *Elul* marks the beginning of the *Selichot* days.

7. *Tishri*–Libra–the first and second of *Tishri* constitute Rosh Hashanah; the third of *Tishri* is the fast of *Tzom Gedalyah*; the tenth of *Tishri* is Yom Kippur; the fifteenth of *Tishri* is the first day of Sukkot, followed by Shemini Atzeret and Simchat Torah.

8. *Cheshvan*–Scorpio–there is no holiday in *Cheshvan*.

9. *Kislev*–Sagittarius–the twenty-fifth of *Kislev* is the beginning of Chanukah.

10. *Tevet*–Capricorn–the tenth of *Tevet* is the fast of Asarah BeTevet.

11. *Shevat*–Aquarius–the fifteenth of *Shevat*, *Chamishah Asar (Tu) Bishvat*, is the New Year of the Trees, *Rosh Hashanah La'ilanot*.

12. *Adar*–Pisces–the thirteenth of *Adar* is the fast of Esther, *Taanit Esther*; the fourteenth of *Adar* is Purim (in Jerusalem, the fifteenth).

Full and Deficient Months

Each month of the Jewish year has approximately 29½ days. Because we count a month by full days and do not reckon half days,[3] a system has been devised whereby the months are alternately 29 and 30 days. A 29-day month is called *chaseir*, deficient, and a 30-day month is called *malei*, full.

The following rule applies: *Nisan, Sivan, Av, Tishri,* and *Shevat* are always full (30 days).

Iyar, Tamuz, Elul, Tevet, and *Adar,* are always deficient (29 days).

In some years, *Cheshvan* and *Kislev* are both full months; in other years, both are deficient.

In an intercalated year, *Adar* I is full and *Adar* II is deficient.[4]

※※※※※※※※※※※※※※

The Rule of AT-BASH

An interesting mnemonic has been conceived that facilitates the instant determination of the day of the week on which a certain holiday will fall. It is the system of א״ת-ב״ש, AT-BASH, whereby א״ת, AT, is made up of the first and last letters of the *alef-bet*, ב״ש. BASH is composed of ב, *bet*, the second letter of the *alef-bet*, and ש, shin, the one before the last letter. Continuing in the same fashion, we combine *gimel* and *reish* to form ג״ר, GAR; *dalet* and *kuf* to form ד״ק, DAK; *hei* and *tzadi* to form ה״צ, HATZ; and *vav* and *pei* to form ו״פ, WAP.

AT, א״ת, tells us that the first day of Passover (א) and the subsequent Tishah Be'Av (initial ת, *tav*) always fall on the same day of the week.

BASH, ב״ש, tells us that the second day of Passover (ב) and the subsequent Shavuot (initial ש, *shin*) always fall on the same day of the week.

GAR, ג״ר, tells us that the third day of Passover (ג) and the subsequent Rosh Hashanah (initial ר, *reish*) always occur on the same day of the week.

DAK, ק'ר, tells us that the fourth day of Passover (ר) and the subsequent *Keriat Hatorah* (initial ק, *kuf*, and meaning Simchat Torah) always fall on the same day of the week

HATZ, צ'ה, tells us that the fifth day of Passover (ה) and the subsequent Tzom (the Fast of Yom Kippur, צ, initial *tzadi*) always fall on the same day of the week.

WAP, פ'ו, tells us that the sixth day of Passover (ו) and the *preceding* Purim always fall on the same day of the week.

P'LAG, פל'ג, tells us that Purim (initial pei, פ) and the Lag Ba'omer following it always occur on the same day of the week.

Another famous calendar rule is: *Lo ADU Rosh velo BADU Pesach*, "Rosh [Hashanah] cannot fall on ADU, and Pesach cannot fall on BADU." This means that Rosh Hashanah can never occur on the days designated ADU, אד'ו: *alef*, א – 1, Sunday; *daled*, ר – 4, Wednesday; vav, ו – 6, Friday. Pesach (Passover) can never fall on the days designated BADU, בד'ו: *bet*, ב – 2, Monday; *daled*, ר – 4, Wednesday; *vav*, ו – 6, Friday.

✛✛✛✛✛✛✛✛✛✛✛✛✛

Blessing the New Month

On the *Shabbat* before the new month begins, the Blessing of the New Month is recited in the synagogue, after the Torah reading. It is said standing, so as to evoke the memory of the sanctification of the new month by the *Bet Din*, when everyone was standing.[5]

First, the prayer *Yehi Ratzon*, "May it be Your will," is said. This is the prayer that the talmudic sage Rav would say after concluding the *Shemoneh Esrei*,[6] a plea for "long life, a life of peace, a life of goodness, a life of blessing, a life of sustenance, a life of physical health, a life in which there is fear of heaven and fear of sin, a life in which there is no shame or humiliation, a life of wealth and honor, a life in which we will have love of Torah and fear of heaven, a life in which our heartfelt requests will be fulfilled for the good. *Amen Selah*." After *Yehi Ratzon*, it is the custom to announce the *molad*, the time at which the new moon will appear over Jerusalem

The *chazzan* then lifts the Torah scroll, and the congregation and the *chazzan* say, *Mi she'asah nissim*, "He who performed miracles for our forefathers and redeemed them from slavery to freedom, may He redeem us soon . . .," concluding, *chaverim kol Yisrael*, "may all Israel become friends." We pray for a speedy redemption so that we may be able once again to sanctify the new month on the basis of visual sighting, as in the days of the *Bet Hamikdash* (Temple).[7]

We end with the phrase, "may all Israel become friends," for the final redemption will come only when Israel is united.

The *chazzan* then announces the day(s) of *Rosh Chodesh*.

On the *Shabbat* before *Rosh Chodesh Tishri*, the Blessing of the New Month is omitted.

❈❈❈❈❈❈❈❈❈❈❈❈❈❈❈

Selected Laws of *Rosh Chodesh*

Fasting is prohibited on *Rosh Chodesh*, and funeral eulogies are not delivered.

Half-*Hallel* is recited in the morning service, and *Yaaleh Veyavo* is inserted in the *Shemoneh Esrei* and in *Birkat Hamazon* (Grace after Meals).

On weekdays, four persons are called to the Torah to read Numbers 28:1–15. When *Rosh Chodesh* falls on *Shabbat*, two Torah scrolls are taken out. In the first, the weekly portion is read, and in the second, the *Maftir* is read from Numbers 28:9–15. The *Haftarah* is *Hashamayim kis'i*, "The heaven is My throne" (Isaiah 66:1–24), which presages the celebration of *Rosh Chodesh* in the future, "And new moon after new moon, and *Shabbat* after *Shabbat*, all flesh shall come to worship Me" (66:24).

After the Torah reading, a special *Mussaf* prayer for *Rosh Chodesh* is said – on weekdays as well as on *Shabbat*.

(For a detailed discussion of the laws of *Rosh Chodesh*, *Shulchan Aruch, Orach Chaim* 417–425 and *Kitzur Shulchan Aruch* 97 are available in English translation.)

✳✳✳✳✳✳✳✳✳✳✳✳✳✳

Women and *Rosh Chodesh*

Although we are permitted to do work on *Rosh Chodesh*, women customarily are more stringent in this regard than men, and they do only work that needs to be done. The reason goes back to the time the children of Israel made the Golden Calf.

" 'The men came to take off their wives' earrings' (Exodus 32:2), to make the Golden Calf, but the women refused to hand over their jewelry. They told their husbands, 'We will not listen to you, to make an abominable idol that has no power to save!' God rewarded women in this world by giving them a greater measure of observance of *Rosh Chodesh*. And He rewards them in the World to Come, giving them the power of constant renewal, which is the symbol of *Rosh Chodesh*."[8]

✳✳✳✳✳✳✳✳✳✳✳✳✳✳

Israel Is Like the Moon

The Jewish people are likened to the moon. The moon has no light of its own but receives its brightness from the sun. So too the Jewish people are totally dependent on God to bestow His benevolence on them and make fortune shine on them. Indeed, God is characterized as "the Light of Israel" in the verse "The Light of Israel will be fire and its Holy One flame" (Isaiah 17:10).[9]

✳✳✳✳✳✳✳✳✳✳✳✳✳✳

The Jewish People Equated with the Moon

Our Festivals are fixed according to the appearance of the moon, for the moon symbolizes the Jewish people. After reaching fullness, the moon gradually diminishes to a point where we cannot see it anymore. Everyone thinks that it has ceased to exist, but then it begins to shine again and grow steadily. So, too, the Jewish people, even when they have declined to their lowest point and seem to be beyond recovery, will rise again to illuminate the world.

Shemot Rabbah 15

❋❋❋❋❋❋❋❋❋❋❋❋❋

A Sin Offering to God

On *Rosh Chodesh*, one goat was offered "as a sin offering to God" (Numbers 28:15). The sages of the Talmud (*Chullin* 60b), noting that only the sin offering of *Rosh Chodesh* is described as "a sin offering to God," present the following remarkable insight:

When God created the universe, the sun and the moon were of equal size, but the moon complained, saying, "Two kings cannot wear the same crown," implying that it wanted to be larger than the sun. In response, God made the moon smaller. Said the Holy One, blessed is He, "Let the sin offering of *Rosh Chodesh*, the day of the new moon, be an atonement for Me for making the moon smaller." Therefore, only the sin offering of *Rosh Chodesh* is called "a sin offering to God." It is as though God were asking forgiveness for making the moon smaller.

❋❋❋❋❋❋❋❋❋❋❋❋❋

Eleven Offerings

On *Rosh Chodesh*, eleven offerings were presented in the Temple: two bulls, one ram, seven lambs, and one goat.

These eleven offerings correspond to the eleven days that the solar year is longer than the lunar year, the solar year having 365 days and the lunar year 354.

The underlying thought may be that the shorter cycle of the moon is a reference to a cosmic imperfection that will be corrected in messianic times, when the moon's primeval splendor will be restored and its luminescence will equal that of the sun. Since the moon symbolizes Israel, we bring the eleven offerings to atone for the moon's—and our own—deficiency, in the hope that *Mashiach* will come soon and reinstate both the moon and the Jewish people to their former glory.

Rabbeinu Bachyah on Numbers 28:11

※※※※※※※※※※※※※

Israel's History Like the Lunar Cycle

The moon changes from crescent to full and back again in about thirty days. From the first of the lunar month until the fifteenth, the moon waxes; from the fifteenth on, it begins to wane until, on the thirtieth day, it disappears from view.

The lunar cycle is reflected in the history of the Jewish people. Like the waxing moon, which reaches fullness in fifteen days, there were fifteen generations from Abraham to King Solomon. With Abraham, the light of Israel began to shine, reaching its zenith in the reign of King Solomon. Like the waning moon, after King Solomon, the monarchy went into decline. And fifteen generations after Solomon, under King Zedekiah, the radiance of the House of David disappeared altogether and the First Temple was destroyed by Nebuchadnezzar, as it says, "In the ninth year of King Zedekiah of Judah, in the tenth month, King Nebuchadnezzar of Babylon moved against Jerusalem with his whole army, and they laid siege to it" (Jeremiah 39:1).

Rabbeinu Bachyah on Genesis 38:29, 30

※※※※※※※※※※※※※

Sanctification of the Moon: *Kiddush Levanah*

The Sanctification of the Moon is a prayer in which we greet the *Shechinah* (Divine Presence) and thank God for renewing the moon every month. We read in the Talmud, "When you welcome the new moon with a blessing at the proper time, it is as though you welcomed the *Shechinah*" (*Sanhedrin* 42a). For by going outdoors, viewing the moon, and reciting the *berachah*, we testify to the fact that God is the Creator and the Power that guides the galaxies in their immutable orbits. But while the stars and planets are compelled to fulfill their tasks at God's behest, we serve God of our free will and, like the moon, renew ourselves each month, attaining greater attachment to Him.

We begin by reciting Psalm 148:1–6, which contains the verse "Praise Him, sun and moon; praise Him, all bright stars."

✸✸✸✸✸✸✸✸✸✸✸✸✸

Jacob Compared with the Moon

We recite three times the phrase "Blessed is your Molder, blessed is your Maker, blessed is your Owner, blessed is your Creator." The initials of the four divine attributes – Molder (*Yotzreich*), Maker (*Oseich*), Owner (*Koneich*), Creator (*Bore'eich*) – together form the name *Ya'akov* (Jacob). Jacob is associated with the moon, for both the moon and Jacob are described as small. The moon is called "the smaller light to dominate the night" (Genesis 1:16); Jacob is characterized as Rebeccah's "younger [literally, smaller] son" (Genesis 27:15) (*Kol Bo*).

✸✸✸✸✸✸✸✸✸✸✸✸✸

Selected Laws of *Kiddush Levanah*

Kiddush Levanah should be said preferably at the conclusion of *Shabbat*, under the open sky, and with a *minyan* (ten adult males).

Kiddush Levanah should not be said before three days after the new moon and no later than fifteen days after the new moon.

Kiddush Levanah should not be recited on Friday night or on *Yom Tov*, unless these nights represent the last opportunity for saying *Kiddush Levanah* before the fifteenth-of-the-month deadline.

Since with *Kiddush Levanah* we are greeting the *Shechinah* (Divine Presence), it should be said joyously and while standing.

(For a more detailed treatment of the laws of *Kiddush Levanah*, *Shulchan Aruch*, *Orach Chaim* 426 and *Kitzur Shulchan Aruch* 97:7–15 are available in English translation.)

※※※※※※※※※※※※※※

A Closing Word

With the discussion of *Rosh Chodesh*, our journey through the Jewish year and its Festivals has come full circle. But living through a Jewish year is by no means an exercise of "going around in circles," an endless mechanical chase after futility. Rather than a circle, the Jewish year is a rising spiral in which each full turn brings us closer to the center. For each *Yom Tov* elevates us, infuses us with renewed spirit, invigorates and rejuvenates us, bringing us a step closer to our Source. And when the year has run its course and we arrive again at the same point on the calendar, we are on a higher plane of the spiral of life and a little nearer to its Center, the Creator.

For, as Rabbi Eliyahu Dessler, the great sage of the *Mussar* movement, put it, each *Yom Tov* is a way station on our journey through life where we stop to restore ourselves and take on a new supply of inspiration and spiritual nourishment.

And while the holidays breathe new life into us, the *Shalosh Regalim* (the Pilgrimage Festivals) also serve to bolster our bond with *Eretz Yisrael* as expressions of gratitude to God for a bountiful harvest: Passover, the Festival in the month of standing grain; Shavuot, the Reaping Festival; and Sukkot, the Harvest Festival. Mentioning the

Omer and the *Bikkurim* (First Fruits), praying for dew and rain to fall in *Eretz Yisrael*, taking in hand an *etrog* that grew in *Eretz Yisrael*, and announcing the hour of the *molad*—the time the new moon will appear over the skies of Jerusalem—all these rituals conjure up cherished images of *Eretz Yisrael* and heighten our yearning for *Eretz Yisrael*.

Year after year, the spiral of Jewish history winds a circuitous path toward its culmination in the coming of *Mashiach*. Multitudes of Jews who have lain dormant or were forcibly deprived of their heritage are waking up to discover the rich treasures of the Torah and the sweetness of living the Torah way of life. The *Yamim Tovim* are a key to Judaism, for they present a delectable platter of the manifold facets of Jewish life. In the observance of the Festivals, Jewish history is reenacted; by way of *mitzvot*, the Jewish outlook on life and philosophy becomes a tangible experience—we can see, hear, smell, taste, and touch them. The *Yamim Tovim* give us a boost, making us new and better human beings.

Like the new moon emerging from darkness, the Jewish people are arising from a long night of suffering and estrangement from the Torah and are marching toward a bright future, when "nations shall walk by your light, kings, by your shining radiance" (Isaiah 60:3). The *ikveta deMeshicha*, the "approaching footsteps of *Mashiach*," are on the horizon. May we soon see the day of his arrival, when we will once again rejoice on the *Yamim Tovim* by going up to the *Bet Hamikdash*, "when the earth shall be filled with knowledge of God as water covers the sea" (Isaiah 11:9).

APPENDIX

Biographical data of the authors quoted in this book. Authors are listed alphabetically according to the name by which they are best known.

Abarbanel, Rabbi (Don) Yitzchak (1437–1508), leading figure in Spanish Jewry at the time of the expulsion in 1492. Author of extensive commentary on the Torah.

Rabbi Aharon Friedman of Sadgora (1877–1913), author of *Kedushat Aharon*. Great-grandson of Rabbi Yisrael of Rizhin.

Rabbi Aharon Kotler (1892–1962), illustrious talmudist, founder of the Lakewood *Yeshivah*, and foremost leader of Torah-observant Jewry in his day.

Rabbi Aharon (Perlow) of Karlin, Rabbi Aharon II (1808–1872), leader of Karlin-Stolin *chasidim*.

Alshich. See Rabbi Moshe Alshich.

Apter *rav*. See Rabbi Avraham Yehoshua Heshel of Apta.

Ari, Arizal, Ari Hakadosh. See Rabbi Yitzchak Luria Ashkenazi.

Rabbi Aryeh Yehudah Leib Alter, the Gerer *rebbe* (1847–1905), author of *Sefat Emet*. Leader of largest chasidic grouping in Poland.

Avnei Nezer. See Rabbi Avraham Borenstein of Sochatchov.

Rabbi Avraham Borenstein of Sochatchov, the Sochatchover *rebbe*
(1839–1910), author of the famous responsa *Avnei Nezer*. Son-in-law of the
legendary Kotzker *rebbe*.

Rabbi Avraham, the *Maggid* of Trisk (1806–1889), grandson of Rabbi Na-
chum of Chernobyl.

Rabbi Avraham Weinberg of Slonim, the Slonimer *rebbe* (1804–1884), author
of *Be'er Avraham*.

Rabbi Avraham Yehoshua Heshel of Apta (1755–1825), author of *Oheiv
Yisrael*, one of the classic chasidic texts.

Rabbi Avraham Yitzchak Kamai became Rabbi of Mir, Poland, in 1917. Son
of Rabbi Eliyahu Baruch Kamai, *rosh yeshivah* of the *Mirrer Yeshivah*.

Baal Haturim. See Rabbi Yaakov Baal Haturim.

Baal Shem Tov (1698–1760), founder of *Chasidut*.

Rabbi Bachyah ben Asher (c. 1340), known as Rabbeinu Bachya. Great
Torah commentator and kabbalist.

Rabbi (Rabbeinu) Bachya. See Rabbi Bachya ben Asher.

Rabbi Baruch of Mizhbozh (1753–1812), celebrated chasidic leader.
Grandson of the Baal Shem Tov.

Belzer *rebbe*. See Rabbi Shalom of Belz.

Berditchever. See Rabbi Levi Yitzchak of Berditchev.

Bet Yosef. See Rabbi Yosef Karo.

Bratzlaver. See Rabbi Nachman of Bratzlav.

Chafetz Chaim. See Rabbi Yisrael Meir Hakohen Kagan.

Rabbi Chaim Halberstam, popularly known as the Divrei Chaim
(1793–1876), prominent chasidic leader in Poland. Ancestor of the present-
day Bobover *rebbe* and Klausenburger *rebbe*.

Rabbi Chaim Soloveitchik, popularly known as Reb Chaim Brisker
(1853–1915), towering Torah scholar. *Rosh yeshivah* (dean) of the *yeshivah* of
Volozhin.

Rabbi Chaim Tirer of Chernovitz (c. 1760–1816), early trailblazer of *Chasidut*,
author of *Beer Mayim Chayim*.

Rabbi Chaim Vital (1543–1620), kabbalist, disciple, and spiritual heir of the
Ari Hakadosh. Author of *Etz Hachaim* and many other works.

Rabbi Chanoch of Alexander (1798–1870), disciple of Rabbi Simchah Bunam
of Pshis'cha and *chasid* of the Kotzker *rebbe* and the *Chidushei Harym*. In 1866
he became the *rebbe* of the thousands of Alexanderer *chasidim*. (Alexander is
the name of a town in central Poland.)

Chatam Sofer. See Rabbi Moshe Sofer.

Chidushei Harym. See Rabbi Yitzchak Meir Alter of Ger.

Damesek Eliezer. See Rabbi Eliezer Hager of Vizhnitz.

Rabbi David Abudraham (13th–14th century), author of a commentary on the prayers.

Rabbi David Kimchi, popularly known as Redak (1160–1235), author of important commentary on the Bible.

Diveri Chaim. See Rabbi Chaim Halberstam.

Rabbi Dov Ber of Mezritch, known as The Great *Maggid* (c. 1704–1772), succeeded the Baal Shem Tov as leader of the chasidic movement. Author of *Maggid Devarav LeYaakov*.

Dubner *Maggid*. See Rabbi Yaakov Krantz.

Rabbi Eliezer Hager of Vizhnitz (1891–1946), author of *Damesek Eliezer*.

Rabbi Elimelech of Lizhensk, known as the No'am Elimelech (1717–1786), one of the early masters of Chasidism and a disciple of the *Maggid* of Mezritch. Mentor of many outstanding chasidic leaders.

Rabbi Elimelech of Rudnick (d. 1850), great-grandson of Rabbi Elimelech of Lizhensk. Student of Rabbi Naftali Tzvi of Ropshitz.

Rabbi Eliyahu Dessler (1892–1953), profound thinker and leading contemporary spokesman of the *Mussar* movement of ethical revival. Author of *Michtav Me'Eliyahu*.

Rabbi Eliyahu Lapian (1876–1970), one of the foremost exponents of the *Mussar* movement. Author of *Lev Eliyahu*.

Rabbi Eliyahu of Vilna, the Vilna *Gaon* (1720–1797).

Gaon of Vilna. See Rabbi Eliyahu of Vilna.

Hafla'ah. See Rabbi Pinchas Horowitz.

Kotzker *rebbe*. See Rabbi Menachem Mendel Morgenstern of Kotzk.

Koznitzer *Maggid*. See Rabbi Yisrael of Koznitz.

Lev Eliyahu. See Rabbi Eliyahu Lapian.

Rabbi Levi Yitzchak of Berditchev (1740–1810), student of the *Maggid* of Mezritch and Rabbi Shmelke of Nikolsburg. Famous as the great defender of the Jewish people. Author of *Kedushat Levi*.

Maggid of Mezritch. See Rabbi Dov Ber of Mezritch.

Maharal. See Rabbi Yehudah Loew of Prague.

Maharil. See Rabbi Yaakov Moelin.

Maimonides. See Rabbi Moshe ben Maimon.

Malbim, abbreviation of Meir Leib ben Yechiel Michael (Weiser) (1809–1879), author of a monumental commentary on the Torah. Served as chief rabbi of Romania.

Rabbi Meir Leib ben Yechiel (Weiser) Malbim. See Malbim.

Rabbi Meir of Premyshlan (1780–1850), prominent chasidic leader.

Rabbi Meir Simchah Hakohen (1843–1926), author of the classic Torah commentary *Meshech Chochmah* and *Or Same'ach*, a commentary on *Mishneh Torah* by the Rambam.

Rabbi Meir Yechiel of Ostrowtza (1851–1928), author of *Or Torah*.

Me'iri. See Rabbi Menachem HaMeiri.

Rabbi Menachem HaMeiri (c. 1249–c. 1306), Talmud commentator. Wrote commentary on Psalms.

Rabbi Menachem Mendel Morgenstern of Kotzk, the Kotzker *rebbe* (1787–1859), one of the famous chasidic masters, a follower of the *Chozeh* of Lublin and Rabbi Simchah Bunam of Pshis'cha. His commentaries were published in *Emet Ve'emunah*.

Mesillat Yesharim. See Rabbi Moshe Chaim Luzzatto.

Rabbi Mordechai Ashkenazi (c. 1240–1298), author of the *Mordechai*.

Rabbi Mordechai Yaakov Breisch (1895–1976), rabbi of Congregation Agudat Achim, Zurich. Author of *Teshuvot Chelkat Yaakov*, an authoritative work of responsa.

Rabbi Mordechai of Lechovitz (1742–1810), chasidic leader with thousands of followers in Lithuania. Promoted settlement in *Eretz Yisrael* by *chasidim*.

Rabbi Moshe Alshich (1508–1593), classic Torah commentator and kabbalist. Author of *Torat Moshe*.

Rabbi Moshe Chaim Efraim of Sadilkov (c. 1748–1800), grandson of the Baal Shem Tov. Author of *Degel Mechaneh Efraim*.

Rabbi Moshe Chaim Luzzatto (1707–1747), ethicist and kabbalist. Author of *Mesillat Yesharim*.

Rabbi Moshe Cordovero (1522–1570), leading kabbalist and exponent of the concepts in the *Zohar*. Author of *Tomer Devorah*.

Rabbi Moshe of Kobryn (c. 1784–1858), chasidic *rebbe* and student of Rabbi Mordechai of Lechovitz.

Rabbi Moshe ben Maimon (Maimonides), known as the Rambam (1135–1204), greatest codifier of *Halachah*, commentator and philosopher. Author of *Mishneh Torah* and *Moreh Nevuchim*.

Rabbi Moshe ben Nachman, the Ramban (Nachmanides) (1195–1270), one of the great Torah commentators.

Rabbi Moshe Sofer (1762–1839), outstanding halachist and Torah commentator, rabbi of Pressburg, leader of Hungarian Jewry. Known as Chatam Sofer, the title of his work.

Rabbi Nachman of Bratzlav (1772–1811), founder of Bratzlav *Chasidut*. A great-grandson of the Baal Shem Tov, his thoughts were published under the title *Likutei Moharan*.

Rabbi Naftali Tzvi Horowitz of Ropshitz (1760–1827), one of the great
chasidic masters.

Rabbi Nassan David of Shidlovtza (1814–1866), grandson of the Yid Hakadosh of Pshis'cha.

Rabbi (Rabbeinu) Nissim, popularly known as the Ran, the initials of his
name (c. 1290–c. 1375), halachist and talmudic commentator.

Rabbi Noach of Lechovitz (1774–1833), eminent chasidic leader.

No'am Elimelech. See Rabbi Elimelech of Lizhensk.

Oheiv Yisrael. See Rabbi Avraham Yehoshua Heshel of Apta.

Rabbi Ovadiah Seforno (c. 1470–1550), celebrated Torah commentator.

Rabbi Pinchas Horowitz, popularly known as the Baal Hafla'ah (1730–1805),
rabbi of Frankfort-on-the-Main. Author of *Hafla'ah* and *Panim Yafot*.
Brother of Rabbi Shmuel Shmelke of Nikolsburg.

Rabbi Pinchas of Koretz (1728–1791), one of the great chasidic masters and a
disciple of the Baal Shem Tov.

Rambam. See Rabbi Moshe ben Maimon.

Ramban. See Rabbi Moshe ben Nachman.

Ran. See Rabbi (Rabbeinu) Nissim.

Rashi, acronym of Rabbi Shlomoh Yitzchaki (1040–1105), author of the most
important commentaries on the Bible and Talmud. His commentary on
the Torah was the first Hebrew book printed.

Reb Chaim Brisker. See Rabbi Chaim Soloveitchik.

Rebbe Reb Bunim. See Rabbi Simchah Bunim of Pshis'cha.

Redak. See Rabbi David Kimchi.

Sar Shalom. See Rabbi Shalom Rokeach of Belz.

Rabbi Samson Raphael Hirsch (1808–1888), brilliant leader of German Or-
thodox Jewry. Author of a monumental commentary on the Torah.

Sefat Emet. See Rabbi Aryeh Yehudah Leib Alter.

Seforno. See Rabbi Ovadiah Seforno.

Rabbi Shalom Rokeach of Belz, known also as Sar Shalom (1779–1855),
revered chasidic leader and founder of the Belzer dynasty.

Shelah. See Rabbi Yeshaya Horowitz of Prague.

Rabbi Shlomoh Yitzchaki. See Rashi.

Rabbi Shlomoh Yosef Zevin, author of *Hamo'adim Bahalachah* and editor of
Talmudical Encyclopedia.

Rabbi Shmuel Borenstein, the Sochatchover *rebbe* (1855–1926), son of Rabbi
Avraham Borenstein, the Avnei Nezer. Author of *Shem Mismuel*.

Rabbi Shmuel Shmelke of Nikolsburg (c. 1727–1778), early chasidic master.

Shulchan Aruch. See Rabbi Yosef Karo.

Rabbi Simchah Bunam of Pshis'cha (1762–1827), trailblazer of new approach in *Chasidut*, a fusion of fervent prayer and in-depth Torah study. Disciple of the *Chozeh* of Lublin and the Yid Hakadosh of Pshis'cha.

Rabbi Simchah of Vitry (died 1105), halachist, outstanding disciple of Rashi. Author of *Machzor Vitry*.

Rabbi Simchah Zissel Ziv of Kelm, popularly known as the *Alter* (Elder) of Kelm (1824–1898), leading *rosh yeshivah* and teacher of *Mussar* (Torah ethics).

Rabbi Shneur Zalman of Liadi, known as the Baal HaTanya (1745–1813), a disciple of the *Maggid* of Mezritch. Originator of *Chabad Chasidut*, also known as Lubavitcher *Chasidut*.

Tanya. See Rabbi Shneur Zalman of Liadi.

Targum Onkelos. Authorized Aramaic translation of the Torah by Onkelos (c. 90 C.E.). *Targum Onkelos* can be found in most standard *chumashim* alongside the Torah text.

Rabbi Tzadok Hakohen of Lublin (1823–1900), influential thinker of the chasidic movement. Author of *Pri Tzaddik*, *Resisei Laylah*, and other works.

Rabbi Uri of Strelisk, popularly known as the Seraph of Strelisk (died 1826), a disciple of Rabbi Elimelech of Lizhensk.

Rabbi Yaakov Baal Haturim, son of the Rosh (c. 1275–c. 1343), author of *Arba'ah Turim*, the comprehensive Code of Jewish Law. He also wrote a commentary on the Torah.

Rabbi Yaakov Emden (1698–1776), author of *She'eilot Yavetz* and *Siddur*.

Rabbi Yaakov Krantz of Dubna, known as the Dubner *Maggid* (died 1804), famous for his parables.

Rabbi Yaakov Moelin (c. 1365–1427), leading halachic authority in regard to customs and synagogue ritual. author of *Teshuvot Maharil*.

Rabbi Yaakov Yitzchak Horowitz of Lublin, known as the *Chozeh* (visionary) of Lublin (1745–1815), one of the great chasidic masters.

Yaarot Devash. See Rabbi Yonatan Eybeschutz.

Rabbi Yechezkel Shraga Halberstam of Shiniava (1815–1899), eldest son of the Divrei Chaim of Sanz and a dynamic chasidic leader. Author of *Divrei Yechezkel*.

Rabbi Yehudah Hechasid (c. 1150–1217), kabbalist and ethicist. Author of the seminal *Sefer Chasidim*.

Rabbi Yehudah Loew of Prague, known as the Maharal (1525–1609), preeminent thinker and kabbalist.

Rabbi Yerachmiel of Pshis'cha (1784–1839), son of Rabbi Yaakov Yitzchak of Pshis'cha, the Yid Hakadosh.

Rabbi Yeshayah Horowitz of Prague, known as the Shelah, the title of his work, an acronym for *Shenei Luchot Habberit* (1565–1630), towering talmudist and kabbalist.

Rabbi Yisrael of Chortkov (1854–1934), grandson of the famous Rabbi Yisrael of Rizhin.

Rabbi Yisrael ben Eliezer. See Baal Shem Tov.

Rabbi Yisrael Friedman of Rizhin (1797–1850), leading chasidic *rebbe*. Great-grandson of the *Maggid* of Mezritch and progenitor of the chasidic dynasties of Sadgora, Boyan, Husiatyn, Buhush, and Chortkov.

Rabbi Yisrael of Koznitz, known as the Koznitzer *Maggid* (1740–1808).

Rabbi Yisrael Lipkin of Salant. See Rabbi Yisrael Salanter.

Rabbi Yisrael Meir Hakohen Kagan (1839–1933), undisputed Torah leader of his generation. Author of *Mishnah Berurah* and *Chafetz Chaim*.

Rabbi Yisrael Salanter (1809–1883), founder of the *Mussar* movement, a movement promoting self-improvement through self-analysis and devotion to God.

Rabbi Yitzchak (Don) Abarbanel. See Abarbanel.

Rabbi Yitzchak Luria Ashkenazi (1534–1572), foremost kabbalist.

Rabbi Yitzchak Meir Alter, the Gerer *rebbe* (1799–1866), author of *Chidushei Harym* and founder of the Gerer dynasty.

Rabbi Yitzchak of Radvil (1741–1825), son of Rabbi Yechiel Michel of Zlotchov, the Zlotchover *Maggid*.

Rabbi Yitzchak of Volozhin (died 1849), son and successor of Rabbi Chaim of Volozhin.

Rabbi Yonatan Eybeschutz (1690–1764), rabbi of Hamburg, eminent author of *Yaarot Devash* and many other works.

Rabbi Yosef Karo, the Bet Yosef (1488–1575), author of the *Shulchan Aruch*, Comprehensive Code of Jewish Law.

Rabbi Yosef Yozel Hurwitz of Novardok (1848–1920), *rosh yeshivah* of the chain of Novardok *yeshivot*. Leading spokesman of the *Mussar* movement. Author of *Madregat Ha'adam*.

Rizhiner. See Rabbi Yisrael Friedman of Rizhin.

NOTES

Chapter 1

1. *Seder Olam* 6.
2. *Minhagei Mahari Tirnau, Minhag Rosh Chodesh Elul.*
3. *Pirkei d'Rabbi Eliezer*, ch. 46. Also in *Machzor Vitry*, p. 362.
4. *Minhagei Yeshurun*, 139.
5. *Rosh Hashanah* 10b.
6. *Pesachim* 4b.

Chapter 2

1. *HaRokeach.*
2. *Rosh Hashanah* 11a.
3. *Mishneh Torah.*
4. Quoted in *Iturei Torah.*
5. *Midrash Tanchumah, Parashat Vayeira.*

6. As in the phrase *tero'em beshevet barzel*, "Smash them with an iron rod" (Psalm 2:9).
7. *Pesikta Rabbati*, ch. 15, and *Shir Hashirim Rabbah* 5:3.

Chapter 3

1. From the *Unetanneh Tokef* prayer.
2. Jeremiah, ch. 40 and 41.
3. *Rosh Hashanah* 18b and *Nedarim* 12a.
4. The present responsum is quoted from *The Responsa Anthology* by Avraham Yaakov Finkel (Northvale, NJ: Jason Aronson Inc., 1991).

Chapter 4

1. *Yoma* 73b; *Shulchan Aruch, Orach Chaim*, ch. 612-615.
2. *Pesachim* 54a; *Nedarim* 39b.
3. *Tomer Devorah.*
4. Chasidism teaches that the universe is filled with divine sparks of holiness – *nitzotzot hakedoshim*. No corner of the universe is without the presence of sparks of sanctity that are giving life to all existence. Even evil contains a spark of goodness, for without this spark it could not exist. It is the historic mission of the Jewish people to release these imprisoned sparks through the performance of *mitzvot*.

Chapter 5

1. *Mishnah Berurah* 619:1 (*Shaar Hatziun*, 4).
2. *Machzor Vitry.*
3. Jerusalem Talmud, *Yoma* 1:1
4. *Mishnah Berurah* 621:1, n. 2.
5. *Mishnah Berurah* 621:4, n. 14.

Chapter 6

1. *Commentary on the Pentateuch.*
2. Zechariah 14:1–21; Ezekiel 38:18–39:16.

3. Jerusalem Talmud, *Rosh Hashanah* 4:8.
4. There were twelve generations from Adam to Noah, enumerated in Genesis 5, and ten generations from Shem (Noah's son) to Abraham, listed in Genesis 11:10–27.
5. *Minhagei Mahari Tirnau*, Sukkot.
6. Hirsch, *Commentary on the Pentateuch*, Leviticus 23:36.
7. *Sefer Chasidim*, par. 453.
8. *Midrash Shir Hashirim* 1.
9. *Midrash Rabbah*, Bereishit 8:2.
10. It is interesting to note that the same thought is attributed to the *Vilna Gaon*.

Chapter 7

1. Hasmonean may mean "man from Chashmonah," a town mentioned in Numbers 33:29. Some say it is a title of honor, cognate of *chashmanim* (Psalm 68:32), which the Septuagint – the Greek translation of the Bible – renders as "ambassadors."
2. The history of *Eretz Yisrael* under Syrian/Greek domination is recorded in the Books of Hasmoneans, which are known also as the Books of Maccabees 1 and 2. These writings are part of the Apocrypha (books not included in the Bible).

   Additional sources are *Antiquities* and *The Jewish Wars*, both by Flavius Josephus (c. 38–100 C.E.), a Jewish historian and main source of much of our knowledge of ancient Jewish history. Josephus was a military commander in the Galilee during the war against the Romans until he was captured in 67 C.E. He is considered reliable and is occasionally quoted by the great commentators. Rashi cites his works fourteen times, for example, in *Berachot* 43a, *Yoma* 23a, and *Bava Batra* 3b.

   Much information about the Syrian/Greek occupation is contained in *Tzemach David*, a historical chronicle by the eminent historian Rabbi David Ganz (1541–1613).

   A more recent source is the monumental *Dorot Harishonim*, an authentic history of the Jewish people by Rabbi Yitzchak E. Rabinovitz (Pressburg, Frankfurt, Jerusalem, 1897).

   Toledot Am Olam, by Rabbi Shlomoh Rottenberg, is a comprehensive compilation of all the historical data culled from the Bible, the Talmud, and *Midrashim* as well as from the above mentioned sources.

3. *Shibbolei Haleket* 199.
4. *Gittin* 57; *Eichah Rabbati* 1:50; Josephus 19; *Tzemach David* 1:610; Hasmoneans 2:7.
5. A compilation of the laws of Chanukah can be found in the *Shulchan Aruch, Orach Chaim* 671–684. An abbreviated version is provided in the *Kitzur Shulchan Aruch*, available in English translation.
6. *Esther Rabbah* 2:1.
7. *Megillah* 12; *Esther Rabbah* 7:13.
8. *Megillah* 7a.
9. 1313 B.C.E.
10. *Megillah* 7a.
11. *Chullin* 139.
12. *Pathways to the Torah*, B44, B45.
13. *Esther Rabbah* 8:7.

Chapter 8

1. *Netivot al Hatorah.*
2. The sages ordained that a second day of *Yom Tov* is to be observed outside *Eretz Yisrael* on Pesach, Shavuot, and Sukkot—the so-called *Yom Tov sheini shel galuyot*. On Rosh Hashanah, a second day is observed even in *Eretz Yisrael.*

Chapter 9

1. This comment is found in the end of the Ran's commentary on *Pesachim*.
2. *Seder Tefilot.*
3. *Emor* 97.
4. Hirsch, *Commentary on the Pentateuch*, Leviticus 26:13.
5. *Sanhedrin* 56b.
6. From the *Adon Olam* prayer.
7. In ancient times, the *Bet Din* (rabbinic court) in *Eretz Yisrael* determined the day on which the new month would begin on the basis of testimony of witnesses who had seen the appearance of the first sliver of the new moon. Because the Festivals are celebrated on prescribed days of the month (e.g., Passover on the fifteenth of *Nisan*, Yom Kippur on the tenth

of *Tishri*), it was, in effect, the *Bet Din* that fixed the day on which the Festivals would occur.

8. *Pesachim* 117a.
9. *Pesachim* 117a.
10. *Rosh Hashanah* 32b.
11. *Arachin* 10b.
12. Quoted in *Yalkut Me'am Lo'ez*.
13. Quoted in *Yalkut Me'am Lo'ez*.
14. The prohibitions against (1) idol worship; (2) murder; (3) incest; (4) robbery; (5) eating the flesh of a living animal; (6) cursing God's Name; and (7) the command to institute courts of law (*Sanhedrin* 56a).

Chapter 10

1. The revelation at Mount Sinai occurred on the fiftieth day after the Exodus.
2. The three elements of *Tanach*, the Holy Scriptures. *Tanach* is the acronym formed by *Torah, Nevi'im, Ketuvim*.
3. *Sefer Matamim*.
4. *Maharil, Hilchot Shavuot, Rema* 494:3.
5. *Rema* 494:2, 3.
6. Quoted in *Shavuos Anthology*.
7. First century C.E.

Chapter 11

1. *Rosh Hashanah* 24a, 25a.
2. *Yalkut Bo* 191.
3. *Megillah* 5a.
4. *Rosh Hashanah* 19a; *Bechorot* 58a.
5. *Magen Avraham, Orach Chaim* 417.
6. *Berachot* 16b.
7. *Minhagei Yeshurun* 70.
8. *Pirkei deRabbi Eliezer*, ch. 44; *Shelah*, p. 74a; Taz on *Shulchan Aruch, Orach Chaim*, ch. 417.
9. Seforno on Numbers 28:11.

GLOSSARY

Aggadah   Nonlegal portion of the Talmud.

Akeidah   Binding of Isaac.

Alef-bet   Hebrew alphabet.

Amud   Reader's stand in synagogue.

Anussim   Jews forced to convert to Christianity who secretly continued to observe Judaism.

Apocrypha   Semisacred books not included in the Bible.

Arba Minim   Four Species taken in hand on Sukkot.

Aron Hakodesh   Holy Ark containing the Torah scrolls.

Avodah   Service of the High Priest on Yom Kippur.

Baal teshuvah   Returnee to Torah observance.

Berachah   Blessing.

Bet Din   Rabbinical court.

Bet Hamikdash   Holy Temple in Jerusalem.

Bet midrash   House of study; a hall for Torah study.

Bimah   Reader's platform.

Birkat Hamazon   Grace after Meals.

Chametz   Leaven.

Chanukah Dedication; Feast of Lights.

Chasid Adherent of Chasidism.

Chasidism The movement of spiritual reawakening within Judaism.

Chatan Torah Groom of the Torah.

Chazzan Cantor.

Chol Hamoed Intermediate days of *Yom Tov.*

Chumash Five Books of Moses.

Dreidl Spinning top, a Chanukah custom.

Eretz Yisrael Land of Israel.

Erev **Yom Kippur** The day before Yom Kippur.

Geulah Redemption.

Grager Noisemaker used on Purim.

Hallel Psalms of praise, Psalms 133–118, recited on the new moon.

Hashem God.

Havdalah Blessing over wine at the conclusion of *Shabbat* and the Festivals.

Heichal Sanctuary.

Hellenists Jews who adopted the Greek language, culture, and ideals.

Kaddish Prayer recited by mourners.

Karet Divine punishment by premature death.

Kedushah Prayer of sanctification.

Kiddush Sanctification; ceremonial blessing over wine, recited on *Shabbat* and the Festivals.

Kiddush Levanah Blessing over the new moon.

Lag Ba'omer The thirty-third day of the counting of the *Omer.*

Maariv Evening prayer.

Maror Bitter herbs on the *seder* plate.

Marranos Jews forced to convert to Christianity who secretly practiced Judaism.

Mashiach The Messiah, a descendant of King David, who will redeem the Jewish people, rebuild the Temple, and usher in the messianic era.

Megillah Scroll of the Book of Esther.

Midrash Homiletic interpretaion of the Scriptures.

Mikveh Pool of water used for ritual purification.

Milah Circumcision.

Minchah Afternoon prayer.

Minyan Quorum for prayer of ten adult men.

Mishkan Tabernacle.

Mishlo'ach manot Gifts of food on Purim.

Mussaf Additional prayer.

Mussar Movement of ethical revival through introspection.

Nes nistar Hidden miracle.

Neshamah yeteirah The extra soul every Jew acquires on *Shabbat*.

Niggun Wordless melody.

Nitzotzot hakodesh Sparks of holiness, a kabbalistic concept.

Pesach Passover.

Pikuach nefesh Saving an endangered life.

Piyut Liturgical hymn.

Rosh yeshivah Dean of a *yeshivah*.

S'chach Covering of the *sukkah*.

Se'udah Festive meal.

Seder Passover service conducted in the home on the first two nights of Passover.

Sefirat Ha'omer The counting of the *Omer*.

Sefirot Spheres, emanations, a kabbalistic concept.

Selichot Prayers of supplication.

Septuagint Greek translation of the Bible.

Shacharit Morning prayer.

Shechinah Divine Presence.

Shechitah Ritual slaughter.

Shehecheyanu Thanksgiving blessing.

Shem Hameforash The ineffable Name of God.

Shemittah Sabbatical year.

Shemoneh Esrei Eighteen Benedictions of daily prayer, *Amidah*.

Shevarim Sobbing sound on the *shofar*.

Shir Hama'alot Songs of Ascent, Psalms 120–134.

Shirah Song of the Sea.

Siyum Completion of a tractate in the Talmud.

Sukkah Booth erected for Sukkot.

Sukkot The feast of Tabernacles.

Tefillin Phylacteries.

Tekiah Long, clear blast on the *shofar*.

Teruah Nine short staccato blasts on the *shofar*.

Teshuvah Repentance.

Tevilah Immersion in a *mikveh*.

Tzaddik Righteous man, chasidic *rebbe*.

Tzitzit Fringes, tassels; see Numbers 15:38.

Viduy Confessional prayer.

Yamim Noraim Days of Awe, Rosh Hashanah and Yom Kippur.

Yeshivah Talmudical college.

Yetzer hara Evil inclination, carnal nature.

Yetzer hatov   Good inclination.
Yom Hadin   Day of Judgment, Rosh Hashanah.
Yom Kippur   Day of Atonement.
Yom Tov   Festival or holiday.
Yovel   Fiftieth year, jubilee year.
Zero'a   Shankbone on the *seder* plate.

BIBLIOGRAPHY

Sources are listed alphabetically by author or title, according to how they are best known. Some works were published posthumously.

Abarbanel, Rabbi (Don) Yitzchak. Commentary on the Torah. Venice, 1579.

Agadah uMachashavah beYahadut. Meir Meisels. Tel Aviv, 1960.

Alshich, Rabbi Moshe. *Torat Moshe,* commentary on the Torah. Belvedere, 1597.

Arba'ah Turim. Rabbi Yaakov Baal Hatarim. Pieve de Sachi, 1475.

Baal Shem Tov. See *Sefer Baal Shem Tov.*

Bachya, Rabbeinu. Commentary on the Torah. Naples, 1492.

Be'er Avraham. Rabbi Avraham Weinberg of Slonim, the Slonimer *rebbe.* Jerusalem, 1970.

Be'er Hagolah. Rabbi Yehudah Loew of Prague, the Maharal. Prague, 1598.

Be'er Mayim Chayim. Rabbi Chaim Tirer of Chernovitz. Chernovitz, 1836.

Bet Aharon. Rabbi Aharon of Karlin-Stolin. Brody, 1875.

Bet Rebbi. Rabbi Chaim Meir Heilman. Berditchev, 1900.

Chashavah Letovah. Rabbi Chanoch of Alexander. Pietrkov, 1929.

Chelkat Yaakov. Rabbi Mordechai Yaakov Breisch. Jerusalem, 1951.

Chidushei Harym. Rabbi Yitzchak Meir Alter, the Gerer *rebbe.* Warsaw, 1870–1876.

Chochman Umussar. Rabbi Simchah Zissel of Kelm. New York, 1957.

Choker Umekabel. Rabbi Moshe Chaim Luzzatto. Shklov, 1785.

Chorev. Rabbi Samson Raphael Hirsch. Frankfurt am Main, 1926.

Damesek Eliezer. Rabbi Eliezer Hager of Vizhnitz. Jerusalem, 1949.

Darkei Chaim. Rabbi Chaim Halberstam of Sanz. Cracow, 1923.

Degel Machaneh Efraim. Rabbi Moshe Chaim Efraim of Sadilkov. Koretz, 1811.

Devarim Areivim. D. B. Ehrman. Munkatch, 1903.

Divrei Chaim. Rabbi Chaim Halberstam of Sanz. Lemberg, 1875.

Divrei Shmuel. Rabbi Shmuel of Slonim. Jerusalem, 1974.

Dover Shalom. Thoughts of Rabbi Shalom Rokeach, the Belzer *rebbe.* Collected by Rabbi Avraham C. S. B. Michelson. Przemysl, 1910.

Emet Ve'emunah. Rabbi Menachem Mendel Morgenstern of Kotzk, the Kotzker *rebbe.* Jerusalem, 1940.

Entziklopedia Talmudit. Rabbi Shlomoh Yosef Zevin. Jerusalem: Yad Harav Herzog, 1947.

Eser Orot. Y. Berger. Warsaw, 1913.

Eser Tzachtzachot. Y. Berger. Pietrkov, 1910.

Etz Hadaat Tov. Rabbi Chaim Vital. Zolkova, 1866.

Finkel, Avraham Yaakov. *The Great Chasidic Masters.* Northvale, NJ: Jason Aronson Inc., 1992.

———. *The Great Torah Commentators.* Northvale, NJ: Jason Aronson Inc., 1990.

———. *The Responsa Anthology.* Northvale, NJ: Jason Aronson Inc., 1990.

Gevurot Hashem. Rabbi Yehudah Loew of Prague, the Maharal. Cracow, 1582.

Ginzei Yisrael. Rabbi Yisrael of Chortkov. New York, 1965.

Hamanhig. Avraham Ibn Yarchi. Constantinople, 1519.

Hamo'adim Bahalachah. Rabbi Shlomoh Yosef Zevin. Jerusalem, 1944.

Harokeach. Rabbi Elazar of Worms. Fano, 1505.

Hirsch, Rabbi Samson Raphael. *Commentary on the Pentateuch.* Franfurt am Main, 1867.

———. *Commentary on Psalms.* Frankfurt am Main, 1914.

Imrei Kadosh. Rabbi Uri of Strelisk. Lemberg, 1891.

Imrei Shefer. Rabbi Naftali Tzvi Horowitz. Lemberg, 1884.

Irin Kadishin. Rabbi Yisrael Friedman of Rizhin, the Rizhiner. Warsaw, 1880.

Iturei Torah. Compiled by Rabbi Aharon Yaakov Gruenberg. Tel Aviv, 1991.

Kad Hakemach. Rabbi Bachya ben Asher. Constantinople, 1515.

Kantor, Rabbi Mattis. *The Jewish Time Line Encyclopedia.* Northvale, NJ: Jason Aronson Inc., 1989.

Kedushat Aharon. Rabbi Aharon Friedman of Sadigora. Warsaw, 1913.
Kedushat Levi. Rabbi Levi Yitzchak of Berditchev. Slavita, 1798.
Kehilat Moshe. Moshe Kohen of Tchudanov. Lemberg, 1793.
Kitzur Shulchan Aruch. Rabbi Shlomoh Ganzfried. Ungvar, 1864.
Kol Simchah. Rabbi Simchah Bunam of Pshis'cha. Breslau, 1859.
Leket Yosher. Compiled by Yosef of Muenster. Berlin, 1903.
Lev Eliyahu. Rabbi Eliyahu Lapian. Jerusalem, 1972.
Likutei Amarim. Tanya. Rabbi Shneur Zalman of Liadi. Slavita, 1796.
Likutei Maharil. Rabbi Yehudah Leib of Zalkilkov. Lemberg, 1868.
Likutei Moharan. See Rabbi Nachman of Bratzlav.
Machzor Vitry. Rabbi Simchah of Vitry. Berlin, 1889.
Madregat Ha'adam. Rabbi Yosef Yozel Horowitz of Novardok. Pietrkov, 1922.
Maggid Devarav LeYaakov. Rabbi Dov Ber of Mezritch. Koretz, 1781.
Maharil. Rabbi Yaakov Moelin. Sabionetta, 1556.
Maimonides. See Rabbi Moshe ben Maimon.
Mekor Chaim. Rabbi Chaim Halberstam. Bilgoray, 1912.
Meshech Chochmah. Rabbi Meir Simchah Hakohen. Riga, 1927.
Mesillat Yesharim. Rabbi Moshe Chaim Luzzatto. 1740.
Michtav Me'Eliyahu. Rabbi Eliyahu E. Dessler. Israel, 1955.
Midor Dor. Compiled by M. Lipson. Tel Aviv, 1929.
Midrash Rabbah on the Torah. Constantinople, 1512.
Midrash Shocher Tov. Midrash on Tehillim (Psalms). Constantinople, 1512.
Migedolei Hachasidut. Rabbi Mattityahu Yechiel Gutman. Bilgoray, 1930.
Minhagei Mahari Tirnau. Rabbi Yitzchak Tirnau. Venice, 1566.
Minhagei Maharil. Rabbi Yaakov Moelin, the Maharil. Sabionetta, 1556.
Minhagei Yeshurun. Rabbi Avraham Eliezer Hirschowitz. Vilna, 1899.
Mishnah Berurah. Rabbi Yisrael Meir Hakohen Kagan. Warsaw, 1892–1898.
Mishnat Rabbi Aharon. Rabbi Aharon Kotler. Jerusalem, 1987.
Mishneh Torah. Rabbi Moshe ben Maimon, the Rambam. Mantua, 1566.
Mordechai. Rabbi Mordechai Ashkenazi. Riva di Trenta, 1558.
Rabbi Moshe ben Maimon, the Rambam. *Moreh Nevuchim (Guide of the Perplexed).* Naples, 1492.
Rabbi Nachman of Bratzlav. *Likutei Moharan.* Compiled by Rabbi Natan Sternherz. Ostroh, 1798.
Nagid Umetzaveh. Rabbi Yaakov Chaim Tzemach of Safed. Amsterdam, 1712.
Netivot al Hatorah. B'nei B'rak: Arachim, 1991.
No'am Elimelech. Rabbi Elimelech of Lizhensk. Lemberg, 1788.
No'am Siach. Rabbi Aharon Kotler. Jerusalem, 1988.
Ohel Elimelech. Complied by Rabbi A. S. B. Michelson. Pshemishl, 1910.

Ohel Torah. Rabbi Menachem Mendel Morgenstern of Kotzk, the Kotzker *rebbe.* Lublin, 1909.

Ohel Yaakov. Rabbi Yaakov Krantz, *Maggid* of Dubna. Josefov, 1810.

Or Hameir. Complied by Rabbi Reuven Margolis. Lemberg, 1926.

Or Torah. Rabbi Meir Yechiel of Ostrowtza. Pietrkov, 1921.

Or Yesharim. M. S. Kleinman. Pietrkov, 1924.

Or Yisrael. Rabbi Yitzchak Blazer. Vilna, 1900.

Or Yitzchak. Rabbi Yitzchak of Radvil. Warsaw, 1961.

Or Zarua. Rabbi Yitzchak ben Moshe of Vienna. Zhitomir, 1862.

Otzar Dinim uMinhagim. Rabbi J. D. Eisenstein. New York: Hebrew Publishing Co., 1917.

Otzar Maamarei Chazal. Rabbi J. D. Eisenstein, 1947.

Otzerot Yosef. Rabbi Yosef Engel. Vienna, 1921.

Pardes Yosef. Rabbi Yosef Patznovsky. Pietrkov, 1931–1939.

Pathways to the Torah. B'nei Brak: Arachim.

Pesikta Rabbati. A midrashic work. Prague, 1653–55.

Pesikta Ze'irta. A midrashic work. Venice, 1546.

Pirkei d'Rabbi Eliezer. Attributed to the *Tanna* Rabbi Elizer ben Hyrkanos. Constantinople, 1514.

Pri Tzaddik. Rabbi Tzadok Hakohen of Lublin. Lublin, 1901.

Rambam. See *Mishneh Torah.*

Redak. Torah commentary by *Rabbi David Kimchi.* Venice, 1517.

Rokeach (also called *HaRokeach*). Rabbi Elazar of Worms. Fano, 1505.

Seder Hadorot. Rabbi Yechiel Halpern. Karlsruhe, 1769.

Seder Hadorot Hechadash. Rabbi Menachem M. Bodek. Lemberg, 1865.

Seder Olam. Attributed to the *Tanna* Rabbi Yosi ben Chalafta. Mantua, 1514.

Seder Tefilot. Rabbi David ben R. Yosef Abudraham. Lisbon, 1489.

Sefat Emet. Rabbi Aryeh Yehudah Leib Alter, the Gerer *rebbe.* Pietrkov, 1905.

Sefer Baal Shem Tov. Brooklyn, NY, 1950.

Sefer Chasidim. Rabbi Yehudah Hechasid. Bologna, 1538.

Sefer Hachasidut. Yitzchak Raphael. Tel Aviv, 1955.

Sefer Matamim. Rabbi Yitzchak Lipitz. Warsaw, 1889.

Shaarei Chaim. Rabbi Chaim Sofer. Munkatch, 1893.

Shavuos Anthology. Rabbi Tzvi Rotberg. Brooklyn, 1896.

Shelah. Rabbi Yeshayah Horowitz of Prague. Amsterdam, 1648.

Shem Mishmuel. Rabbi Shmuel Borenstein of Sochatchov. Warsaw, 1929.

Shemen Hatov. Thoughts of Rabbi Shmuel Shmelke Horowitz of Nikolsburg. Compiled by Rabbi A. S. B. Michelson. Pietrkov, 1905.

Shibbolei Haleket. Rabbi Tzidkiyahu ben Rabbi Avraham Harofeh. Venice, 1546.

Shulchan Aruch. Rabbi Yosef Karo. Venice, 1564.
Siach Sarfei Kodesh. Y. K. K. Rakatz. Lodz, 1928.
Siddur. Rabbi Yaakov Emden. Altona, 1745.
Siddur Rashi. Rabbi Shlomoh Buber. Berlin, 1911.
Sifran shel Tzadikim. Rabbi Elazar Dov. Warsaw, 1914.
Siftei Tzaddikim. Rabbi Michael Levi Rodkinson. Lemberg, 1876.
Simchat Yisrael. Thoughts of Rabbi Simchah Bunam of Pshis'cha. Compiled by Rabbi Yisrael Berger. Pietrkov, 1911.
Talmud, tractates *Rosh Hashanah, Yoma, Sukkah, Megillah, Pesachim, Shabbat, Sotah, Chagigah.*
Tanchumah, Midrash. Rabbi Tanchuma bar Abba. Constantinople, 1520.
Tehillot Hashem. Rabbi Eliyahu Hakohen Haitamari. Salonica, 1839.
Teshuvot Maharil. Rabbi Yaakov Moelin. Venice, 1549.
Tiferet haYehudi. Thoughts of Rabbi Simchah Bunam of Pshis'cha. Pietrkov, 1912.
Tiferet Uziel. Rabbi Uziel Meisels. Warsaw, 1863.
Tiferet Yisrael. Rabbi Yehudah Loew of Prague, the Maharal. Prague, 1593.
Toledot Am Olam. Rabbi Shlomoh Rottenberg. Jerusalem, 1967.
Tomer Devorah. Rabbi Moshe Cordovero. Venice, 1589.
Torat Avot. Rabbi A. Y. D. Lewin. Lemberg-Pietrkov, 1912.
Torat Chesed. Rabbi Shlomoh Yavetz. Belvedere, 1597.
Torat Moshe. See Alshich, Rabbi Moshe.
Torat Moshe. Rabbi Moshe Sofer. Pressburg, 1895.
Tur Orach Chaim. Rabbi Yaakov ben Asher. Pieve de Sachi, 1475.
Tvuat Shor. Rabbi Efraim Zalmon Hirsch Schor. Lublin, 1615.
Tzemach David. Rabbi David Gans. Prague, 1592.
Tzofnat Pane'ach. Rabbi Yosef di Trani. Venice, 1648.
Rabbi Yaakov Emden. *Siddur*. Altona, 1745.
Yaarot Devash. Rabbi Yonatan Eybeschutz. Karlsruhe, 1779.
Yalkut Me'am Lo'ez. Rabbi Yaakov Culi. Jerusalem, 1984.
Yamim Nora'im. Compiled by Shmuel Yosef Agnon. Tel Aviv-Berlin, 1938.
Yeshuot Yisrael. Rabbi Yisrael Friedman. Tarnow, 1904.
Yitzchak Alfasi. *Hachasidut*. Tel Aviv, 1977.
Yitzchak Raphael. *Sefer Hachasidut*. Tel Aviv, 1955.
Zohar. *Tanna* Rabbi Shimon bar Yochai. Mantua, 1558.

INDEX OF SAGES

(According to the name by which they are best known.)

INDEX OF SCRIPTURE

20:12, 192
20:14, 197
20:15, 192
20:17, 202
20:18–21, 187, 199
23:16, 201
24:7, 190, 196
25:8, 122
25:31–40, 101
32:2, 221
34:1, 3
34:5, 201
34:6, 8
34:22, 201

Leviticus

8:33–35, 168
15:28, 165
Ch. 16, 70
16:15, 71
16:17, 74
16:30, 53
Ch. 18, 70–71
18:5, 71
19:3, 192
23:1–41, 117–118
23:4, 215
23:9, 10, 166
23:14, 163
23:15, 101
23:15, 16, 161
23:24, 13
23:27, 50, 54
23:40, 86, 88
24:1–2, 117
25:2–7, 101
25:3–4, 168
25:8–34, 101

Numbers

5:6, 66
7:1, 8:4, 116
23:4, 142
28:15, 222
28:26, 201, 208, 209
29:1, 25, 41
29:12, 34, 68
29:35, 95
29:36, 99
33:29, 117

Deuteronomy

4:20, 146
5:15, 146
5:19, 204
8:8, 101, 168
11:12, 14
16:1, 141, 216
16:3, 150
16:10, 201
16:14–15, 88
19:15, 18
26:17–19, 128, 137
29:9, 12
30:2, 12, 60
31:18, 134
34:5, 105

Joshua

6:20, 24

1 Kings

3:15, 100

INDEX OF SUBJECTS

Index of Subjects

Catholicism, forced conversions to, 63-64

Chametz
evil tendency, 149
matzah differentiated from, 149
removal of, 147
search for, 152-153
smuggling of, 148

Chanukah, 107-123
Bet Yosef question, 118-119
chasidic interpretation of, 120
cleansing the Temple, 122-123
customs of, 116
festival of family, 120-121
historical background of, 108-112
Jewish survival and, 107-108
laws of lighting the *menorah*, 114-115
lights of, 119
Ma'oz Tzur, 121-122
message of the lights, 114
miracle of the oil, 121
no *Megillah* for, 137
observances of, 116
Purim and, 136
tales of heroism and martyrdom, 112-113
Talmud and, 113
thirty-six lights, 119
Torah references to, 116-117
why eight days, 117-118

Charity
Erev Yom Kippur, Ten Days of *Teshuvah*, 48-49
Rosh Hashanah and, 33-34

Cleansing the Temple, Chanukah and, 122-123

Conceit, *Kol Nidrei*, is worse than sin, 71

Conversions, *Kol Nidrei*, 63-64

Crusades, *Omer*, mournful period of *Sefirat Ha'omer*, 167

Culture
Chanukah and, 108-110
Holy Days and, xxi-xxii

Dairy food, Shavuot and, 200
Dancing, Sukkot and, 104
Day of Judgment (Rosh Hashanah), 15. *See* Rosh Hashanah (Day of Judgment)
Day of new beginnings, Rosh Hashanah and, 14-15
Day of rejoicing, Rosh Hashanah and, 17
Days of Awe, 1-12
acronym of Elul, 3
to behold God, 6-7
even before *Selichot*, 11-12
every day is *Elul*, 10
finding the way, 10
the fish are trembling, 9-10
lesson from a peasant, 9
like a lamp, 12
to live in the house of God, 5-6
no ulterior motive, 6
prayers of supplication (*Selichot* service), 7
preparation for, 2-3
Psalm 27 and, 4-5
repentance (*teshuvah*) and, 1-2
repentance (*teshuvah*) for the entire year, 11
serve yourself, 9
sounding the *shofar* during *Elul*, 4
standing before God, 12
Thirteen Attributes of Mercy, 7-8

Index of Subjects

263

new moon, festivals, and *Shabbat*,
215
peace among heavenly bodies,
214
rule of AT-BASH, 218–219
Sanctification of the Moon
(*Kiddush Levanah*), 224
second day of *Yom Tov*, 215–216
selected laws of *Kiddush Levanah*,
224–225
sin offering to God, 222
women and, 221
Rosh Hashanah (Day of Judgment),
13–43
acceptance of God as master,
32–33
Akeidah and, 35
apple dipped in honey, 19
Avinu Malkeinu (Our Father, Our
King), 33
break your stubborn heart, 43
a broken heart, 26–27
charitable treatment and, 33–34
day of judgment, 15
day of new beginnings, 14–15
day of rejoicing, 17
divine scales of justice, 16–17
ego smashing and, 41
eye of a needle, 41–42
faith is the answer, 22
fear of angels, 39–40
God's concealment, 22–23
Golden Calf and, 35–36
greatness of a *Baal Teshuvah's*
prayer, 42
greeting for, 19
Hallel omission, 23–24
hidden spark, 23
inscribe us in the Book of Life, 16
the King, 20

language of heaven, 37
like a fish, 40
like a fly, 37
Malchuyot, Zichronot, Shofarot,
31–32
man's sustenance, 18
meaning of, 13–14
meireishit (from the beginning), 14
Psalm 130, 20–22
Rabbi Amnon story, 37–39
remembering and forgetting,
34–35
Satan and, 18, 26
secret code, 31
shofar sounding and, 24–25,
27–28, 29–30
strategy of evil inclination, 41
Tashlich and, 40
tekiah-shevarim-teruah-tekiah, 30–31
Torah reading on, 28–29
wake up from sleep, 25
wicked and the good, 36
yoma arichta (one long day), 19–20
zodiac sign (Libra), 16
Rule of AT-BASH, *Rosh Chodesh*,
218–219

Sanctification of the Moon (*Kiddush
Levanah*), *Rosh Chodesh*, 224
Satan
Rosh Hashanah and, 18, 26
Ten Days of *Teshuvah*
(repentance), 47–48
Scales of justice, Rosh Hashanah
and, 16–17
Seder
egg on the *seder* plate, 158–159
four cups, 159
Passover and, 154–155